This book is dedicated to Eleanor Brownell,
who truly is the best mom in seventeen counties.
Oh, how I love you so!

Praise for *Elusive Mommyhood*

"In a powerful blend of intimate memoir and compelling journalism, Ginanne Brownell tackles the many clichés and misunderstandings surrounding IVF and surrogacy, and also offers the reader a nuanced and empathetic view of the painful struggles infertility can bring. She manages to clarify, with honesty, humor and compassion, a topic that is increasingly commonplace, and yet still deeply misunderstood. A must-read for anyone searching to deepen their understanding of a topic too often treated superficially."

—Claire Shipman, Peabody Award–winning journalist and *New York Times* best-selling author

"A forensic look at one of the toughest, and most nuanced, ethical quandaries of modern times. Ginanne threads her own experiences of surrogacy into the history and science behind a process that is helping thousands of people to become parents, giving the book a deeply personal feel. If you think you have a view on surrogacy, infertility, or women's rights, read this book—then think again."

—Emma Haslett, journalist, author, and co-host of the *Big Fat Negative* podcast

"The journey to becoming a mother has never been more varied than it is at this moment in time—and Ginanne Brownell impressively sheds light on an increasingly important part of this conversation: surrogacy. Through the lens of her own moving story, and weaving in eye-opening research and insight from those on the inside through her journalistic rigor, she pulls back the curtain on a mysterious world still in its infancy but growing at pace. [This world is] still filled with as many misconceptions and complexities as [it is with] connection and joy; [it] stretches from the celebrities of California to the clinics of India and the law courts of her home state of Michigan. Whether surrogacy—or any aspect of fertility or parenthood, for that matter—has touched you or not, this is a breathtaking read in which page after page will leave you looking at life and love and legacy with a fresh perspective."

—Lauren Clark, health journalist

Elusive Mommyhood

To Sen. Chang —
    Thanks for all
the work that you
do for Michigan families!
    Best —
        Gi nevene

Elusive Mommyhood

An
Investigative Reporter's
Personal Journey into
IVF and Surrogacy

Ginanne Brownell

MISSION POINT PRESS

Published by Mission Point Press
2554 Chandler Rd.
Traverse City, MI 49696
(231) 421-9513
MissionPointPress.com

ISBN: 978-1-965278-11-6

Cover illustrations by Aurelie Baudry Palmer

Library of Congress Control Number: 2024921572

Printed in the United States of America

Contents

Introduction

This book helped change the law.

Or to put it more precisely, the research and work I have done on this global investigation into in vitro fertilization (IVF) and surrogacy led directly to me becoming an activist. And that activism, in turn, just changed the antiquated surrogacy laws in my home state of Michigan, a place that has played an integral role in the history of global surrogacy. As one of the leaders of the Michigan Fertility Alliance, we worked with several prominent US family and reproductive rights organizations to help craft legislation, the Michigan Family Protection Act (MFPA), which was signed into law by Governor Gretchen Whitmer on April 1, 2024.

That law not only makes surrogacy now legal in Michigan—there had broadly been a civil and criminal ban on surrogacy—but it gives protections for all children born through assisted reproduction, including IVF, in the Great Lakes State. Since 1988 that hasn't been clear—and it's been unfair on the parents, surrogates and, arguably most importantly, the children.

Does the subject of surrogacy make you feel uncomfortable? If so, you aren't alone. That's because it's a cultural anomaly, a term first coined by twentieth-century British anthropologist Mary Douglas. She said that the way we organize our thoughts are by categories. Every bit of information we process we filter through classifications defined by our culture. Things that are out of place, therefore, are cultural anomalies. She used the example of hair. Hair is supposed to be on your head, that's where it belongs. But if you find hair in your soup, it's gross because it's not supposed to be there. While there is no difference between hair on your head and hair in your soup, it's out of place in your broth. We as humans crave things in their right setting. But when something blurs and makes us question our fundamental categories, it upsets the applecart.

Surrogacy does just that. It jumbles up all our notions of things like body and motherhood. We know what a body is and what it's for. But with surrogacy, suddenly something that comes from one woman's body is in another woman's body, and what that woman has in her body "belongs" to another woman. We know what a mother is, but surrogacy comes along and defies that too: a woman carrying the baby is not the mother and the woman who isn't carrying the baby is the mother. And the woman who gives the genes? She might be the mother, but she might not be the mother. Elly Teman, an Israeli American anthropologist who has studied surrogacy for over two decades, told me that people are uncomfortable with surrogacy because it jumbles up the basic categories that give us cohesion, organization, and order in life.

Initially, I felt the same way because, let's face it, surrogacy has an image problem. All I knew about surrogacy was what I had read in the media: either stories of surrogacy going horrifically wrong in places like India and Thailand or of wealthy celebrities like Elton John and David Furnish, Angela Bassett and Courtney B. Vance, and Nicole Kidman and Keith Urban, all of whom could afford a practice that was seemingly astronomical in price and out of reach for average people. But after suffering through years of infertility, my then-husband and I had run out of other options. So, in 2015 when my gay middle-class Israeli friends told me they were pursuing surrogacy to have a family, it opened my mind a bit more that it could be a possibility for us too.

Thanks to technological advances like IVF, the trend for having children later in life and the softening of cultural attitudes, there has been a major boom in surrogacy over the past several years. Since the world's first surrogacy contract was signed in Michigan in 1976, hundreds of thousands of children have been born globally via surrogacy. Initially it was all through traditional surrogacy, where the surrogate was also the egg donor, an ethical minefield that exploded during the mid-1980s with the Baby M case in New Jersey. But after 1986, when the world's first baby was born via a gestational carrier—meaning the surrogate is not related to the child and the egg either comes from the intended mother or a separate donor—again, in my home state of Michigan, that's become the preferred practice globally. And unlike what we see and read in the media, the vast majority of families that are created or expanded through surrogacy are not Silicon Valley billionaires or Bollywood superstars. They're just normal people who are desperate to have or expand their families, scrimping and saving to fund their surrogacy journey.

Compensated cross-border surrogacy is legal in most US states (16% of intended parents working with gestational carriers in the US are not American residents[i]), Ukraine, and Georgia (and, until recently, Russia), while countries like South Africa, most Australian states, and Britain allow non-compensated surrogacy for their citizens. In Canada, meanwhile, surrogacy is non-compensated and open to both locals and foreign nationals. The term non-compensated is somewhat of a misnomer, as in Britain, for example, pretty much every surrogate receives some kind of compensation, which sometimes gets called "reasonable expenses."

A number of countries that used to be in the surrogacy game, including India, Thailand, and Russia have made cross-border surrogacy illegal in the past few years (though as of May 2024, Thailand is planning to lift their ban on cross-border surrogacy). With high profile cases like Baby Gammy (Thailand) and Baby Manji (India), the world's media helped shape a narrative that surrogacy was a practice that exploited women and left many children stateless. Unfortunately, as is the case in several countries that have eventually banned surrogacy for one reason or another, surrogates as key stakeholders were never asked their opinions on the subject. Currently there's a lot of debate and discussion by both those in the surrogacy world and a handful of multilateral organizations to come up with international regulations or a framework on surrogacy similar to The Hague Adoption Convention.

Even over the course of the four years it has taken me to write this book, several countries have looked at unilaterally changing or amending their laws. Realizing their surrogacy statutes were rather antiquated, Britain, for example, in 2020 finished an eighteen-month consultation process on surrogacy. The Israeli Supreme Court in 2021 annulled a law that made it illegal for same-sex couples to have children via surrogacy while the Mexican Supreme Court in 2022 declared that their legislature should advance legal regulation of surrogacy. Under new plans drawn up in Ireland in the end of 2023, international surrogacy arrangements would be recognized in the country for the first time and Denmark has passed new pro-surrogacy regulations that will go into effect in early 2025.

Heather Jacobson, a sociologist at the University of Texas in Arlington who has written extensively on American surrogates, told me that we should stop using the word surrogacy as a blanket term globally. "They are surrogacies," she said. She added that it's inaccurate and misleading to compare surrogacy practices in countries like Israel, Britain, and most US states (all of which have strict laws and/or legal rulings in place) to surrogacy in places like Laos, Colombia, Kenya, and Ghana, where surrogacy may be practiced but with few, if any, statutes on the books, a possible legal and ethical minefield. While surrogacy is less expensive in these countries—as there are certainly valid conversations around how to make surrogacy more accessible and more equitable for couples from all races, ethnicities, and backgrounds—there are grave concerns over the perceived exploitation of women, the majority of whom teeter on the poverty line. Those who work in the surrogacy and assisted reproduction space raised great concern when, in early 2024, Pope Francis made a blanket statement against global surrogacy, missing the point that surrogacy in one part of the world can be vastly different in another.

While going through my IVF and surrogacy journey, I was keen to read a book that was a wide-ranging look not only in terms of personal stories by normal people who experienced surrogacy firsthand but also an overview of the fascinating yet controversial global surrogacy and IVF landscape. And there was nothing out there—it was either all heady academic meanderings or personal narratives that were more guidebooks than memoirs. Surrogacy is a fascinating, multilayered, and textured subject but one that has yet to be written about in a comprehensive global manner. My hope for this book, then, is to be that resource: the backdrop of my personal story of my struggles with infertility mixed with investigations into all these things that I mention above that I've done through research and interviews with surrogates, doctors, judges, policymakers, campaigners, feminists, anthropologists, sociologists, egg donors, lawyers, clinicians, journalists, activists, academics, intended parents, psychologists, and children born through surrogacy.

As a journalist, I have used my tools to examine all this with a critical eye, and as a mother—I have twins who were born via a surrogate in Illinois in 2018—with a personal view as well. Since starting work on this book, I have, as I stated above, become an advocate and an activist for legal, safe, ethical, transparent surrogacy that gives agency to surrogates, intended parents, and for the children born through this practice. Just as menopause and abortion are controversial subjects that are now being tackled in books, I think it's high time surrogacy and IVF also got a look in as well.

Chapter One

My Elusive Mommyhood

In all my days, I will never forget that ham and cheese panini.

It's not because it was the best thing I had ever tasted—in fact I remember it being a bit soggy as it had been wrapped in tin foil right out of the toaster—but it was because that sandwich came to symbolize a bridge between my old life and the beginning of my new one. When I had purchased it in the sterile hospital cafeteria, I was still just me: a journalist, traveler, expat, aunt, wife, daughter, sister, friend, and infertile woman. But once back in the maternity ward waiting room and three bites into that panini, my life changed forever. The phone rang next to where I was sitting with my older brother. "Answer it," he said, barely looking up from the thick political tome he was reading, underlining points he liked with a pen. He often reminded me of my father, who had died fourteen years previously and had been the most stoic, thoughtful, and intelligent of men. Along with my mother, my dad had been a true role model of a parent.

I hesitated, putting the sandwich down as a greasy string of its melted cheesiness landed on my black button-down shirt. No one else was in the waiting room so we knew the call must be for me. "Hey Ginanne, great news, your twins have arrived," said Susan LeBlanc, the jovial maternity nurse who still had specks of a Massachusetts accent in her voice even though she'd lived in central Illinois for several decades. My brother looked over at me, waiting. "What's wrong with them?" I asked immediately, believing that because of all the horrible, sad luck my husband and I had had over the years with infertility, it couldn't be possible that they were now here on the planet—and robust. "They are gorgeous, they are healthy, come over and meet them," she said. In this most significant and consequential of life's moments, all I could think to say was, "But I just got a ham and cheese sandwich." She let out a chuckle, having obviously dealt before with new parents who were in shock when their bundles of joy arrived. "Well then finish it up quick because they need you," she said and then hung up. I put the phone down, shook my head and said to my brother, "Okay, let's go." On the way out of the waiting room I binned the panini. My old life over, my new life awaiting me down that hallway.

My brother took a great video of the moment they wheeled out my children to me. A gorgeous boy, Ransom, and sweet girl, Lexie[2], whose faces were slick with erythromycin ointment—a prophylactic treatment every American baby gets at birth to prevent infection—and their heads covered in pink-and-blue striped hats. (My daughter's one had a cute bow at the front.) I'd had nine months to get my head around the concept of becoming a mother: hearing from Julie Hudelson Schmidgall, our surrogate, about how the embryo transfers had gone at our clinic in Los Angeles when the blood tests came back confirming that she was pregnant with twins; flying in from London to go to the twenty-two-week scan with her at this same hospital complex in Peoria; and getting to see them move in utero for the first time.

Yet now that they had been born, it just seemed incredibly otherworldly and unbelievable. After a few minutes of awkwardly holding each of them I said to the nurses, "It's totally surreal now they are my responsibility, so Julie gets to relax now, she gets the wine now. This is crazy, you think about this happening and then all of a sudden it happens." Though my commentary was certainly not very brilliant or enlightened, what strikes me most every time I watch this video is just how tense I looked. I nervously flipped and pulled at my hair, completely out of my element, a skittish deer in some massive proverbial headlights. I stayed quite clear of Ransom and Lexie—they were in a see-through plastic moveable crib at this point—and I chattered on nervously to the nurses and my brother.

I checked my phone and saw a text from my husband. He told me he'd landed at Chicago O'Hare after flying last minute from London where we lived. I Facetimed him, showing him the babies. "Little ones," he said with a chuckle, his deep voice heavy with a Balkan accent. The video ends but those next moments are still crystal clear in my mind's eye. As the nurses wheeled the twins toward the nursery to be cleaned up and have a number of tests run, I joked, saying to them, "So where's their mom?" The nurses both smiled at me, and one said, "Honey, *you* are their mom."

Like my children who had just been wrenched out of our carrier's womb, startled and screaming, I had just been yanked into motherhood—and I was just as freaked out as they were.

I went into the newborn nursery and really got a chance to examine them for the first time. They were so tiny and fragile. As I watched Lexie's tiny jittery little heart beating so fast out of her chest—to which one of the nurses gave her droplets of sugar water to raise her blood sugar to calm it down—I thought, "Oh my god, how can I be responsible for these two little humans? How will I keep them alive?"

Six-plus years later, I find it fascinating, humorous, and slightly sad at how completely dazed I was by what had just happened. I had become a mother and, like probably every other first-time mother before me, I felt clueless. I was scared, shocked, perplexed, and over the moon that these two creatures I had yearned for so long had arrived. In my more than thirty years as a journalist, I've reported from more than forty-five countries on six continents doing everything from being helicoptered into a steaming hot war-torn Beirut to trudging around a recently uncovered muddy mass grave in Bosnia and being chased down a hallway in Suva, Fiji, by the country's prime minister. All this to say, not much fazed me anymore. I had developed that journalistic thick skin where I acted blasé at pretty much whatever came my way when I was on assignment. But that was always a cover. Because deep down I was an incredibly Type A person who craved control. One of the things that infertility has taught me—which in hindsight was great training for motherhood—is you never really have control. You may think you do, but it's all a crazy crapshoot.

I often ponder what would I say to that old me on the 2018 video, tugging at my bright green scarf and trying to make light of the situation, as humor has always been my way to assuage even the heaviest of situations. Probably something like: "Hey, it's okay, you got this. It's a huge learning curve but you just have to get on with motherhood. And though nothing can prepare you for it, soon it will all come together if you trust your instincts and embrace the crazy ride." But then again knowing me, or at least the old me, I would have asked a million questions and still been highly skeptical of this unsolicited advice.

Growing up in Flint, Michigan, I never consciously thought about having kids, it just seemed a given that I would at some point become a mom. I figured I would do what my mother did. Have a career—she was one of the first ever female journalists in the newsroom for the *Flint Journal*—and then quit to have babies. It was, at least in the 1970s, what many women from certain backgrounds did. My very driven mother, who throughout my childhood and to this day has served on the board of several volunteer community organizations, told me not long ago that had she lived another life she would have run a Fortune 500 company. I have no doubt that would have been the case.

That's what most of my friends' moms had done too, except my high school friend Michelle. Raised by a single mother who was a waitress, Michelle had big career dreams, and she planted the seed that I could be a mom and have a career too. (She went on to become a lawyer for the US Department of Labor and has one son.) At that time, I didn't really contemplate "having it all"—something that's debated even to this day—I just innocently assumed it would somehow work out because I was a big believer then that my destiny would take me where I needed to go. Looking back that seems to be how I lived a lot of my early life, assuming things would just fall into place without me instigating much effort or planning.

Maybe that made me a typical Gen Xer. Not a slacker per se but not really taking the helm of my own ship. For example, during my senior year of college, where I was a history major only because it was the subject that I got my best grades, my muddled plan was to move to Chicago to work at the Gap while I, "figured things out." But luckily my roommate convinced me to apply for a journalism internship in Washington, DC. With maturity also comes the realization that you sometimes need to grab destiny by the nose ring and lead it in the direction where you want to go. Over the years I had done that with my career—for example, moving to London for graduate school in 1998—and as I barrelled into my mid-thirties, I came to understand I needed to do that with my fertility too.

By that time most of my friends had gotten married. Then they all started having kids. And while I was leading a great life over-all, I could pinpoint exactly what was missing: I wanted to have a baby. When I turned thirty-five, I asked my general practitioner in London if I should freeze my eggs, but she quickly pooh-poohed the idea, saying it was expensive and the technology was not there yet. However, four years later at my annual checkup she said to me, "Remember how I told you not to freeze your eggs a few years ago? Well, forget I said that because the technology has moved on."

When egg freezing first started, there was only about a 10 per-cent chance of it working but as of 2013 doctors were claiming up to an 80 percent success rate with a flash-freezing process called vitrification.[3] That process involves dehydrating the cells, add-ing cryoprotectant to them, which stops ice crystals from grow-ing and disrupting the cell's internal structure, and plunging the test tube into liquid nitrogen at -320F.[4] So, my birthday present to myself the year I turned forty was to freeze five viable eggs, which I joked with my friends were my "in case of emergency, break glass" ones. As Yale anthropologist Marcia Inhorn wrote in her 2023 book *Motherhood on Ice: The Mating Gap and Why Women Freeze Their Eggs*, egg freezing won't fix the reasons why women are having children later in life—career, not finding the right partner, etc.—but that technology does offer some hope of a "reproductive suspension bridge."

A year and change later, I decided to try and have a baby on my own. I had talked with a few women who were friends of a friend of mine who had had babies via sperm donors, and I figured they were cool and dynamic women. So, if they did it, I could too. One of them said to me, "Yes, it is hard at times being a single mom, but you are the one who makes all the decisions and you do not have to compromise on what you believe in when it comes to raising your kid." That really appealed to the control freak in me.

I had found a sperm donor through a clinic in Denmark, a place that had come highly recommended. Though it took me some time to get my head around the idea that I would never know the father of my potential future offspring, I finally acquiesced because I so wanted to have a child of my own. When I took the pregnancy test and saw it was positive, I was elated. But I was not so thrilled when my London gynecologist, Dr. Sara Matthews, strongly recommended I avoid flying for the first trimester. As someone who spent at least two weeks a month on the road for work, it was a bittersweet pill to swallow. It meant that I would not be able to meet my family for a long-planned trip to Florida for Easter, the first of many trips and plans cancelled because of IVF. But I was going to be a mom, so I reprimanded myself for being selfish and instead focused on creating a cute nursery in my mind's eye.

At seven weeks things just didn't feel right, so I went in for a blood test. My instincts were correct—my hCG levels (a pregnancy hormone made by cells in the placenta) should have been a certain number by that stage in the pregnancy and they just weren't there yet. In fact, they were far off from where they should have been. Dr. Matthews said to come back after Easter break and she would have a look again, but she warned me that I should prepare myself. "And try not to stress," she said right before I staggered out of her central London office, completely distraught. I went home, called my mom crying and then booked myself a last-minute Eurostar ticket to Paris. A weekend in the City of Lights was bound to make me feel better.

The next morning, after a loungey breakfast where I avoided coffee but not *pain au chocolat*, I headed off, window shopping for fun and trying to take my mind off my panic. But just as I was leaving one of the shops, I had to sit down. A wave of exhaustion crashed over me like nothing ever before in my life. I had no energy to even care that on one of the poshest shopping streets on the planet, I was crouching down on the sidewalk with my head in my hands. As I watched well-heeled Parisians walk by swinging their shopping bags in the zesty spring air, I just knew that this baby was not meant to be.

Maybe it was already a mother's instinct. Less than a week later, I had a D&C procedure in a perfectly pleasant but sterile hospital room back in London. Since all my friends were away for the holiday, I had to have Dr. Matthews's nurse escort me home. I felt very down and terribly alone. Not long after, that same nurse called to say there had been a mix-up in the laboratory (something about the pathologist and the geneticist getting sent the reverse samples) so they weren't sure why the pregnancy had failed.

Though I was filled with anger and anguish, I decided I was not going to give up. A few weeks later I called Dr. Matthews to say that I wanted to order more hormones and start again in the late summer. But fate is a furtive mistress. Just as I was about to start the fertility treatments again—every morning I felt like a third-rate chemist mixing powders and liquids in vials and then extracting the hormones into the syringes—I re-met my future husband. (We had briefly dated a decade earlier.) Things took off quickly and we decided we wanted to start a family right away. And so began a grueling, long, emotionally shattering two years of several fertility treatments, including flushing my fallopian tubes with dye and being put through temporary menopause to recalibrate my cycle.

We also, of course, tried countless IVF rounds as well, where my belly became a pincushion filled up with angry painful brown, blue, and later, faded yellow bruises. I found tiny comfort in that I was far from alone—according to *The Economist*, every year over a million women go through IVF cycles, which through a cocktail of hormones help the ovaries produce several mature eggs, rather than the monthly one (or two) of a normal cycle. My eggs were then collected with a needle and fertilized with my husband's sperm. Then, if any had made it to blastocyst (five days of cells dividing to form embryos), Dr. Matthews would do an embryo transfer with one or two of them, and the others would be frozen for potential later use.

Considering that a good portion of my job as a journalist is doing thorough research on stories I'm writing, I did surprisingly very little when it came to looking at my chances of IVF working.

According to U.S. Society of Reproductive Technologies (SART), while the likelihood of having a full-term, normal birth weight baby after a cycle is greater than 20 percent for women younger than thirty-five, those rates plummet to about a 2.3 percent chance by the time they are forty-three, which was my age around that time. And a woman's chances of pregnancy success drop the more IVF cycles she does.[5] While there are records that are kept of the number of IVF cycles done and how many live births come from that—worldwide that ratio is four to one—little is tracked of failed IVF treatments. It is, *The Economist* wrote in

2023, an "unusually lonely form of grief" that ends up being a "baffling experience of losing something that could have been but never was."[6] That is so heartbreakingly true, to miss something that hadn't existed.

My last round of IVF I've since come to refer to as my Wimbledon breakdown. Tennis players Rafael Nadal and Thomaz Bellucci were doing a changeover during their first-round match at Wimbledon in 2015 when I felt my phone buzz in my pocket. When I saw it was Dr. Matthews, I jumped out of my seat and raced down some cement stairs, hoping for good news. As tennis fans mingled around in the entrails of Court No. 1, I listened as Dr. Matthews—her Northern Irish lilt cheerful as ever—told me that it might be time to stop doing IVF. The next day was my embryo transfer, and if it didn't work, she said, "I think we need to accept that you have unexplained infertility."[7] As the crowd broke into a rapturous applause over some magical point that Rafa had made on the court, I quietly sobbed in the corner under the cement stairwell. Two weeks later, I took a pregnancy test. It was, of course, glaringly negative.

After being told I could not bear children, my husband and I briefly delved into adoption. A few years earlier when I was still single, I had looked into adopting in part because way back in 2001, I had spent a month volunteering in a state care home in Yaroslavl, Russia. The children ranged from the ages of seven to eighteen, and the experience had been very formative for me. Ever since then the idea of adopting a baby had been something in the back of my mind. But I also understood from my experience in Russia that I didn't have the required skill set to take on an older child because of the complex psychological issues that many of them face.

And so, when I looked at adopting in Britain, I was put off

because most children who come up for adoption are at least toddlers. That meant that they had already been shuttled through the foster care system in their short lives. I also found out through an information seminar I attended for prospective adoptive parents that even though your child lived with you before the adoption was finalized, it could take upwards of a year. That meant that I couldn't travel abroad with the child unless I got the biological parents' permission. So not only could I not take the child on work trips abroad with me but, more importantly, if something happened to my mother or brothers back in the US and I needed to be there for an extended time, it would be a logistical fiasco. When I presented my husband with that option, he was not keen on that either.

We then looked at third country adoption, meaning that though we both resided in Britain—I am a dual US/British citizen while my now ex-husband is Serbian—we would adopt a child from another country. However, I quickly learned that it would be complicated. With this information at hand, we decided adopting from another country would likely be a paper trail of tears. Plus, we already had my five frozen eggs and a few remaining embryos left that we had also frozen right before we got married. It seemed a waste not to continue the painful yet well-trodden assisted reproduction path.

That led us to surrogacy, something I never thought could be an option until our options ran out. All my family and most of my friends were very supportive of our decision. One even said, "Didn't Phoebe on *Friends* have a baby for her brother?" (Yes, she did. Twins in fact.) However, a few of my friends who had children made comments that not only rankled me but hurt me very much as well. Instead of being intrigued and excited about the idea of surrogacy, they told me how expensive surrogacy was going to be and that I should instead look at adoption. (Adoption, of course, can also be a costly and long process.) They offhandedly made adoption—such a complicated process—sound like it was so easy. One friend, who had several children, even told me that since adoption wasn't something we wished to pursue, maybe I wasn't meant to be a mother. I was incredulous and deeply offended, later kvetching to my mother that it was easy to make a throwaway comment like that when you had no trouble getting pregnant and it all happened for free.

What little I knew about surrogacy was through celebrity magazines, actors and billionaires who did photospreads with their expanded families. That implied to me that surrogacy was only open to super wealthy well-connected people. That stereotype is something that I quickly learned is far from being the case. (And one I hope this book will help to smash.) I also had seen a few television shows like *The New Normal* and movies like *Baby Mama* that had surrogacy plots, which are based on more fiction than fact. I didn't think much about it at the time, but pop culture and the media have negatively helped to typecast surrogacy and surrogates. Surrogacy seemed to me like complicated uncharted waters.

I didn't even know where to begin. But with a little sleuthing on the internet, I started investigating the practicalities of what surrogacy meant. First, I learned that to this day, surrogacy remains the most controversial of all fertility treatments.[8] Even the word surrogacy is considered by some to be problematic because it suggests that the surrogate is a substitute or replacement.[9] Secondly, I had to familiarize myself with the different terminologies and definitions. I found that there are two kinds of surrogates: traditional (sometimes called genetic) and gestational. Traditional surrogacy is where the egg also comes from the carrier, while a gestational surrogate refers to a woman who is pregnant with a baby that is not genetically hers.

Surrogacy can be either compensated—meaning that the surrogate receives payment for carrying the pregnancy—or it can be non-compensated, a term that implies that a surrogate is doing a philanthropic pregnancy. (Some call this type of surrogacy "altruistic" but as many will point out, the antonym of that word is selfish and surrogacy carriers, no matter if they are compensated or not, are anything but selfish.) However, in the vast number of non-compensated cases, surrogates do still receive some kind of financial benefit. Whatever the type of surrogacy, it often involves a third party like an agency or a clinic, as well as other specialists such as doctors, lawyers, social workers, and psychologists.

Cross-border surrogacy, which in most cases tends to be compensated, is where an intended parent (IP) goes to another country to pursue surrogacy. This is either because surrogacy isn't allowed in their country (for example, in France, Germany, and Italy) or it's less expensive than in their home country where it's legal (like in the US) or it's legal in their home country but because of their sexual orientation, they have to travel abroad for surrogacy (like in Russia). Some countries where cross-border surrogacy takes place—provinces in Canada being an example—have specific laws that address the practice. Other countries like Ghana, Northern Cyprus, and Colombia don't (yet) have laws but they are places where there has been an uptick in cross-border surrogacy births.

While non-compensated surrogacy is allowed in Britain for its citizens, we decided that it made the most sense to do it in the United States. That was in part because it seemed like they had the most practical laws in place, though I would later learn that surrogacy is legislated by state—versus federal—laws. Being

American, it also helped that there weren't any cultural issues to contend with. I then needed to find an agency considered to be great not only by IPs but also by carriers. Though I had yet to consider all the ethical and legal arguments around surrogacy, it was certainly important for us that whichever surrogate we agreed to work with would need to be very confident, comfortable, and not conflicted with her decision to carry our baby.

A few hours after Ransom and Lexie were born, and once my husband had arrived at the hospital, we wheeled the twins in to see our surrogate Julie. She'd been suffering from a bad sinus infection for the last few weeks and plus it looked like she'd had a clot in her leg (it's one of the common side effects of a multiple pregnancy as well as anemia, gestational diabetes, and high blood pressure).

Lying in her hospital bed drinking water from a straw, she rightly looked pale and exhausted.

We bantered a bit with Chad—her good-natured and kind husband who always seemed upbeat—but we noticed that Julie was fading fast from exhaustion. It was, for sure, an odd experience to bring in my twins to see this woman who had carried, and cared, for them for nine months. They had been her physical responsibility all that time. I had entrusted them to her body, but now they were forever in my charge.

It was, to say the least, a unique changing of the guard.

Chapter Two

A Brief History of the (Surrogacy) World

There might not be a more awkward date in the world than meeting your potential surrogate for the first time.

At least that was what my husband and I felt right before our video chat with Julie and Chad on a Sunday afternoon in the middle of December 2015. One of the lawyers from Circle Surrogacy had sent us an email earlier that morning saying, *"I know you must have some feelings of nervousness and anxiety and I promise that once the conversation gets going, everything will feel much more natural."* I had a good chortle over that line because none of the process up to this point had felt natural in the slightest.

A few months earlier we had signed on with Circle, a Boston-based agency that was also a law firm handling surrogacy match-ups and legal contracts. The reason that we had chosen Circle in the first place was when I was doing research into US agencies, they had received high marks not only from IPs but from surrogates as well. That was important to me because of course an agency—pre-COVID-19 there were an estimated four hundred in the US—was going to treat the intended parents well, as they were the paying clients. But how the carriers were treated was even more telling as that helped show me the ethos and integrity of the agency. Circle had scored well on a few surrogate internet forums I found, including Surrogate Mothers Online (SMO), so I reached out to them.

After a very uplifting video interview with the founders John Weltman and his then-husband Cliff Atkins—the first gay men in the US to become parents through surrogacy—we decided to work with them. We then had to go through reams of paperwork including background and credit checks, speak with a social worker, and send over our medical histories. We also had to get my eggs (those "in case of emergency" ones I had frozen when I was 39) and our two embryos from London over to a clinic in the US.

John had recommended the Pacific Fertility Center (PFC) in Los Angeles, run by Dr. Vicken Sahakian, in part because they were quite cost effective. This was a big consideration as we were going to use a good portion of our savings to afford our surrogacy journey. Dr. Sahakian was a straight shooter, something at first I was taken aback by but later learned to really appreciate. We also had to write a heartfelt letter to our potential surrogate explaining why we had decided to go down the surrogacy path.

The letter started out explaining how my husband and I had met and then went on to discuss our IVF anguish:

> I assumed, once [we] started proper IVF in the autumn of 2014, that I would get pregnant, no problem. We couldn't get pregnant naturally (with help from IVF meds) and in October of 2014, right before our wedding, we did another round of IVF and froze six embryos. I had two put back

in in February 2015, but they did not take, and we put two more in in April. They also did not take. In July, after my doctor put me through temporary menopause for two months to try and stabilize my hormones, we did a fresh transfer of one. That, sadly, did not take either. We sat down with my doctor, and she told us the heartbreaking news—she thought my womb was "inhospitable" and that it looked like I was not able to get pregnant and carry a baby to term.

To say we were devastated would be putting it mildly... I spent a good portion of the summer of 2015 trying to mentally heal from the news. Ever since I was little, I always knew I wanted to have a child. And [my husband] was the same... I adore my nephews, my godchildren and my friends' children, and [my husband] is beloved by pretty much any child who meets him. To be told we could not conceive a baby was one of life's toughest blows. But we started investigating options [and] surrogacy, something we knew about only in passing, became an idea.

Being a journalist, I researched all aspects of surrogacy—from the clinics to the statistics and even the social attitudes to surrogacy (several of our friends, when we told them we were thinking of surrogacy, said "oh, like Sarah Jessica Parker and Nicole Kidman?")... In the end, [we] decided surrogacy was the route we wanted to take on the journey to becoming parents... To complete our family, we would love a child (or two) of our own. When I moved into this house (I was still single when I bought it), I even had a room decorated with a child in mind. The room is ready; we just need a gorgeous, cuddly, delicious baby to put in there.

Matching IPs to surrogates is the primary activity of an agency, and while some agencies have password-protected websites where intended parents can scroll through potential surrogates by themselves, Circle would whittle down our choices for us. There are, of course, a number of ethical quandaries that surrogacy flags (more on this later) and we had discussed a number of them with John and Cliff. For example, they needed to know where we stood on things like selective reduction and genetic testing.

But they also asked us to consider what our expectations were not only in terms of the relationship we would have with the surrogate and her family but also who she was as a person. At first, we didn't really get what they meant since she was going to be a gestational carrier so it's not like it mattered if, for example, she had blonde hair or blue eyes. So, what exactly should we be looking for? Would it matter what her thoughts were on politics? What books did she like to read? What food did she like to eat? Just what exactly was it we were supposed to be looking for?

As luck would have it, I'm very close with a gay middle-class Israeli couple, Ben Peter and Offir Dagan, who worked with an Oregon-based carrier for their surrogacy (their twins were born about fourteen months before Ransom and Lexie). They had cobbled together their savings and done some refinancing, their argument being that instead of saving money to buy a bigger flat, they'd rather hear children's giggles bouncing around their current one. With their usual wit, thoughtfulness, and panache, they interpreted exactly what John and Cliff had meant: you wanted a surrogate that you got along with (obviously) and a similar sense of humor was a bonus.

But you also wanted someone who had some parallel values and beliefs when it came to health and well-being. They, for example, found it imperative that they find a surrogate who didn't eat junk food. As a couple who loves an occasional Quarter Pounder from McDonald's, that wasn't an essential for us. Ben and Offir also wanted to have regular, consistent interaction with their surrogate throughout the pregnancy. Ben told me that you also just had to get that good feeling in your gut that you liked and trusted her. There was something of chemistry to it, they said, not unlike dating.

Dr. Elly Teman, an Israeli American medical anthropologist who has done fieldwork with Israeli surrogates for over two decades, also found that to be the case. Intended mothers she interviewed were "intuitively aware" from the moment they started their search that they needed to find someone who they could closely identify with and who they saw had the potential for a friendly, comfortable, and even intimate relationship. Intended mothers relied mostly on their physical and emotional instincts in choosing who they wanted to have be their surrogate. Just as Ben and Offir had used the word "chemistry" to describe their connection to their surrogate, Israeli surrogates told Dr. Teman that was also how they'd describe what they were looking for with potential intended parents. Sometimes the intended mother and the surrogate both spoke of how they were "destined" to work together.[10] This was all helpful advice that guided our decision.

We wanted to be in good communication with our surrogate, but we didn't feel the necessity to be in constant contact, and we wanted to trust her to be proactive about her health and the health of the baby or babies. I place a heavy value on education, and I was keen to have someone who had some level of higher education, believing she might be more proactive about certain things during the pregnancy. I also very much wanted her to have thought, discussed, and read about the ethical arguments around surrogacy. That was not only from a perspective of curiosity. It was also important for me that our carrier understood and was equipped to deal with the very likely contentious conversations she might have with friends, family, and colleagues when they found out she was a surrogate.

During our video blind date with Julie and Chad, we discussed all of these things. After some initial awkwardness, just as the lawyer had predicted, we then started to get down to brass tacks. Both Julie and Chad were in their early thirties, they had both been married before and between them they had five children. Both had graduate degrees in business and Julie worked as the executive director of a non-profit housing organization. This was, of course, all contrary to the stereotypes of American surrogates that have long been played out in popular culture and media, that of women who are desperate for money and turn to surrogacy as a last-ditch attempt to pay their rent.

Those against surrogacy have long warned that poor women of color would be taken advantage of by wealthy white heterosexual couples desperate to have a child. "What we learn from experience today is that a lot of [US] surrogates are white and tend to be lower middle class, so empirically this has not held true," said Sital Kalantry, who at the time of our interview was a law professor at Cornell University and has written extensively on surrogacy in both the US and India.

Part of that firsthand research comes from academics like Dr. Zsuzsa Berend, a sociology professor at the University of California, Los Angeles (UCLA) and author of *The Online World of Surrogacy*. What she found in doing extensive research on the once-popular web forum SMO—the place I had initially done research about Circle—was that an entirely different picture emerged through polls, stories, and conversations. Almost all American surrogates were white, and their age ranged from their mid-twenties to late thirties. The majority of women were Christian, yet they were "strikingly liberal" on gay issues. "There are many stay-at-home mothers," Dr. Berend wrote in her book, "but the majority work full-time as nurses, teachers, doulas, lab technicians, dispatchers, legal and accounting assistants, paralegals, information technology managers, account managers, office managers, software testers, and massage therapists." A small number of them ran their own businesses.

Of the women that she corresponded with through the forum, all of them considered themselves to be middle class. Informal polls found that most women stated that their family income exceeded $40,000 (excluding surrogacy compensation) and that they had more than a high school degree. Dr. Berend found that while none of the polls were statistically rigorous and that it was impossible to know how many surrogates had responded, "the many polls and posts I have read over a decade in which women discuss their lives, as well as women's writing style and their attention to spelling and grammar, indicate lower-middle to middle-class status, not lower class and financial desperation, as many critics assumed."[11]

This was similar to what another sociologist, Dr. Heather Jacobson, found in research for her book *Labor of Love: Gestational Surrogacy and the Work of Making Babies*. Most American surrogates she interviewed defined themselves as non-Hispanic Caucasians, therefore making surrogacy mostly the terrain of white women. "There was a variety," Dr. Jacobson told me in terms of their financial and class backgrounds. "Some women even came from the professional middle class, whose husbands, for example, were physicians."

Meanwhile in Britain, Paul Morgan-Bentley, the head of

investigations at the *London Times* and author of *The Equal Parent: How Sharing the Load Helps the Whole Family Thrive*, who along with his husband became parents through surrogacy in March 2020, told me that surrogate stereotypes were completely off. He said that at SurrogacyUK events, the not-for-profit organization they worked with, there were a range of women who were surrogates. The sister of one of his colleagues at the *Times*, who is a political writer and "very posh English," is a surrogate and "there are lawyers who have been surrogates, there are academics, people from all walks of life."

That, however, didn't mean there wasn't still quite a big divide between gestational carriers and their IPs. While American surrogates may be middle class, they may be carrying babies for very wealthy couples and those differences sometimes can feel quite incongruous. Dr. Jacobson found that many American surrogates quickly discovered they had little in common with their intended parents outside of their surrogacy relationship. "Differences in social class played a role in that disconnect," she writes. "Though there were several surrogates in my sample who indicated they had similar means as their IPs, most who discussed this topic with me said that their IPs had considerably higher socioeconomic status than they did."[12]

A number of surrogates told her that had it not been for surrogacy, they would have never had reason to interact with their intended parents because they ran in different social circles. This was something Julie told me too when I later interviewed her for this book. "There are people that you meet in life and you're like 'Oh, we are never going to be friends' and there are other people that you meet in life and you are like 'I appreciate people I can be friendly with but I don't have to maintain [the friendship],'" she said to me when I asked her about how she felt after meeting us on that initial video call. "I also kind of had to wrap my head around that, like, you wanting to know me is, sure, us but without your children, we would never have ever for any reason met."

During our initial video chat, which ended up lasting for about two hours once we met their children and we introduced them to our two Labradors, Julie told us she wanted to do surrogacy for a few reasons. One was that Julie, who was originally from Michigan, had a friend from high school who lost her ovaries to cancer. "And as a junior in high school, you don't usually have to think about the fact that you aren't going to be able to have kids," she told us. Julie admitted it was something that stuck with her, this idea of a woman not being able to have children. "Being a mom," she told us, "is one of the things that defines me." In addition, before she started going out with Chad—who had gone to college in Michigan (so this was starting to feel destined!)—she dated a man whose sister had had twins via surrogacy. The two women spoke a few times about that experience and that had also had a profound effect on Julie's thinking.

Julie, it turns out, was not unique in terms of her reasons to become a surrogate. Dr. Jacobson found that one-third of the women she spoke to said that their interest was sparked by seeing family, friends, or co-workers suffer the pain of infertility.[13] Empirical research has found that, at least in Western countries, women also decide to become surrogates because of the desire to do something special and the enjoyment of being pregnant.[14] Kim Kluger-Bell, a psychotherapist who does fertility consulting for a number of clinics in the US, told me that a lot of surrogates "almost feel like it is a calling for them."

Meanwhile, this was something that Israeli surrogate Orit Chorowicz Bar-Am, a children's education specialist, found too among other Israeli carriers that she has corresponded with over the years. While being a surrogate was not any kind of dream of hers, like a large number of other surrogates globally, she truly relished being pregnant (she has two young boys). Orit liked the actual giving birth part as well. "That's what made me think that I have a special quality, a special skill," she said. Though Orit and her husband, a children's theatre director, did not want more kids, she really craved the idea of being pregnant again. "It was very clear to me," she said, "I wanted to experience it another time."

There is a perception that to admit to enjoying being pregnant is odd but to be pregnant for someone else is downright nuts. Many people are befuddled that anyone would want to carry a child for another person, especially if they're strangers. "It's not only about the idea of giving birth to a child and then that child being raised by someone else," Dr. Jacobson told me, "but it's about the process of pregnancy." This is something that's quite difficult for many people to wrap their heads around, this idea that pregnancy and childbirth can be a satisfying experience that many women desire to do again. "I think," she told me, "that is really hard for a lot of people, especially for women."

Julie had told us that her enjoyment of pregnancy was a reason that she wanted to be a surrogate. She'd once had an interesting conversation with a fellow mom where they both admitted to each other how much they had loved being pregnant. Julie asked the other mom that if that were the case and she could help another woman become a mother, why not do surrogacy? "She told me she would never be able to 'let the child go,'" Julie said. "That stuck with me, and I was like, 'No, I do not think I would have that trouble. I don't think that I would be as emotionally attached.' So, I think a surrogate has to have the right personality."

Dr. Teman wrote in an essay on surrogacy that: "Beyond the ambiguity that surrogacy introduces to the concept of 'motherhood', it also starkly reveals that our perceptions of motherhood are socially constructed." She goes on to say that surrogacy exposes a strong assumption in Western culture that women "naturally develop" instinctive bonds of love for babies that they carry and, "that they won't want to give those babies away unless they are desperate for money, forced to do it by their partners, or out of their minds."[15]

That concept of crazy was something that some early psychosocial studies hypothesized and implied; that women who chose to become surrogates were non-traditional thinkers or somehow different from the majority of the population.[16] There is still an assumption by many that women become surrogates out of desperation, force, or mental instability. That's likely in part, again, because of how surrogates are portrayed in films and on television. Lifetime, an American cable channel, for example, has something of an obsession with surrogacy, making films including *The Sinister Surrogate, Sorority Surrogate, The Secret Life of a Celebrity Surrogate, The Baby Swindler* and *The Surrogacy Trap.*

Yet despite all these presumptions, nearly all the studies have concluded that surrogates are not markedly different by any measure to other women and that most are within what psychologists consider "the normal range" of psychological stability, intelligence, and moral standards.[17] They also found that the majority of surrogates actually subscribe to conventional beliefs about gender roles and motherhood and are ardent subscribers to conservative values of having children and being good wives and mothers.[18] When it came to the tricky conversations around attachment to the surro-babies they carried, a number of women in Dr. Berend's study—who might have taglines on their messages like "I'm not the mom, I'm just the stork" or "Their bun, my oven"—said they viewed surrogacy as nine months of intensive babysitting. "I think how they formulated what [surrogacy] is was partly to convince themselves and find a way to talk about it that was easy," Dr. Berend told me.

She said that during her several years researching the SMO message boards, the term "babysitting" developed and grew to become how many of the women described their pregnancies. Interestingly, that was exactly the term that British surrogate Sarah Jones, the director of SurrogacyUK, used when describing her numerous experiences as both a traditional and gestational surrogate. "You either want us weeping over the loss of 'our' baby or cold and heartless, there is no middle ground, there is no way you can love something but not want to keep it," she told me with more than a hint of sarcasm. As a child care provider two days a week for ten hours a day, Ms. Jones has looked after numerous children who are now in early primary school. "Now, it's the same as me stuck in the doorstep when the parent comes to pick them up going, 'No, quite like this one. Now I am going to keep this one,'" she joked. "You can care for a child and love a child and be willing to step in front of traffic for them but not have a maternal bond."

The surrogates that I spoke to for this book not only had the traits of enjoying pregnancy and wanting to do something for someone else, but they also all struck me as being very confident and quite proud that they liked to think outside the box on some things. They weren't lemmings and they were proud of that fact. "Being a surrogate was new ground, it was something that not everyone does, it was something unique," Julie told me when I interviewed her for this book almost five years after our initial meeting. "Now, I won't compare your kids to a car, but I just bought a Maserati. I am only one of ten people in town that have a Maserati and I am the only one who has a Maserati of my type.

I like doing things that are a little bit unexpected. Being a surrogate fit my personality."

Dr. Jacobson confirmed this, finding that many surrogates thrive on the idea of doing something that is seen as not the norm. She writes that they "celebrate their participation" in defying the status quo, and for some surrogates that is done through helping gay couples become parents.[19] In fact, some surrogates only want to work with gay men because they find the relationship to be a lot less stressful because they are seen to come with a lot less baggage. There is not an aura of failure and sadness that many intended mothers come with, be it their infertility or health issues in the past that prevent them from being able to carry a baby. "[Intended mothers] have gone through years of torture by the time they [decide on surrogacy] and gay men, it is so uncomplicated and such happy news," Leslie Morgan Steiner, the author of *The Baby Chase*, told me. "They feel like the surrogate is a goddess, not a competitor, and so it is much easier for gay men, definitely."

There are even some agencies, especially in California, that specialize in working exclusively with gay couples.[20] Minnesota surrogate Briana Mohler, who was thrice the surrogate for Nir Segal and Or Ben-Ezra Segal, another gay middle-class Israeli couple I am friendly with, told me that when she was researching whether to become a surrogate, she made the decision that she only wanted to work with a gay couple.[21] "One of the things that I read over and over again—and maybe it's true, maybe it's not—but sometimes it's hard for the surrogate and the intended mother to bond," she said. "Maybe I would be able to meet a heterosexual couple where that wasn't the view. Or she was just welcoming with open arms but then who knows what could really happen after the baby is born? I just wasn't willing to risk even going down that path with the possibility that it could end in the way of like, 'now the baby's here [don't contact us].'"

Nir, who is a London-based artist, even invited Briana to Israel after their first daughter was born to discuss their relationship during an artist talk at a gallery in Tel Aviv. Her views of wanting to work exclusively with a gay couple created a lot of discussion, and afterwards Nir spoke with a number of women considering surrogacy. "I have said to them, 'it could be something really beautiful and the fact that you cannot get pregnant doesn't mean you don't get to experience something very wonderful and enriching and empowering as a woman,'" he told me as he took a side glance at the baby monitor to make sure their second daughter, born in 2020 during COVID-19, was napping. "A surrogate doesn't come to take something away from you, she comes to enable something in you."

Media stories and pop culture, of course, have also played a factor in why some women decide to become surrogates. (They are likely not watching those terrible Lifetime films.) From Kim Kardashian's surrogacy journey on the reality show *Keeping Up with the Kardashians* to segments on programs like *Oprah* and celebrities talking about their surrogacy journeys in glossy magazines, there's evidence this also plays a role in recruiting surrogates.[22] Evan Ryan, who had two children from different surrogates, told me that their first surrogate became a gestational carrier because of the reality television show *Giuliana & Bill*. The couple—Giuliana Rancic is a celebrity television host and Bill, her husband, is an entrepreneur—chronicled their struggles to have a child on the show. That touched a nerve with Evan's California-based surrogate, making her want to do something similar for another couple. "I almost burst into tears because all I thought was 'I am sitting here with a baby about to be born and now I know it's because of Giuliana and Bill,'" said Evan, the White House cabinet secretary for President Joe Biden; her husband, Antony Blinken, has served as secretary of state under President Biden. "So, it's amazing to me, the power of media."

During much of that initial video conversation with Julie and Chad, I kept talking and babbling, something my husband called me out on a few times. That eventually gave way to some light-hearted banter between all of us. We also talked about the potential issues surrogacy could pose for their families, as I got the impression they had come from somewhat conservative and religious backgrounds. They said it was something they had spent a lot of time talking about and that this was a decision between the two of them and their children. That was all the support they required, as I found out later neither of their mothers were on board with the decision. As we got off the call, I turned to my husband saying, "Oh, I really like them!" Luckily it turned out they liked us too.

My email to them a few days later showed our excitement:

Just wanted to drop a quick note to say we are so pleased (or "chuffed" as the Brits say) that you have decided to be our surrogate.

It's quite funny as I have told a few friends that we have found our surrogates and they keep asking why I am saying it in plural—I guess because I view you as both our surrogates, because you are both doing this together and are on this journey with us. I know it may sound cheesy but I cannot find the words (ha—surprising!) to say how pleased [we both] are.

I am not sure how all this contact works in the beginning, as we are all on a learning curve here. But as [we] stated on

Sunday, we want you both to lead initially on this. We are happy to do as much or as little as you feel you want and need. We are happy to come to whatever appointments you would like us to go to [and] we know you are very busy with jobs, children, marriage, and life in general and don't want to get in the way. So please let us know what your expectations are, and we can go forward.

We then started contract negotiations. To make sure I was equipped in terms of what was in the contract and how this all would look, I started reading a bit more online about surrogacy across the globe. In 1981 when surrogacy was entirely traditional, an estimated one hundred babies were born through surrogacy in the US. By 1986 that number had only risen to approximately five hundred.[23] According to the U.S. Centers for Disease Control and Prevention (CDC) a reported 1,210 attempts of gestational surrogacy were made in 2000, double the number that had been attempted just three years before. Those numbers quadrupled in the early part of the twenty-first century, with the CDC reporting that in the US alone between 1999 and 2013 there were more than 18,000 births through surrogacy arrangements. However, at 2 percent, surrogacy made up only a miniscule part of total assisted reproduction cycles in those years.

There are estimates now that each year in the US about 2,000 babies are born from surrogacy arrangements.[24] John Weltman, who said it took twenty years for Circle to reach 1,000 births but only five years to then double that number, believes that CDC's calculations are much lower than reality because in the US, agencies, doctors, and clinics don't have to report their numbers to any central authority. There is no federal regulating or monitoring of surrogacy in the US and while there are ethical guidelines for practitioners put out by the American Society of Reproductive Medicine (ASRM), compliance is not mandatory.[25] And because birth certificates are not required to list a baby's genetics (nor who gave birth to the child), babies born to surrogates are not typically registered as surrogate births in the US.[26] (That, however, is not the case in countries like Britain.) "Worldwide, those numbers are significantly higher," John told me. "And whatever numbers you see aren't going to be accurate." According to Global Market Insights, a market research consultancy, the global surrogacy industry was worth an estimated $14 billion in 2022. Estimates are that by 2032, that will rise to $129 billion, due to increasing infertility and same-sex couples opting to use surrogacy to grow their families.

Surrogacy, of course, isn't just a modern concept, as it dates all the way back to Biblical times. In the Book of Genesis, Sarah tells Abraham that "the Lord has prevented me from bearing children" and tells her eighty-six-year-old husband to go to her Egyptian maid, Hagar, because "it may be that I shall obtain children from her." Their son, Ishmael, is the first recorded child born via a traditional surrogate. Meanwhile in Hinduism, Krishna—one of the religion's main gods—had a brother, Balaram, born from a surrogate.[27] Throughout further centuries, infertile couples turned to traditional surrogacy in order to have children and there were rumors that in twelfth-century Spain, at least one of the kings used surrogates so he could have a biological heir. (In 1988 all surrogacy was banned in Spain.) These days, however, the American Bar Association (ABA) strictly defines all assisted reproduction—including surrogacy—as, "a method of causing pregnancy through means other than sexual intercourse." So, by these new definitions, Hagar today wouldn't be considered a surrogate.

With the advent of artificial insemination—with the first medical journal report[28] of a successful if ethically corrupt case taking place in Philadelphia in 1884 when an anesthetized married woman was unknowingly impregnated via rubber syringe with the sperm of a medical student during what she thought was a routine gynecological examination[29]—by the 1970s huge leaps and bounds were being made through assisted reproductive technologies (ART). Plus, opinion around infertility was also changing. According to a 1969 Harris poll, a majority of Americans felt that IVF was "against God's will" and the American Medical Association (AMA) in 1972 encouraged a moratorium on all IVF research.[30]

However, two years after the first formal surrogacy agreement was brokered in 1976 by Noel P. Keane—a Dearborn, Michigan-based lawyer who played a key role in surrogacy's history—opinion started to change after the birth in Britain of Louise Brown in 1978. Successfully orchestrated by Dr. Patrick Steptoe and Dr. Robert Edwards, she was the world's first baby born from in-vitro fertilization, which literally means "in glass" as it refers to the biological process of making babies outside the body in a petri dish or glass tube.[31] Hence, Louise was dubbed a "test tube" baby, a term that's rarely used anymore.

Her mere existence was proof that there were alternative ways to conceive a child and her birth brought hope to millions of infertile couples across the globe. Six months after she was born, a new survey was conducted about IVF. Its findings were that more than 60 percent of Americans now supported it. A year later, the United States' National Institutes of Health (NIH) allowed federal funding for IVF research. These shifts in attitudes toward ART, along with a rising number of women entering the workforce and waiting to have children "led to a perfect storm" in the late 1970s that saw the explosion of medical treatment for infertility.[32] Medical visits for infertility tripled from 600,000 in 1968 to more than 1.6 million in 1984, and the use of assisted reproduction rose from nearly 60,000 cycles in 1995 to over 160,000 by 2011.[33]

Today, it's estimated that more than twelve million people on the planet were born through IVF.[34] In Denmark, IVF accounts for 9 percent of live births, the highest proportion for any country, while the average number of cycles undergone per woman is in Israel. Both countries make IVF widely available and almost free.[35] However, for most of the rest of the world, most couples cannot afford IVF. In lower-income countries, a single round of IVF costs between 50 percent and 200 percent of a couple's annual income.[36] In the US, couples whose insurance doesn't cover fertility treatments like IVF, can expect to pay an average of $20,000 a cycle.[37]

Since that first contract back in 1976, Mr. Keane, seeing the commercial potential of surrogacy, assumed the role of broker between IPs and surrogates, placing advertisements in Michigan newspapers offering traditional surrogates a fee. (A number of newspapers refused to place his advertisements because they were worried about the appropriateness of it all while others ran editorials describing him as a charlatan and a baby-trader.)[38] This essentially launched a market "searching for a supply [of surrogates] to meet the demand" that was glaringly apparent.[39] "Thank you, Noel Keane," John Weltman told me sarcastically. "That schlockmeister of surrogacy, it's absolutely frightening what he did. Don't just look at Baby M, there are tons of cases that involve Noel Keane and the horrors that he committed."

The infamous case that John was referring to was that of Bill and Betsy Stern. They were an upper-middle-class New Jersey couple who, via a contract drawn up by Mr. Keane, secured Mary Beth Whitehead, a high school dropout married to a garbage collector, to be their traditional surrogate for $10,000. When the child, a girl called Melissa ("Baby M"), was born in 1986 and Ms. Whitehead was to sign over her parental rights, she refused and ran off to Florida where she hid out for almost three months with the baby. A protracted custody battle ensued, something that I very much remember hearing and reading about in the news as a teenager. My former *Newsweek* colleague Barbara Kantrowitz wrote a cover story for the magazine when the legal battle first began. "A lot of it was a class issue," she told me, recalling that there was much reluctance by the editors to even do the story. "I remember what concerned me the most, and I hope I got that out in the story, was 'are we headed for a future where rich women pay poor women to have their babies?' It felt like science fiction."

In the end, the New Jersey Supreme Court ruled in 1988 that the surrogacy agreement between the couple and Ms. Whitehead was illegal, and her parental rights were reinstated. However, full custody was granted to Mr. Stern with Ms. Whitehead having visitation rights until Melissa was eighteen. According to the *New York Times*, when Melissa did come of age, she then terminated her legal relationship with Mary Beth Whitehead and Mrs. Stern adopted her. After graduating from George Washington University in Washington, DC, Melissa went on to obtain a master's degree at King's College London, whereas of 2020 she was still living with her husband and young daughter. I did reach out to her for an interview, especially as it related to her graduate thesis from King's entitled *Reviving Solomon: Modern Day Questions Regarding the Long-term Implications for the Children of Surrogacy Arrangements*, but I never received a reply.

What made traditional surrogacy so complicated and compromised was that the surrogate was also the genetic mother of the child. This asymmetry made surrogacy a potential ethical and legal calamity because the surrogate had a greater claim on the child than the intended mother.[40] Until the Baby M case, because traditional surrogacy—in a sense—resembled traditional adoption, many legal experts approached the arrangements as such. "Adoption was a known legal quantity; surrogacy was not," wrote Dr. Jacobson. Adoption, therefore, was used as the "legal model for surrogacy because initially there were no state laws, regulations, or litigation precedents" that governed surrogacy arrangements.[41] The Baby M case marked a major turning point in the history of surrogacy in the US not only because of these ethical quagmires it exposed but also it coincided with the beginning of the (mostly) end of traditional surrogacy in the country.

In 1985, a South African-born Cleveland-based gynecologist and reproductive endocrinologist named Dr. Wulf Utian wrote a letter in the *New England Journal of Medicine*. In it, he stated that he had created a baby using a surrogate's uterus, another woman's egg, and her husband's sperm.[42] Before he fell out with the Apartheid government back home, Dr. Utian had been doing most of his research in menopause, being the first to describe way back in 1967 that it was a health-related issue. Dr. Utian told me that because he happened to work at the same hospital in Cape Town as Christiaan Barnard—the first doctor to do a human-to-human heart transplant—Dr. Utian, and his research, benefitted from all the research money the hospital started receiving after that successful surgery. When he arrived in Cleveland in the mid-1970s, Dr. Utian helped to set up a fertility clinic at Mt. Sinai Hospital, which became one of the most successful fertility clinics running in an academic center in the country.

Meanwhile, in 1982 Dr. Elliot Rudnitzky, a New Jersey-based cardiologist, and his wife, Sandye, who had abscesses on her fallopian tubes, had traveled to Britain's Bourn Hall, the clinic that was founded by Dr. Steptoe and Dr. Edwards, for IVF treatment. After treatment there, Sandye got pregnant, and all was going well until the seventh month when she had to have an emergency Caesarean hysterectomy. The baby, Heather, died thirteen days later.[43] A few months after that tragic loss, Dr. Rudnitzky had an epiphany. His wife still had functioning ovaries so he suggested to her that they could create an embryo through IVF and have a surrogate carry the baby. Sandye's reply was, "What doctor would even attempt this?"

"And out of the blue one day I got a phone call from a cardiologist, Elliot Rudnitzky, from New Jersey," Dr. Utian told me in a Zoom call from South Africa where he now spends some of his retirement. "And he said, 'I will be honest with you, you are "U" in the alphabet, so you are the fifth person I am calling.'" Dr. Utian quipped back, "It's unusual for a cardiologist to propose advancement in the field of obstetrics."[44] Dr. Utian thought about the proposition. He had been so close to being the first in the race to create the first IVF baby in the 1970s but, with the birth of Louise Brown, Dr. Steptoe and Dr. Edwards had won it in the end. (In November 2024, a new biopic about the two extraordinary reproductive medicine pioneers was released on Netflix, with Bill Nighy and James Norton starring.)

This proposition by Dr. Rudnitzky, thought Dr. Utian, could be the opportunity for a different kind of first in fertility health care. "It was being done on animals for years," said Dr. Utian about implanting embryos from one to another, "so it was not a unique concept." He told Dr. Rudnitzky that he was interested. But the hospital board said before they could proceed, Dr. Utian needed to get the permission of the local religious leaders, as the hospital had seen protests over their assisted reproduction work. "The rabbi, to my surprise, told us, 'You know it's written in the Torah be fruitful and multiply onto the land so therefore since you are helping people get pregnant, it's kosher,'" Dr. Utian said, adding that while the Catholic bishop never got back to him, years later the bishop's secretary became one of his patients.

In terms of a surrogate, Dr. Rudnitzky said they had a good friend who was willing to be their surrogate. However, she backed out. Not losing hope, Dr. Rudnitzky remembered having read about Noel Keane in a *People* magazine article. They reached out and Mr. Keane helped find them a carrier, who after a few failed attempts, walked away. Undaunted, Mr. Keane found Shannon, a mother of a three-year-old who lived in suburban Ann Arbor, who had previously been a traditional surrogate. The hospital, of course, required psychological screenings on both Shannon as well as Sandye and her husband. They also wanted airtight contracts that considered things from whether the surrogate should take prenatal vitamins to if there was a fetal anomaly, would the couple consider termination? "We actually fell out with Noel because we were very keen about certain rigid ethical issues," Dr. Utian said. "And with all due respect, he skirted to the edge of a lot of that stuff."

The seven-pound, three-ounce baby girl, Jillian Shira, was born in Ypsilanti, Michigan, in April 1986. She not only was the world's first baby born via a gestational carrier, but she was also the world's first baby where a judge ruled that the genetic mother, and not the surrogate, should be listed on the birth certificate. "I didn't have any law to go by," Judge Marianne Battani told me when I asked about her ruling. "It was mostly based on common sense to me. [And] I thought, 'Well, this is the way it is supposed to be.'"

The birth—and the court ruling—were watersheds in changing how surrogacy worked. "There was a lot of excitement from people because suddenly you had this whole group of women out there who had uterine abnormalities or recurrent miscarriages or other reasons why they couldn't carry a pregnancy but they still had eggs and ovaries," Dr. Utian told me, adding that he's still in touch with the Rudnitzkys and even attended her bat mitzvah.[45] "So I mean, we were inundated with phone calls." According to a 2016 CDC report, 95 percent of all surrogacies in the US now are via gestational carriers.

Jill Brand, as she now goes by, is married with her own children, lives in New York City, and is a marketing executive. She told me in her first ever interview, that there was "never a time" that she didn't know the story of her birth. "So, there are two parts of the story—there's my parents, what they went through, which is, to some extent, not my story to tell. I wasn't there," she said over a video call in 2021. "And then there's the part of the story of my own upbringing, which is more my story. But what may surprise you is while I've heard the story a billion times, I don't know all the details. And I think to some extent the story for me is equal parts amazing and beyond a miracle, and then equal parts just me, totally mundane. My parents had a quest to have a biological child and went through a lot of things to try to make that happen. My dad had this idea and sought out clinicians who could help them do it. And Dr. Utian had the guts, the gall, and the resolve to partner with them on it."

Until I started working on this book, I had no idea what a pivotal role my home state of Michigan played in not only the

Baby M case but in states' regulations on surrogacy. When my then-husband and I first started our surrogacy journey, I had originally hoped to find a surrogate in Michigan. The plan was that once the baby or babies were born, I would spend a few months at my mother's home in Michigan while we organized passports, vaccinations, and paperwork to bring our kids back to London.

But in 2015 when I initially asked Circle if they could find me a Michigan-based surrogate, I was told that my beloved state was, at the time, one of five states where surrogacy contracts were not legal (and recently, until the passage of the Michigan Family Protection Act, Michigan was the last holdout state to make surrogacy broadly illegal—but more on that in the final chapter). Since in the US surrogacy falls under both family and contract law, it's therefore regulated on the state versus the federal level. This is similar in Canada, Mexico, and Australia so, for example, in Australia's New South Wales it's been a criminal offense to enter into a compensated international surrogacy arrangement while in Victoria, their neighbor directly to the south, it's not.[46]

When we started doing the contract negotiations with Julie, I was floored that there was a specific clause in her Circle contract that stated she could not travel to Michigan after her first trimester. When I asked why, I was flummoxed by the response: in the Great Lakes State, surrogacy agreements were considered null and void. A party to a surrogacy contract was liable for a fine of up to $50,000 or imprisonment of up to five years.[47] Turns out, Michigan was the first state to broadly make surrogacy a felony way back in 1988.[48] The bill's sponsor, Republican State Senator Connie Binsfeld, who went on to become lieutenant governor, admitted that the legislation had been explicitly aimed at shutting down the Dearborn-based surrogacy agency run by Mr. Keane. "She spent most of her time in the legislature dealing with children's issues, she was kind of like the children's advocate," said Bill Kandler, a longtime Lansing lobbyist.

At the time, there was a lot of talk around the lack of any legislation covering issues related to surrogacy, and how the Baby M case had really opened a lot of legal and ethical cans of worms around not only surrogacy specifically but the ethics of fertility treatments in general. "Hardly anybody knew what IVF was, so [surrogacy] was really out there for people," said Mr. Kandler, who also for a time served as Governor James Blanchard's director of legislative affairs. "People were saying, 'You are kidding me? You can pay people to have a baby?' There was probably some individual who testified against the bill. But overall people were like 'Obviously we want to fix this, it's a disaster.'"

Governor Blanchard, a Democrat who as Michigan governor from 1983 to 1991, signed the 1988 bill into law, remembered just how controversial surrogacy was at the time. "Noel Keane was making money off of charging [people] to arrange a surrogate," he told me in a phone interview in 2022. "It was relatively new and got everybody upset." He added that the debate in the state at that time was very much one-sided. "I don't recall anybody lobbying me on it," he said. "I don't recall any letter writing. I don't remember any controversy over passing the bill or signing the bill or whether they should have a bill. I remember the controversy was all over Noel and making money off this." (Governor Blanchard, who went on to be appointed the ambassador to Canada by President Bill Clinton, told me that he even had friends who years later worked with a surrogate, though he did not say where they lived or where their surrogate was based. "And they had two kids and so they're quite happy about it," he said. "So obviously, it's been relatively popular since.")

In the end, the "Why and how?" behind the 1988 Surrogate Parenting Act was done to stop just one man from profiting from surrogacy contracts. Interestingly, this seems to have been something of a trend with lawmakers in Michigan in the late 1980s and early 1990s: creating legislation to dissuade individuals from taking advantage of loopholes where there was no law. "This law was aimed at Noel Keane doing surrogate [contracts] in Michigan [just as] the legislature passed the 1993 law that was aimed to stop Dr. Jack Kevorkian from doing doctor-assisted suicide in the state," said Robert A. Sedler, a retired Wayne State University law professor who also was one of three lawyers in 1992 who took the state to the Michigan Court of Appeals over the surrogate law.

On the Michigan Senate floor back in 1988, the roll call vote on the 1988 Surrogate Parenting Act was thirty yeas, six nays, two excused and one not voting. (I was pleased to see that Joe Conroy, my state senator at the time and also a family friend, was one of the six nays.) At the time of its signing, it was targeted at both potential surrogates as well as anyone who assisted in developing a compensated contract for surrogacy. When the bill became law, Mr. Keane—through both his Michigan and New York offices—had already handled about a third of the seven hundred or so surrogate arrangements that resulted in births in the US. At the time, Senator Binsfeld was quoted as saying that she hoped this would strongly discourage his operations in Michigan and that was the law's intent. "I think it will really curtail his business in Dearborn," she added. [49]

While it did restrict him doing surrogacy contracts in Michigan, the ambitious Mr. Keane—who loved both Irish music and his 1967 Mercedes convertible—just moved his practice to other states, setting up shell offices in Indiana, Nevada, and California. Dubbed by some as the father of surrogate parenting, he continued his work until his death from cancer in 1997 at the age of 58. He was and still remains, even in death, a controversial figure.

I tracked down one of Mr. Keane's sons, Christopher, a lawyer based in San Francisco, to ask him what he thought of his father's legacy. (Mr. Keane's other son, Douglas, who also lives in the Bay Area, won the 2013 season of the American television show *Top Chef Masters*.) Turns out Christopher and his dad practiced together for a few years in Dearborn and though Christopher never handled any of the surrogacy work—his focus was on child abuse cases—he's very proud of the role his father played in the history of surrogacy. I asked him how his father, who before that first contract in 1976 did mostly wills, divorces, and drunk driving cases, even got involved in working in surrogacy.

Christopher estimates that at least six hundred kids were born thanks to the surrogates and IPs his dad matched up through contracts. "All these kids are descendants of my stubborn crazy Aunt Maureen and my dad," he told me adding, "his relationship with her was the genesis of that." Maureen and her brother were two of five siblings who grew up poor in East Dearborn, the offspring of Irish immigrants. Their father worked on the assembly line at Ford Motor Company and as a former member of the Irish Republican Army back in Ireland, he suffered heavily from PTSD. It was, said Christopher, a traumatized home but in part because of that, Maureen and her brother in particular were very bonded. "She loved him, and he loved her and if she said 'help' he said 'sure,'" recalled Christopher.

At some point in the mid-1970s Maureen, who worked in local politics and who eventually made a run for mayor of Dearborn, had met a couple who couldn't have children. "She was the sort of person where if she saw someone who had a problem, she would try to fix it, so I guess she marched [the intended father] into my dad's office," he said. "I am sure he said something like 'What the fuck? What do you want me to do with this?' and I can almost guarantee my dad got one of his young [law apprentices] to do it. The idea of him sitting still and writing up a contract is not possible for me to conjure up."

Mr. Keane, who was always full of energy and new business ideas, was something of a man-about-town in Dearborn. He would go every day to the same donut shop to catch up with his friends who were ex-cops and he had great relationships with many of the local lawyers and judges in town. Those strong relationships also meant that when that contract came up in 1976, he got his legal buddies to represent the different sides in the case. "It was like a friendly court case because nobody was opposed to it, they needed a judicial ruling," Christopher said. "Then once he got publicity, I think he figured out it could be a business."

That business soon exploded and people from across the globe came to him to set up not only surrogacy contracts but to match IPs with surrogates. "When I was doing an internship in 1987 in London at the Houses of Parliament, my parents came to visit me and we ended up going to Germany to visit some family who had a castle," recalled Christopher. "My mom and dad were not fancy people, but this lady was a baroness, and they had a baby [thanks to] my dad."

When I asked him about the 1988 law in Michigan, Christopher told me that he didn't think that his dad was against the legislation per se to make the law clear. "That is not my recollection at all, he was not saying, 'stay out of it,'" Christopher said. "But any time you mix religion or mix a woman's uterus with something, then everybody gets in their political camps and all reason gets chucked out the window."

The law in Michigan was not without controversy, with the state's chapter of the American Civil Liberties Union (ACLU) filing an appeal stating that the law was unconstitutional (it was overruled by the appellate court in September that same year). "The government has absolutely no business intruding into the very private and sometimes heartbreaking decisions that families must make when they are afflicted with infertility," said Howard Simon, who at the time was the executive director of the Michigan ACLU. "The state of Michigan should be open to new advances in technology for dealing with infertility, not shut its eyes like some Luddite."[50]

Elizabeth Gleicher, now a Michigan Court of Appeals judge, along with Mr. Sedler and another attorney, were the three lawyers who took on the case for the ACLU. When I asked her if today the ruling would be the same, she said she wasn't sure. "There has been a change in the way judges think about these issues," she said. "I doubt that the court could leave its analysis with the baby selling rap, because we've seen that that hasn't caused a revolution in baby selling and commodification of babies around the country. What has happened is that a lot of beautiful families have been created. And that's the evidence, not the wholesale destruction of the American family."

At the time, however, those against surrogacy hailed the strong steps that the Michigan legislature—and the courts—took. "This turns children into a product and it turns women into breeders," said Jeremy Rifkin, who was then the co-chairman of the now-defunct National Coalition Against Surrogacy. When the bill was signed into law, Mr. Rifkin said that it marked the beginning of the end of commercial surrogacy in the US. "Michigan is the biggest state in the country for surrogate brokering," he told the *Los Angeles Times*. "Now, we think that within two years, surrogacy will be ended all over this country."[51] How wrong his forecast turned out to be.

When I asked Christopher—who it turns out was college fraternity brothers with a number of guys I grew up with—what he thought about that misbegotten forecast, he chuckled a bit. "My dad was the person who started it all, someone else could have done it but he had the combination of personality, the Irish street hustle to weather the storm, and it was just kind of the right mix," he said. "All the families he helped create was his legacy. I am sure your experience of happiness with your kids, imagine that not happening?"

He had no idea how close that was to being the case.

Chapter Three

This One Time at a Taylor Swift Concert...

All day I had been mulling Julie's email over in my mind.

As I unsuccessfully tried to hide from the sizzling February sun, traipsing around with my translator Dawit to several of the magnificent twelfth-century rock-hewn churches of Lalibela, I worked hard to keep shoving away sentences that floated through my head as a reply. Dawit had been going on all morning about the church paintings (I had been travelling across Ethiopia for over a week with him and I now was very familiar with their symbolism and references) and standing on the top of the volcanic tuff that the Church of St. George had been carved out of, I had reached my breaking point. As I opened my mouth to ask him if we could keep moving to find some shade, a fat fly flew into my mouth. I spit it out with disgust and contempt. Here I was in Lalibela, a place I had dreamed about coming to for years, and yet I was in a foul mood getting unwanted protein from an insect as angst churned away in my stomach.

Later on, sitting outside on the balcony of my hotel with resplendent views of the green Western Ethiopian Highlands, I sipped my glass of refreshing *tej*—a locally made honey wine— and watched as the cursor on my computer blinked incessantly at me. I had reread Julie's email at least three times by now, contemplating what she had written. After initial greetings, she cut right to the chase, her directness something I later came to learn was at the forefront of her personality:

> *I wondered what your plans were specifically involving your relationship and surrogacy [and] I didn't know if surrogacy was something that was going to cross your path again anytime in the near future, or if you pushed it off for a while.*

She went on to say that she and Chad had been excited to have met us over Skype those few months back in late 2015 and that she hoped that my husband and I were going to be able to work out things in our relationship. I swirled a bit of the *tej* around in my mouth and forwarded the email to my husband because I simply didn't know what to reply. Marriage is hard on the best of days but when things get really bad, it can feel like the Seventh Circle of Hell. From the start, my husband and I had a very tumultuous relationship. We were both fiercely independent, outgoing, and opinionated people who had each lived on our own for most of our adult lives. Plus, we hadn't been spring chickens when we got married—I was forty-three and my husband turned forty on the midnight after our nuptials in Belgrade in November 2014. We also came from two very different cultures, which meant that things I was sensitive to didn't really seem to show up on his radar. Throw in the stresses and strains of infertility, and the combination was like a dropped match on gunpowder.

The foundations of our marriage started to crack almost right away, when eleven months after our wedding and three months after my Wimbledon meltdown, we had had a massive blowout in the rental car parking lot at LAX when we arrived after a long-haul flight from London. The whole reason we were going to California was to get more of my eggs with Dr. Sahakian for our yet-to-be-picked surrogate. By the time we landed, my husband, who was a nervous flier, was in a horrendous mood in part because he wanted to buy cigarettes and couldn't find anywhere that sold them in the airport. The fight culminated in him grabbing his bag and saying he was going to take a flight straight back to London. Frustrated, exhausted, hormonal, and pissed off beyond belief, I plugged the hotel address into the satnav and took off. A few hours later, tail somewhat between his legs, he showed back up. It was not a great start to our trip.

A few days later, I injected myself in a restroom at the Staples Center at a Los Angeles Lakers game during Kobe Bryant's last season. I had to do the trigger hormone, Ovitrelle, at exactly 8:30 p.m. so that it would start my eggs on their thirty-six-hour journey, winding their way down to where they needed to be for the retrieval that happened to coincide with my birthday. My husband couldn't bring himself to shoot me in the butt so while it was a rather awkward angle to do in a bathroom stall, I had become so used to doing these over the years that I just zipped down my pants, shot myself, popped the used needle into my bag, and went to grab some buttery popcorn.

Earlier that year, during the same IVF cycle as my Wimbledon drama, I had to give myself an Ovitrelle shot during a Taylor Swift concert in Hyde Park. Just as Tay-Tay (as my kids now call her) was bounding down the stage in our direction, I shouted into my friend's ear that I'd be back in ten minutes. As I walked against the thronging crowd in Hyde Park on that midsummer's evening, I headed toward the looming two-story sound deck that looked like it might have a private dark corner. At exactly 9:00 p.m. I needed to inject myself. But to my horror, I realized I didn't have the actual syringe. Since I had to keep the serum cold, earlier in the day I had taken the hormone out of the box so it wouldn't be so bulky in my purse and had enveloped it around a bag of frozen peas. But I had accidentally thrown the needle out with the box, which I was supposed to screw on right before I injected the shot. Luckily, I hadn't tossed out a needle from a different injection I had taken earlier in the day. Having no other option, I screwed it on, made sure no one was looking, and injected myself to the opening strains of "Clean." This is obviously not recommended protocol and Dr. Matthews, my gynecologist, didn't find it amusing when I later regaled her with the tale.

A day and a half after the LA Lakers injection, we arrived at the clinic for the egg retrieval around 8:00 a.m. Though initial scans done in London by Dr. Matthews had shown there were only three eggs, we got our hopes way up when, during a scan at PFC a few days before the retrieval, there looked to be several more. It seemed that we'd be spoiled for choice with genetic material, and I was greedily counting on not only the five original frozen eggs and the two embryos flown in from London, but maybe there could be several more embryos we could use as well. I floated off into the la-la-land of general anesthesia in a great mood. After I revived and slowly got dressed, wolfing down a few crackers to stabilize my blood sugar, one of the nurses came in. She said things had gone well and they'd contact us soon to let us know how many viable eggs they retrieved.

After a long nap back at the hotel, we went for a stroll and had a nice birthday dinner—my forty-fourth—with a few of my friends who lived in LA. A few days later we received an email from the clinic saying that one of the embryos was growing and they were hoping to take it to blastocyst (on day five an embryo evolves into about seventy to one hundred cells). It would then be frozen and later implanted into our surrogate. They said they'd reach out if anything changed. To celebrate the news, we headed off to Joshua Tree National Park for a hike. As we walked through the glorious desert landscape of those twisted discomforting trees, we talked about maybe coming back next month to try another round of IVF. We left California the next day in great moods. Six weeks later we had our first Skype date with Julie and Chad. And then soon after, things started to really go downhill.

In early January 2016, I sent Circle an email telling them that we needed to put our surrogacy on hold:

It is with a heavy heart that I have to say that [we] have decided to take a break. Not to get into things too personal, but I think all the IVF and other pressures of our first year of marriage have all played a toll. We are hoping this will be a temporary break, while we work things out. But at this time, we both feel that pursuing surrogacy at the moment is not the best move for anyone. I am not sure if I should contact [Julie and Chad] directly or if [Circle] would do that. They are a lovely couple and we would have loved to have worked with them but obviously it is not the appropriate time to pursue having a baby.

Callie Kolkind, our coordinator who has also been a surrogate herself, told us that we should contact Julie and Chad directly. We had not signed a contract with them yet, but Circle recommended a personal touch from us would be appropriate. Crying through bitter tears, I sent them an email and Julie replied back quickly saying they understood. A month later, I went to Ethiopia on a work trip while my husband met friends to go skiing in Bulgaria. We were trying to work things out by going our separate ways. As it turned out, for a number of reasons Ethiopia proved to be the tonic that I needed to clear my head and really think about my marriage.

After several days spent working on a few stories in Addis Ababa, I took off for Aksum—the ancient Ethiopian capital which is not only the fabled home of the Ark of the Covenant but also supposedly the resting place of the Queen of Sheba—before heading to the Simien Mountains. On our drive we passed men walking camels packed with things to sell and girls herding donkeys who carried packs of flour and jerry cans of water from local wells. During a pit stop in one village that was holding its weekly goat market, a young mountain girl asked Dawit if I was a man or a woman because I was wearing trousers, this after another woman in a market in Mekelle asked me how I "got permission" from my husband to travel solo.

While the Simien Mountains National Park is 412 square km in size, it's just a portion of the entire mountain range, which looks like a combination of the Grand Canyon on steroids with the occasional lushness of mountains I've seen in Bosnia and Canada. The beauty and vastness of the mountain ledge outcrops, which seemed to go on for eternity, took my breath away and put my problems in perspective. During that drive we came across sloping fields full of geladas (also known as the bleeding-heart baboon) quietly eating grass and wild thyme—their tranquil munching sounding like a gentle babbling brook. We passed very young shepherd boys and girls responsible for their families' sheep and goats. One shy little girl, in a green-and-black shawl, watched her flock as she sat on a boulder all by her lonesome. She told Dawit she was five.

On our second day where we stopped by a small village holding a feast in the honor of Virgin Mary, we were invited to the house of a local farmer to have coffee and *injera*, a sour spongy fermented flatbread eaten with every Ethiopian meal. Their home was typical of the village, with a thatched roof, dirt floors, and walls made from mud, dung, and straw. The couple and their two small children slept in the same bed, which was about two meters off the ground, and at night their donkey and goats slept underneath in the space for both warmth and safety.

Though the farmer dominated the conversation, I tried to engage his wife by asking her how old she was. She whispered that she didn't know but thought maybe she was about twenty-five. She looked at least a decade older, and I could tell she was melancholic and nervous around her husband. I thought to myself as she stirred the coffee beans in a large round pan, her head bowed down in an attempt to disappear into the dark shadows, how blessed I was to have a choice not only in terms of who I married but if I wanted to get married in the first place.

Millions of women across the globe didn't have the privilege to question their relationships. They just got on with it because there was no other option. And here I was taking a mental break from my marriage traipsing across this Ethiopian landscape. After saying our goodbyes, we headed toward the Jinbar Waterfall. It was a twenty-five-minute rocky trek, past rhododendron, overgrown Queen Anne's Lace, Abyssinian wild roses, and a few olive trees. A local guide we had to hire tore off a twig from an olive tree and started chewing on it, telling me that it served as a toothbrush for locals. He said that in the mountains, if you liked a girl, you would chew on the twig in front of her. If she liked you, she would say that the twig made your teeth nice and white. If this exchange took place, it meant you could begin dating. I liked this mating ritual, but I didn't have the heart to tell him it was the complications that came after that proved to be the real test.

It was a few days later, sipping my *tej*, that I forwarded the email from Julie. My husband replied quickly, saying we should be as forthcoming as possible: that we were trying to figure things out and that once we knew what we were doing, we hoped to work with them. As I watched as thick-billed ravens swooped through the sky, the echoing sound of their wings pumping with air to carry them along, I sent Julie my reply:

We are working on our relationship [and] making a con-certed effort to understand each other better, communi-cate more openly, etc. [Can] I get back to you on this once we have had a long discussion? We really liked you both and thought it would be/could be a great match. My regret on holding off surrogacy was that we might not work with you (which sounds weird saying "work with you" but you know what I mean).

Anyway, hope all is well and again, lovely to hear from you. This trip has been amazing in many regards, and also very sad to see so many gorgeous and sweet kids who live in horrible, impoverished situations. One man even jok-ingly (not funny to me) asked if I would adopt his daughter because he was so poor, he could not provide well for her.

Throughout the rest of my trip and over the next several weeks once I got back to London, Julie and I exchanged a few emails. In hindsight, I think our deeply personal marital troubles helped to create a bond between us all. We had to be open to these strangers about what was going on in our marriage and it created a sort of odd yet important intimacy, something that would put us in good stead later on. I told Julie about the farmer's wife who had made me coffee and how fortunate we were to live in cultures where we had choices and options as women.

Julie had had all her children quite young but then decided to divorce her husband when things turned sour. I also told her that I was never under the illusion that many people fall into, the trap that having children can somehow mend a marriage. My husband and I both understood that having kids would be tough, so we tried to create a strong basic infrastructure before we added on another component that included yucky diapers and lost sleep.

By the middle of March, we decided to work things out. After a conversation with a social worker at Circle (they obviously wanted to make sure things were really okay between us), we reached back out again to Julie. She agreed that she was still keen to be our surrogate and so began a number of protracted negotiations over contracts: everything from what were the expectations of expenses related to things like paying for her gas to drive to a doctor's appointment to would she agree to doing an amniocentesis (she did, if it proved to be necessary for the health of the child). Though we didn't fully understand or appreciate it at time, it was a lucky thing that Julie lived in Illinois because it's one of the states that has the most surrogacy-friendly laws in the US.

In the decades since Michigan became the first US state to make surrogacy contracts illegal, the federal government has been hesitant to impose any kind of sweeping law on surrogacy. That's meant that surrogacy has grown in a fragmented and "highly disparate fashion" with each state following and maintaining a mix of laws.[52] That in part harkens back to the early history of surrogacy in the US where there were two waves of regulations and laws. That first wave in the latter part of the 1980s saw legal bans along with civil and criminal penalties in several states (like Michigan), something of a knee-jerk reaction to the Baby M case.[53]

Those bans were also in response to the prevailing feminist viewpoint at the time: surrogacy was both exploitative of women and it also defined women by their reproductive capabilities. But starting in the mid-1990s, a second wave of legislative and legal rulings swept across the US, making surrogacy both more regulated and more permitted. That was largely because the concerns that surrogacy would not only be exploitative to the carriers but would also be psychologically damaging to children and society just never came to pass.[54] Bans on surrogacy did not end the practice and American surrogates, most of whom were gestational versus traditional carriers, were reporting positive experiences. Also, the arguments against surrogacy were seen as "too similar to other arguments against reproductive freedom" for women.[55]

Steven Snyder, a Minnesota-based family formation lawyer who has also served as the chair of the Assisted Reproductive Technologies committee of the American Bar Association, told me that the US Constitution and the Bill of Rights have both played a role in shaping American surrogacy laws and rulings. He has argued that certain amendments (the 14th, 15th, 19th, and 26th) together create a broad "panoply of individual liberties and rights."[56] Also, personal autonomy and individual freedoms are concepts that are deeply entrenched in the social consciousness of Americans (just look, for example, at the fiery debate over guns). That bolsters the argument of many surrogates who say they can do whatever they like with their bodies. Mr. Snyder and other legal scholars also like to point to Supreme Court of the United States (SCOTUS) rulings that they believe have also helped shape surrogacy in America. For example, in *Skinner v Oklahoma*, the ruling was that the 14th Amendment does protect the law to procreate and that it's a fundamental human right.[57] This has been interpreted by many that the US government cannot restrict individual procreative decisions without a strong case and any attempts by Congress to regulate surrogacy might face constitutional limitations.[58]

This has all led to three approaches to surrogacy by states: some have laws that directly address surrogacy (like Illinois), some only have legal rulings (like Pennsylvania and Ohio), while others have no laws either way (like Minnesota). However, every determination of parentage for a child born through surrogacy in the US is subject to some sort of legislative or judicial oversight. That's one of the reasons why many foreign national IPs are drawn to having their babies in the US. "A lot of people with a concern for things being done legitimately and in an appropriate way go to the US," John Pascoe, a retired chief justice of the Family Court of Australia who has written extensively on surrogacy, told me in 2020. "For me, part of the US system I do not like and agree with, but there is a system. It does provide protections [and] broadly across the U.S., you have judicial oversight, judges are not corrupt and are not stupid."

Since I did not have much of a clue about law, I asked our attorneys at Circle about the clause in the contract stating that Julie could not travel to Michigan after her first trimester. My concern was if we brought the baby (or babies) back to Michigan after they were born and the state somehow found out they had been born through surrogacy would they take the babies away and would I have to pay a fine or even face jail time? Our lawyer reassured us that it would not be an issue because there is something called the Comity Clause in the Constitution, which essentially means one state has to respect the legal rulings of another.

So the transfer of parentage—which can either be done pre-birth or post-birth—granted in one state is given full faith and credit by all other states. That's even if that other state has a different policy on surrogacy.[59] I let out a very audible "phew" when I read that email. Years later when I asked Judge Marianne Battani—the Michigan judge who ruled in 1986 that Jill Rudnitzky should have her biological parents listed on her birth certificate and not the surrogate—if she realized how groundbreaking that ruling was, she chuckled softly. "I considered the woman carrying the child as the incubator," she said, adding that she based her ruling on common sense. "And I really thought that because she had no relationship to the child."

However, most countries around the world to this day would disagree. That's because they adhere to the Roman-law principle of parental determination called *Mater semper certa est* ("The mother is always certain") and *Pater est quem nuptiae demonstrant* ("The Father is he to whom marriage points"). Before IVF, it was always certain who the mother was since she was the one who gave birth to the child. Paternity, meanwhile, was assumed if the woman was married, however, there's a reason why the cringeworthy milkman jokes are still in circulation. But once a baby could be created in a petri dish, using either the intended mother's egg or an egg donor's, and another woman who was not biologically related to the baby could give birth to it, the mother therefore wasn't always certain. "It's antiquated," Maud de Boer-Buquicchio, the former UN Special Rapporteur on the sale of children, child prostitution, and child pornography, who during her time in that position published two reports on cross-border surrogacy, told me.

And while most people I interviewed for this book agreed with me that this Roman law is not only out of date but also rather sexist—as many countries like Ireland and Germany legally accept the biological connection of the intended father to a surrogate-born baby but not the biological connection of the intended mother—it's still the main law on the books globally around surrogacy. "Genetic mothers in Europe, in almost every country, don't get any rights unless they do a secondary step [like adoption]," said Dean Hutchison, the former chair of the American Bar Association's ART committee, "or in some countries they never get rights."

That means a surrogate who gives birth to a child and her husband, if there is one, are considered the child's legal parents and "there is no way to legally pre-empt" this determination.[60] Most of the US views this differently in part because of the Uniform Parentage Act (UPA), a best practice legal framework for establishing parentage determinations based on marriage, birth, or genetic relations. "Thus," writes Steven Snyder in an academic paper on surrogacy, "the United States does not concur that the mere biological fact of giving birth presumptively or necessarily determines a child's legal parents."[61]

After we got that clarification that we would not face any legal problems bringing a surrogate-born baby back to Michigan, the contract negotiations got back on track. In the meantime, Julie flew out for an appointment with Dr. Sahakian in LA, where she had lived years before. She admitted to me that while she was not stoked for the pelvic exam, she was excited to go back to Tender Greens, one of her favorite restaurants in Santa Monica. It ended up becoming something of a ritual that every time she had to go out to LA for an appointment, afterwards she and Chad would head there for a kale salad and a falafel with mashed potatoes. While she was busy chowing down on her vegetarian delights, my husband and I were writing up our surrogacy wills. If we both happened to die while Julie was pregnant, we needed to state who would get custody of the baby and who would be responsible for paying her compensation. It was not the most pleasant thing to work on but we knew it was important, so we named my brothers and my husband's sister as legal guardians.

One of the most controversial aspects of surrogacy is the compensation. Those against surrogacy have long argued that the practice would only draw in women who were financially vulnerable. And while this is arguably true in developing countries where there is surrogacy—more on this later—in Western countries like the US it hasn't developed in this way. Partly that's because when agencies interview potential carriers—with legitimate ones using guidelines from the ASRM[62]—they make sure that the women are not going to be economically dependent on surrogacy. That rules out most women who are on government assistance because compensation might jeopardize those benefits. Also, a potential surrogate in economic distress could be anxious, creating negative impacts on the pregnancy.

Being reliant on public assistance is also seen as potentially something that could create strain in the surrogate/IP relationship. "It somehow got embedded in the American psyche that women who are surrogates are welfare queens who want to be pregnant and do nothing," said Jennifer White, the co-founder of US surrogacy agency Bright Futures Families. "I mean, that could not be further from the truth." Judith Daar, who at the time that I interviewed her chaired the ASRM's ethics committee, touches on this in her book, stating that US agencies and clinics avoid engaging women who are on public assistance because it calls to mind the "oft-argued critique" that compensated surrogacy is unfair to poor women. "The exploitation argument highlights that the surrogate is typically (far) less wealthy than the intended parent(s)," she writes, "and thus the practice is called out as expressly and dangerously exploitative of women who are coerced into the arrangement because of their dire economic circumstances."[63]

Legitimate agencies, therefore, are extremely hesitant to take on surrogates who say that money is their chief motivating factor. The marketing and PR used by agencies to draw in potential surrogates and to weed out those who are undesirable is to emphasize the gift-giving nature of being a carrier.[64] "By arguing that surrogacy is a gift," wrote Dr. Heather Jacobson, "the market attempts to obscure both the work involved in and the income generated from surrogacy." Dr. Zsuzsa Berend found in her research that while American carriers did say that money had initially been an incentive to do surrogacy, over time that became much less important. Part of that came from them learning about the process and the risk. That proved to also be the case among many Israeli surrogates and some Indian surrogates who worked in garment factories in Bangalore.[65]

Sharmila Rudrappa, an associate professor of sociology at the University of Texas at Austin, found that Indian carriers felt that surrogacy was "more meaningful for the women than other forms of employment." And because babies "were life-affirming in ways garments are obviously not" surrogacy allowed these women to "assert their moral worth."[66] Meanwhile a longitudinal study on British surrogates done by researchers at the University of Cambridge discovered only one carrier who said she did it for the money. "She was absolutely adamant that that was the only reason anyone would do it," Vasanti Jadva, who led the research, told me. "She was the outlier, everybody else said they did it to help somebody else."

Surrogacy, of course, requires an extraordinary amount of commitment. "It is a ridiculously long process, three to six months even just to get cleared before you are even matched with IPs," said Ms. White. "You are getting nothing for those months." It then takes another four to six months to be given the go-ahead for an embryo transfer and then if the transfer does not work, that's a year where there has essentially been no compensation. "So, it really does actually take people who are giving, really committed personalities and that money cannot be the driving factor in it," she said.

American surrogates also have to go through criminal checks, home studies, and explorations into every aspect of their lives before they are approved. "It is not a fly-by-night decision," said Richard Vaughn, a California-based family formation lawyer who focuses his practice solely on surrogacy. "I find it demeaning and insulting to women that critics of surrogacy assume these women do not know what they are doing." Mr. Vaughan told me that he fervently believes that women should be paid for their extraordinary commitment of time and sacrifice. "You don't hang up your uterus at five o'clock and say, 'I'm done,'" he said, adding that if you calculate the amount that a US surrogate receives—the average is around $35,000—and divide that by 24 hours a day for 280 days it comes out to barely $5 an hour. "So to say that $35,000 is exploitation, they are just ignoring the other side of the coin."[67]

Way back when we had our first conversation with Julie and Chad about surrogacy, they told us that they both highly prioritized education. So, while compensation was not a driving factor for them in their decision, they did want to set up an education nest egg for their children. This ended up being one of the reasons we really warmed to Julie and Chad in the first place. Three years after Julie had delivered Lexie and Ransom, she told me that her children's education was one of the chief factors for her doing surrogacy. "I ultimately paid for their private school education with my surrogacy money," she said. "So, my children fueled your children [and vice versa]. My goal in mind was that this was something that I could do for somebody else. But it was also something I was doing for my family."

The difference between compensated surrogacy—banned in countries like Germany, France, and most Australian states—and non-compensated surrogacy has become quite muddied over the years. Natalie Gamble, a British lawyer who has worked on surrogacy cases for over two decades, has argued that the terms are very complicated, very loaded and different people mean different things by them. "In terms of 'altruistic' surrogacy, what most people understand that to mean is the surrogates are motivated by the desire to help someone and there is no financial benefit for them," she told me. "In reality, some of the restrictions around 'altruistic' surrogacy in [Britain] and elsewhere are more about whether the intermediaries can profit and whether they are regulated, which is a different issue. [So] are we talking about compensated or uncompensated in the terms of the surrogate? Or are we talking about commercial or non-commercial in the terms of the third parties involved?"

"Altruistic" surrogacy implies that surrogates receive no payment or just "reasonable expenses." But Ms. Gamble, who also founded the British surrogacy agency Brilliant Beginnings, said the line between what is a reasonable expense and what is compensation is never clear, and many gestational carriers in Britain receive something to acknowledge their inconvenience or compensation beyond their out-of-pocket expenses, and over-all the amounts paid can be upwards of £30,000. She told me that she gets very frustrated with the lack of transparency about what is going on. "Let's be honest about this," Ms. Gamble said, "it may be badged as expenses but that may not entirely be the reality."

Steven Snyder, meanwhile, told me that he doesn't think there is even such a thing as "altruistic" surrogacy. "I don't think it's appropriate to argue for non-commercial surrogacy because," he said, "it's the commercial nature of it that puts the proper profes-sionals in the safeguarding positions that they need to be in to make the process stable." He went on to clarify the terminologies: "compensated" surrogacy is where the money goes directly to the surrogate while "commercial" is where people like IVF phy-sicians, lawyers, psychologists, and agency owners also get paid. "If you're going to make agencies non-profit," Snyder said, "then the IVF physician should be non-profit, the lawyer should be non-profit, and the psychologist should be non-profit." Whether they agree with it or not, there are many in the global surrogacy space who in general appreciate how the US compensated surrogacy system works because it's at least calling a spade a spade. "In some ways," Ms. Gamble said, "having an element of compensa-tion makes it feel fairer and more balanced [because] if the sur-rogate and her family are not receiving any obvious benefit, the parents can feel very beholden."

Several days after Julie's falafel fest in Santa Monica, Dr. Sahakian's office in LA was sent a legal clearance from Circle stating that we had all agreed up to three transfers together. It stipulated that they had to be done within eighteen months and that we could do two embryos per transfer. The idea of twins scared us when we were negotiating this part of the contract, but we also figured doing a transfer of two embryos gave us a better chance each time of having a child. That we had even progressed to this point had taken a long time—not just for us but for Julie as well. She told me that by the time she and Chad finally made the decision to do surrogacy she had researched a number of agencies before she decided on Circle. "I thought for five years that I wanted to be a surrogate before I actually pulled the trigger," she said. "I did not have reservations, I was able to read contracts, I could say I understood a decent amount of it, or I knew to ask questions of what I did not know. That is how I live my life and I don't want to get into something blindly."

While there are not many rules for IPs in the US in terms of an agency taking them on as clients, there are many for potential surrogates (though they do, of course, range from agency to agency). First and foremost, they require that a potential surrogate must have birthed and mothered a child, with most agencies and clinics preferring also to work with women who have not had complicated pregnancies. (Interestingly, British agencies like SurrogacyUK sometimes work with "child-free surrogates" who according to Sarah Jones are women who don't have their own children, have no intention of having their own children, "but would like to experience pregnancy.") One of the reasons for that is it's seen to minimize the possibility that the carrier might want to keep the baby. "Here the ghost of Baby M can be seen to continue to haunt surrogacy, as agencies attempt to avoid similar cases," wrote Dr. Jacobson. "The hope is that because surrogates have previously given birth, they will understand what is involved in motherhood and enter into a surrogate arrangement with their eyes wide open."[68]

Red flags go up for agencies when potential surrogates have substance abuse issues (or their partner/husband), those who have higher BMIs, are on antidepressants, or have police records.

Agencies, of course, hope to get high-quality gestational carriers on their books. Circle, for example, receives about 1,500 applications a month but John Weltman told me they only accept about 1.5 percent of potential surrogates. "We are less than any other agency," he said. While some US agencies take on between 20 percent to 30 percent of surrogates who apply, Mr. Weltman told me he could fill his IP waiting list if he began taking even 5 percent of carrier applicants. "It is about quality to me," he said. "It always has been."

Unfortunately, because at the moment there is only self-regulation within the surrogacy industry, there are unscrupulous agencies that don't follow ASRM carrier guidelines. That means potential surrogates who have been turned down by legitimate agencies will pop up somewhere else. "I see surrogates on Facebook, and they'll say, 'This agency took me even though others declined me' and I will know why I declined her, but I cannot say anything publicly," said Ms. White. "It's hard because you see [these agencies] are taking advantage of people and putting people at risk."

After all the starts and stops with our contracts, once we all signed, we decided to begin right away. In June my husband flew out to LA to give sperm for the five frozen eggs (the idea was that the eggs would be unfrozen and mixed with fresh sperm to create embryos for a fresh transfer). I met him in Northern Michigan a few days later and we had a relaxed vacation on the stunning beaches along Lake Michigan. The summer before, after being told my womb was inhospitable, I had mended myself by sinking my feet in the wet sugar sands and staring out past the sea-foam green and turquoise waters to the distant and sometimes desolate horizon. But in the summer of 2016, as I scampered down the golden ridged dunes, past the itchy blonde dune grass and the baby's breath—its thickly sweet aroma the perfume for so many childhood memories—and charged straight into the vast freshwater lake, there was a great bursting hope in my heart. Maybe just maybe that next summer I could be floating with my baby in these healing waters.

Back in LA, three embryos had been created out of the five thawed eggs. Of those three, only one made it to an early blast, which we were told meant that the cells of the other two had not completely differentiated. That embryo of only fair quality had been transferred in Julie on July 11, but the hope was that because her lining and blood work looked good—and she was relaxed after an acupuncture session—it might attach to her womb wall and thrive. They also told us the other two embryos were still growing and if they made it to blast, they would be refrozen in case we needed another transfer. They would let us know their progress the next day. It wasn't the best news, but we were hopeful. The next afternoon, I took my husband to the airport in Traverse City to drop him off for his flight back to London. He was going back for a work project while I was going to spend a few more weeks with my family.

Traverse City has become something of a foodie hub in the US these days and one of the standout stars is The Cook's House, situated on a residential street filled with nineteenth-century lumbering mansions. It was hard to get a reservation there but knowing several weeks in advance that I'd be dropping him off at the airport, I was able to get a much-coveted booking for dinner. It was a lovely warm July 2016 evening and as I was taken to my table next to an open window, I noticed that just in view was Little Fleet Bar.

In the summer, its parking lot is opened up to about a dozen mouth-watering food trucks and I could hear the lively music and conversation spilling out and wafting through the window. After ordering a starter salad of locally grown vegetables and tomatoes and their house specialty, hay-smoked whitefish, as a main, I took a long sip of the local white wine I had ordered and sat back. After watching a hipster couple walk down the sidewalk toward the food trucks, I picked up my phone to see I had an email from PFC. The email from Dr. Sahakian's assistant stated that the other two embryos did not develop but that they still had the two frozen embryos in storage.

I sat up in my chair and reread the email.

And then I called my husband, who at that point had arrived in Chicago from his Traverse City puddle jumper. "So, we should have three frozen embryos, right? Because we had the two flown in from London and then the one from last November's retrieval in LA," I said, trying to remain calm as the waiter brought my salad. My husband replied that yes, that was the case, so I emailed PFC and got a quick reply, in hot pink font, stating that those November embryos did not blast and they weren't able to fertilize any from that cycle. I was flabbergasted and reread the email from November where we were told there was one embryo.

I quickly replied back:

[Our] confusion (and shock) from today was that we had never been told that the embryo that was created in LA last November had not blasted. We had heard that it had developed . . . that there was one from the number of eggs taken out and mixed with [my husband's] sperm (per the email to us in November). Our understanding (because we were not told otherwise) was that that one as well had been frozen. No one had followed up to say that it had never developed . . . so we understood it had been frozen and that we had

three in total (the two from London and the LA one). There seems to have been miscommunication . . . and that was the shock. That for a number of months we thought we had three "in the bag" but now just have those two (plus the one that was created last week and put in [Julie] yesterday).

The emails flew back and forth between LA, Chicago, and Traverse City for the next thirty minutes. The whitefish that I had so looked forward to, laying picked over on my plate, my appetite gone and me in a growing state of torment and anxiety. We had not gone back to California in December 2015 because we had figured that it was not only expensive but since we had three embryos plus five eggs that should be more than enough. And yet psychologically, because we now had only two embryos left, it felt like our chances had been depleted significantly. Dr. Sahakian via the frenzied emailing apologized profusely that there was miscommunication about the "third" embryo that had never really existed as a possibility.

I paid the bill for the meal that I barely touched and headed to my car. I didn't cry on that forty-five-minute drive back to the house, but I sure did yell and have several angry imaginary conversations with Dr. Sahakian. "It's bullshit," I shrieked hysterically at my steering wheel, blasting at it with my fist as I sped through the silent birch and pine woods that had always before brought some kind of medicinal Zen for me. Like so much of this journey so far, I went from feeling like I had some element of control—getting my eggs frozen, taking the hormone shots on time, being diligent about picking the right surrogate for us—to having no control whatsoever. We were at the whim of doctors, DNA, and destiny, and it was tearing my soul apart.

Ten days later, after a long and eventually proactive

conversation with Dr. Sahakian, we were informed via email by his assistant that Julie's blood work had shown she wasn't pregnant.[69] What's interesting to me now is that I'm sure I must have wept and maybe went for a walk, again, along that restorative Lake Michigan shoreline. But I honestly don't remember, and I'm not sure why. Maybe it was because I had gotten so used to the negative, sad information that always seemed to come my way when trying to create a life that I just maybe blocked this one out. I think your brain can only muster so much hurt and this one has completely faded into the recesses of my memory. My "in case of emergency, break glass" eggs had proved useless, like a fire extinguisher that when called upon couldn't put out a blaze.

I returned to London at the end of July, and we asked if Julie could do another transfer after her next normal period (another peculiar part of surrogacy is that you get to intimately know another woman's menstrual cycle even though she lives thousands of miles away). Luckily, she was up for it and was still in good cheer despite the last transfer not working. I also sent an email to our coordinator, Callie, about the possibility of working with donor eggs. I hadn't really gotten my head around this idea yet, but I wanted to feel like we had a Plan B if our embryos didn't take the second time around. I didn't know then that our journey hadn't even really started yet.

Chapter Four

I Left My Heart in Bagamoyo

The tempestuous waves on the Indian Ocean were a foreshadowing of the emotional roiling that would take place later that night in my mind and my stomach.

I had arrived in Bagamoyo, Tanzania, earlier on a September day from Moshi, a town that sits in the shadow of Mount Kilimanjaro, nicknamed "Kili" by both locals and those who have the gumption to climb it. The day before, I had done a day hike up part of the mountain, something that had been pitched to me as an easy stroll that would take me up to the first base camp. It turned out to be one of the hardest physical things I had ever put my body through, as it was like climbing steep and uneven stairs for seven hours in equatorial humidity. On my Sunday morning flight the next day, I was achy and sore but overall, I felt proud not only because of pushing myself to do something so difficult but also because of the work I had been doing in Moshi.

I had gone to Tanzania to do research on girls' education and the barriers they face to stay in school. The idea had grown out of conversations I'd had with young girls in Ethiopia, Senegal, and Nepal who told me they had found themselves at a crossroads when it came to their schooling. While they'd had access to primary education as younger girls, things changed once they became adolescents. For some, it simply boiled down to having to travel long distances—sometimes through unsafe or desolate areas—to get to school. For others, their families could not afford the hidden tuition fees that included everything from school uniforms and books to sometimes even small bribes to teachers.

There were also social and cultural barriers that many adolescent girls faced, from having to help around the house to the fact that in the developing world, one in nine girls is married before the age of fifteen. I had spent that week in Moshi talking to several teenage girls about these issues, as well as doing some volunteer work within a school helping teachers prepare their students for their final English exams. I'd then flown on to the coastal city of Bagamoyo where I was going to be spending a few days visiting schools with representatives of Camfed, a British-based organization that supports vulnerable young women with their education. This reporting trip was the perfect remedy for distraction because Julie was now almost eight weeks pregnant.

After the failed transfer in early July, she had gone back to LA about six weeks later for another transfer with our last two embryos that were both Grade One, the best possible score. About ten days later, we got news from PFC that blood tests from Julie's doctor back in Illinois indicated that she was pregnant. We were cautiously optimistic. Right before I left for my trip to Tanzania, Julie had an ultrasound that showed that there was one fetus, and it was the exact size it should be at that stage. However, a heartbeat had not yet been detected. But as Dr. Sahakian's assistant told us in an email, it was possible it was still a heathy pregnancy and the heartbeat might be seen the next week, which coincided with me arriving in Bagamoyo.

After checking in at my hotel, I headed over to look at the view of the ocean. There was no beach to speak of and with it being high tide and windy, there wasn't much to see except the palm fronds blowing. Nearby moored dhow boats bobbed ferociously up and down in the white-capped water. I closed my eyes and took in the salty scent, promising myself to be mindful in the moment. "Don't obsess about Julie" had so far been my mantra of the trip. But no matter how much I said that over and over to myself, she had constantly been on my mind.

Julie had always been very good about being in touch and we would send each other messages every few days just to check in. But she had been conspicuously quiet all weekend. When I got back to the room after my salty ocean stroll, I sent her another cheery text to tell her about my Kili hike. I was trying not to be paranoid but between being used to bad luck over anything to do with fertility and maybe also some kind of premonition, those turbulent Indian Ocean waves had sent me into a deep malaise.

Within ten minutes, she replied back. She hadn't been in touch because she had started spotting earlier in the weekend and had called the doctor. One of the reasons we had initially decided to work with Julie was that she seemed very proactive about many things, including her health. She hadn't wanted to tell us in case it was nothing, but she got checked and tests confirmed that she had miscarried. My heart sank. After asking if she was okay and how she was doing mentally (she said she was fine and resting), I lay down on the double bed, numb. The mosquito netting had been opened around my bed by housekeeping and I absentmindedly started playing with it, watching the white net billow as dusk ominously danced into my room. My mind then started racing, and I tried, desperately, to control my breathing.

What had I ever done to make this happen? Was I some kind of terrible person who deserved all this dreadful misfortune? Was it karma coming back to haunt me? Why had my ovaries betrayed me and sent out only batches of sorrowful follicles that spoiled instead of basking in the warm glow of a womb? My poor eggs only ever seemed able to survive as embryos for eight weeks. They were good for nothing more. I already knew my large and dismal womb was like Miss Havisham's rotting Satis House, decayed and covered over in proverbial cobwebs. Yet it seemed that even out of my body, my genetic material was soaked in feebleness and futility. The overly familiar self-loathing that was borne out of my infertility had grabbed hold of me with its full fractious force. (I discovered only later that my feelings of worthlessness are very common feelings in women suffering from infertility.)

As I listened to the melodic whirl of the fan overhead, I ground my hands into the skin over my pointless ovaries. I angrily kneaded away at the physical representation of my heartache and desperation. I kept thinking I should call my husband, my mother, my brothers. But I couldn't. I just kept pressing down and down until I couldn't physically take the pain anymore. I gasped and screamed out. My two miscarried dreams—one that had died in me and one that had died in Julie—I would never know. Never would I ever get to hear their cute deep giggles or wipe away their tears. I could never help those babies with their homework or walk with them along my Lake Michigan. I would never see my face in theirs or hear their sweet voices calling out for me on a playground. I simply wasn't destined to be their mom.

The mental anguish was so deep and so desolate that it felt

like my soul had cracked open. The sorrow spilled out of me, swirling up to the ceiling fan, where it was then flung across the room. My heartache hit the walls violently, oozing down to the floor. Stronger, it seemed, than me, it army-crawled back over to the bed and crept up through the mosquito netting, finding me once again. I lay for hours lamenting over never having a biological child. All my hopes destroyed in one text message. I was physically so far removed from my own reality and everyone I loved, and yet that distance also gave me room for my pain and somehow it also brought me some solace as I drifted off, finally, to sleep. Back home in London I would have been consumed by my misery for weeks but in Tanzania, where everyday realities were so disparate from my own, it brought me the perspective I needed at that time.

I hit the ground running the next morning, casting aside my pounding grief as I headed off to meet the Camfed team. Nothing ever cleared my head like on-the-ground reporting, and after we had a perfunctory meeting with the local government's head of education, we dropped in on the first school. Resplendent in khaki skirts and starched white head coverings—along Tanzania's Swahili Coast there is a large Muslim population—the girls came into the classroom shy yet curious. These girls came from some of the most extreme situations and were delighted to receive provisions that included shoes, notebooks, sanitary napkins, solar lights and, for a few, mattresses.

I got a chance to speak with some of the girls and their grateful mothers, who had come to pick up these life-enhancing items. These women, dressed in bright colorful dresses of oranges, yellows, and pinks, put the packets on their heads and started heading home. A few told me that they had never had the opportunity to go beyond primary school—not surprising to me as 76 percent of girls in Tanzania never get to secondary school—so they knew how important it was for their daughters to stay in school. I walked and chatted with a few of them, noting that a number of solar lights had been left in the sand outside one of the classrooms, charging up in the bright coastal sun.

In the afternoon we went to another school where I sat in a small colorful library with a group of fourteen-year-old girls, including one bashful teen named Fatima. Maybe it was her silence and her awkwardness—tugging on her white headscarf repeatedly throughout the session and frequently wringing her hands—that made me hone in on her a bit more than the others. She told us that her favorite classes were biology and physics. She then said something that truly caught my attention.

When I asked about her morning routine, she explained that she got up each day at 5:00 a.m. She would do housework before she woke up her nine-year-old sister, got her breakfast, and then send her off to primary school. After school, Fatima would walk the fifteen minutes home to start preparing dinner, which was usually *ugali,* a dish made from maize that resembles polenta. She and her sister would then do their homework using their solar lights. "Sounds like you do a lot at home—do your parents work early so that they have to leave home before you are awake?" I asked her.

She shyly looked at her feet, re-adjusted her headscarf and then told me in a powerful voice that they lived alone. Her parents had split up and her father worked several hours away as a security guard on a game reserve. Her mother, meanwhile, had remarried and moved to Dar Es Salaam where she worked in a tuck shop. Though this is something that happens with frequency across the developing world, I was still dumbstruck by not only her perseverance to stay in school but also that she understood that education was likely her only chance for a better life. Fatima told me when she grew up, she either wanted to be a soldier, like her uncle, or a doctor. When I asked her if she ever had any downtime to just sit in the grass and look up into the azure sky, she told me, "No, I have no time to watch the clouds."

That afternoon, reviewing my interview notes, I let my mind wander back to my conversation with Fatima. On the one hand I understood that her mother had to make sacrifices for survival (she always sent money back to the girls), but it also pained me that a girl so young and at such an exposed stage in her life was forced to take on such a heady responsibility. Without a parent to guide her, it threw up all sorts of concerns about making appropriate life choices. The exploitation of women and young girls was rife across Africa and with Julie's dire news from the night before constantly in the back of my mind, it got me thinking how surrogacy played out in countries like Tanzania.

I had read a few stories over the years where some surrogates were treated abysmally and that there were some dodgy—and even tragic—situations that arose because of lack of regulations. Even though surrogacy was less expensive in countries outside the US—it can cost upwards of $100,000—we had purposely never looked at cross-border surrogacy in countries like Ukraine, Mexico, India, or for that matter, Tanzania, because I had grave concerns around the vast economic disparity between IPs and surrogates. For a woman keen to make a lot of money in a relatively short period of time—in India through surrogacy a woman could earn $7000 in nine months versus it taking seven years to make that amount as a casual laborer or a cook[70]—I could understand how being a gestational carrier could appeal.

From the 1980s onwards, cross-border surrogacy became more and more popular. First, the technology was advancing in leaps and bounds. Second, laws were becoming more permissive in US states like California and Florida, while in a number of countries across Europe, there were either no laws on the books or, like in Britain, surrogacy was allowed only for heterosexual couples.[71] Also for couples that were either priced out of surrogacy at home—or it was illegal in their home country—international surrogacy gave them an option. In 1987 one of the first known international surrogacy cases happened when a nineteen-year-old Mexican woman, Arellano Munoz, crossed the US border illegally to be impregnated with her husband's cousin's sperm. The mother of three later argued that she did not understand the terms of the contract.[72]

Two years later, the ethically sketchy California-based Bionetics Foundation announced that it would be opening a surrogacy center in the Philippines. It was marketed toward middle-class American couples who, instead of paying a US surrogate between $10,000 and $15,000, could save money by paying an Asian woman only $2,000 to have their baby.[73] Meanwhile in 1995, newspaper ads for surrogacy began appearing in Poland. They subtly solicited Polish women to be surrogates for couples in Germany, Belgium, and Holland, promising them the rough equivalent of two years of an average Polish salary. In 1997 in India, a woman desperate to get medical treatment for her paralyzed husband said she would carry a baby for 50,000 rupees, the equivalent today of about $650.[74]

Of course, that kind of money could be life changing. "Some of the women I have met [in the US] who are surrogates don't have to do it to survive, it's, 'it is nice we get some luxury goods we would not normally get,'" Prof. Kalantry told me in 2020. "But for women who are doing it [in places like India] 'my husband had an accident,' 'I need a house,' 'I need to marry my daughter,'

'I need an education,' so it's basic goods they are doing it for."
She added that while Western women most often do surrogacy
because they like being pregnant and view their surrogacy as a
gift, that was not what women in India were saying. "'Yes, we like
it, and we are making money from it,'" said Prof. Kalantry, para-
phrasing Indian surrogates, "'but we wouldn't be doing it if we
had the money not to do it.'"

With that carrot-and-stick scenario, I could imagine how dubi-
ous agencies might therefore take advantage, not sufficiently
explaining the risks to a potential carrier's health that can be
associated with IVF pregnancies. Research has shown that some
international agencies don't do the proper due diligence on mental health screenings that legitimate agencies in the West require.
One journalist who has done investigative reports into surrogacy
in several countries across the globe told me that she heard a
story of one surrogate in Ukraine who, after giving birth to the
baby, committed suicide by jumping out of the hospital window.

I was also troubled because during all my years writing on
girls' education, I had seen firsthand how high levels of poverty
coincide with poor access to quality education. What that meant
was that many potential surrogates in developing countries
likely would not understand some of the legalese in a contract,
if they even had the capacity to read them. Prof. Kalantry told me
that in India some contracts were only in English, so even those
who could read Hindi weren't able to understand what they were
signing.

Meanwhile, there were cases where surrogates were never
even given copies of their contracts to know their rights and
what was expected of them. One even had it expressly written
in the contract that the Indian surrogate would not be allowed
to keep a copy.[75] Meanwhile in Mexico, many women in Tabasco,

Cancun, and Mexico City were given only brief verbal explanations of their contracts.[76] If they had questions, no one was made available to answer them, with one lawyer telling a surrogate that she had to obey the doctors and if she didn't like it, "don't sign."[77]

Oftentimes the same agency or clinic personnel that explained the contract to the surrogate were also the IPs' legal advisors. Just like in India, a number of Mexican surrogates were not given copies of their contracts or offered the chance to renegotiate its terms.[78] "A lot of contracts are in English [and] then they are given to sign having never really read them," said Isabel Fulda Graue, the deputy director of Mexico's leading legal defense and advocacy organization Grupo de Información en Reproducción Elegida (GIRE). "Or while the contracts are explained to them very clearly by the agency, they have no way of negotiating the different aspects of them."

Mexican agencies have been also known to obstruct communication between surrogates and IPs, stating to each that the other had no interest in establishing contact. The reality, meanwhile, was agencies prevented parties from meeting because they both might uncover irregularities like respect of payments.[79] Several surrogacy contracts in the state of Tabasco did not allow for surrogates to terminate their pregnancies even if their lives were in danger, despite the fact that the state's criminal code does not penalize abortion when the woman's life and health were at risk.

The global surrogacy landscape is truly a patchwork, with countries broadly taking five different approaches to it: prohibitive, tolerant, regulatory, free-market, and medical.[80] The prohibitive approach does as it sounds, with surrogacy prohibited in any form. An example of this would be Spain and Germany. The problem with this approach is that while these countries may succeed in protecting their own citizens from potential exploitation, "the price of this protection is paid" by people in other jurisdictions. So these prohibitive jurisdictions "uphold their own moral principles," while turning a blind eye to what happens elsewhere and then claim "the moral high ground when knowing full well that the undesired practices take place elsewhere and the 'results' are then accepted is, at best, cynical."[81]

The tolerant approach, seen in places like England (not inclusive of the rest of Britain), Hong Kong, and Australia, are countries that do not regulate surrogacy but "exercise control over its effects."[82] Israel, New Zealand, and South Africa, for example, use the regulatory approach where not only is surrogacy tolerated but it is actively facilitated. The free-market approach, which includes US states like California, and Ukraine, do not regulate who can enter into a surrogacy arrangement, permitting instead for private compensated surrogacy arrangements to be enforced.[83] The final approach, medical, is currently practiced in jurisdictions including Japan and South Korea where surrogacy is regulated by medical/ethical guidelines but are non-binding and unenforceable.

As of 2017 there were fourteen countries that allowed both compensated and uncompensated surrogacy, and of those a few countries—including the US, Georgia, Ukraine, and some states in Mexico—also permitted cross-border surrogacy. While fifty countries prohibited any and all forms of surrogacy, twenty-one countries permitted only uncompensated surrogacy for their citizens, with Canada allowing cross-border uncompensated surrogacy as well (except Quebec, which for the moment, bans all types).[84] Another seventy-two countries had undeterminable policies.[85] Tanzania, along with thirty-seven other countries like Kenya, Laos, Poland, and Iran, have no regulations relating to surrogacy. So that would mean that young women just a few years older than Fatima could technically be surrogates. But with no rules, it could create serious legal, financial, and health care heartaches if problems arose. "To be honest," said one journalist who has reported on a number of cross-border surrogacy scandals, "if it is in a Third World-ish country, it will be absolutely riddled with bad cases."

Up until a few years ago India, Thailand, Nepal, and Mexico had thriving surrogacy markets.[86] Yet each of these countries, which saw an explosion in surrogacy over a short period of time combined with a dearth of surrogacy laws and statutes, also quickly saw their international surrogacy markets implode due to global coverage of abusive practices. In Thailand—where surrogates were paid up to $10,000—because of its high-quality health care facilities, personnel, and its relatively low costs, for a time was a global hot spot.[87] It was estimated in 2015 that there were thirty fertility clinics in the country working on between 3,000 and 4,000 surrogacy cases a year. The country's fertility industry was valued at around $125 million.[88] That, however, was the last year that international surrogacy was allowed because of a few shocking cases.

The first involved Mitsutoki Shigeta, a twenty-eight-year-old son of a Japanese billionaire, who fathered thirteen children, using nine Thai surrogates. In late 2014, police found nine children, whose ages ranged from two weeks to two years, in the care of twenty-four-hour nannies in a luxury Bangkok apartment. (Four other children were also found to be fathered by him).[89] The children were placed in foster homes while he petitioned the court for custody. Campaigners raised concerns over the case, stating that it was "way outside the norm for cross-border surrogacy" and highlighted that the practice needed stronger regulation.[90]

In 2018, Mr. Shigeta was awarded custody of all thirteen

children. In an even more distressing case, a story broke in July 2014 that a child—Baby Gammy—with Down syndrome had been abandoned in Thailand by his Australian intended parents. The couple took his healthy twin sister back home but left the boy with his twenty-one-year-old Thai gestational carrier, Pattaramon Janbua. Baby Gammy's father, David Farnell, who was later found to have been convicted of child sex offenses when he was younger, claimed that no couple would want to raise a baby with Down syndrome.[91]

The scandal received such international outcry that the military government that ruled Thailand at the time began the process of drafting a new law intended to put an end to commercial surrogacy altogether. It was signed into law by King Rama IX in April 2015. With international surrogacy illegal, for now, in that corner of Southeast Asia, some agencies moved their business to Cambodia. But just a year later in 2016, after a few nefarious cases emerged, surrogacy was criminalized there by using existing human trafficking laws. According to a New York Times piece, "Dozens of surrogates have been arrested, accused of trafficking the babies they birthed."[92] Now the business of surrogacy has moved on to a third country, Laos, where there are currently no laws whatsoever. According to Stephen Page, an Australian lawyer who focuses his work on cross-border surrogacy, some Thai surrogates will get impregnated in Cambodia and then go to Laos to have the babies. So cross-border surrogacy is still very much happening in Thailand, just in more illicit ways.

India, meanwhile, had such a booming international commercial surrogacy industry that for several years it was the world's largest market for fertility tourism.[93] The country had a long history in fertility treatments, dating back to the late 1970s when the world's second IVF baby, Kanupriya Agarwal, was born in

Calcutta just a few months after Louise Brown. Though the practice of commercial surrogacy had been ongoing since 1997 with the commissioning of India's first surrogate, as part of a larger effort to promote medical tourism in 2002 the country legalized surrogacy.[94] One of the country's pioneers of surrogacy was Dr. Nayna Patel, the founder of Gujarat's Akanksha Fertility Clinic. She was so well-known that she was featured not only on a 2007 segment on *Oprah* but also as the protagonist in the Israeli documentary *Google Baby*.

That was in part because Dr. Patel, who charged between $15,000 and $20,000 per surrogacy, had assisted a grandmother to deliver twins for her British-based daughter in 2004. "Lots of people were commenting on it, good and bad, because the grandmother delivered the grandkids," Dr. Patel told me in a video interview. "More people started reaching out to me and I met couples and saw how desperate they were. We were offering all services under one roof."

As surrogacy grew in India—with both heterosexual and gay couples coming from across the globe to have babies—so too did the market. It jumped from $445 million in 2008 to upwards of between $1 and $2 billion by 2012, where that year 10,000 foreign clients visited the estimated 800 fertility clinics in the country.[95] The Indian Council of Medical Research (ICMR) even speculated it might grow to be a $6 billion a year industry. However, though the ICMR issued guidelines on surrogacy in 2005 and many fertility clinics followed them, they were neither tough nor mandatory.[96] That was because there was no statute at the federal or state level on surrogacy. And just like what had happened in Thailand, a number of troubling high-profile cases started springing up that garnered global attention.

The first was the case of Baby Manji, a baby girl born in July

2008 whose Japanese parents got divorced when their surrogate was still pregnant. The egg had come from a donor and the intended mother decided she no longer wanted to parent the child. Because Japan only recognizes the birth mother as the legal mother, the child could not obtain a Japanese passport. And under an Indian law from 1890 called the Guardian Wards Act, single men could not adopt girls in India.[97] In the end, her paternal grandmother was finally able to get temporary custody and travel back with her to Japan in the end of 2008.[98] Another high-profile case involved German twins, Nikolas and Leonard Balaz, who were also born in India in 2008. Since German law prohibits surrogacy, the embassy would not issue the boys a passport, rendering them stateless. After a protracted two-year legal battle, they were finally issued visas and their parents then initiated proceedings to adopt them under German law.

These concerns over exploitation and statelessness eventually led the Indian government in 2015 to ban all international surrogacy. Prof. Kalantry told me that throughout the whole political process, not a single surrogate was ever asked her opinion. In 2022 the Surrogacy (Regulation) Act, 2021, went into effect. That law broadly makes it so that only non-compensated surrogacy is allowed for married heterosexual Indian couples, but the carrier would have to be a close relative of the couple.[99] That law now also aims to make compensated surrogacy unenforceable, and it makes sure that only accredited surrogacy facilities can perform surrogacy-related medical procedures. They are also, rightly so, prohibited from pressuring women to be surrogates by "deceptive advertising of other means."[100]

Lopamudra Goswami, an Australian-based Indian psychologist whose doctoral research examined surrogacy in India, told me in an interview before the bill passed that she was doubtful

India would ever give up on surrogacy altogether. "There is a massive billion-dollar business around it, India has invested a lot in the fertility industry, and they benefit massively from it," she told me. Plus, in a country where "my sister-in-law's sister's husband's sister is also my relative so she can be my surrogate," she believes the loopholes could make the law fragile.

However, Lavanya Regunathan Fischer, a German-based lawyer who works on family law cases in India, feels that India did the right thing because, "it was such a mess that the only way they could regulate it was to shut it down completely." Though she believes that it "changes who can be a family and I am really upset by that," in many ways the law addressed a lot of the problems. "What happened was that surrogacy basically shut down for everyone, except for Indian citizens who could not have their own children," she told me in an interview in early 2024. "So, it was a very narrow group of people."

As I closed my notebook in the late afternoon sun in Bagamoyo, I noticed I had a niggling feeling in the pit of my stomach. All day I had pushed aside my heartache as I spoke with the schoolgirls. But now that I was back at the hotel and all I could hear were the giggles of kids jumping in the pool, I had an urgent need to get out of there. The thought of another night in that room, so filled up with recent memories of my anguish and sorrow that it felt suffocating, thoroughly depressed me. It felt like I had lost a piece of my heart that night before in Bagamoyo and the thought of being far away from there felt like some kind of step in the right direction. So I checked out early and headed to Dar es Salaam. That evening over dinner at a beachside restaurant, I called and texted with a number of friends and family to tell them about the miscarriage. To say it out loud meant that it had happened. It was all a part of my reckoning.

The next day I headed for a work trip to Kenya—where there are no surrogacy laws on the book and surrogacy is happening with more frequency—and on the drive in from the airport, my taxi driver queried if I had children. While it was a natural small talk question, it struck me tight in the chest. I had to take a moment to breathe. Looking out the window watching the red clay dust kick up as a *boda boda* driver flew by on his motorbike, I tried to stop my throat from choking with my response. "No, I can't have kids," I finally said with a melancholic smile. "Aw, so you are barren," the good-natured if obtuse man said as he grinned at me in the rear view of his mirror. "Because of that, you know, if you were Kenyan, your husband could take another wife." I am not sure if that comment was meant as matter of fact or just to lighten the mood, but I let out a bemused chuckle. What a long, strange trip this had so far been.

His comment reinforced to me that views on infertility and surrogacy across the globe are far from uniform. The backgrounds and motivations of women like Julie in the US and Orit in Israel are quite different from women in places like Kenya, Mexico, and India. Vasanti Jadva from the University of Cambridge's Centre for Family Research told me it's difficult to compare surrogacy across different countries and make assumptions by looking through the lens of just one cultural context. "I have met other academics from different countries, and we can all be sitting in one room," she said, "and somebody is talking about surrogacy as being really harmful and some negative experiences for the surrogate like exploitation. And [my colleagues and I] are just looking at each other going, 'That is not what surrogacy is like in the UK.'"

Israel, where all IVF is paid for by the state, is a case in point. First legalized in 1996, surrogacy is tightly regulated by the state and all contracts must be pre-approved by a government committee. All parties must be Israeli citizens or permanent residents, they must be the same religion and they cannot be related to each other.[101] Everyone involved also has to go through comprehensive medical and psychological screenings and, according to Orit, surrogates are interviewed for about an hour by two of the members of the government's surrogacy panel.

The paperwork is also quite bureaucratic. "If you pass that part of the process," she said with a laugh, pulling at her graying upswept bun, "it shows that you are very organized, and you know how to handle your time." Originally, Israeli surrogates had to be single and raising at least one child. As Elly Teman wrote in her book *Birthing a Mother*: "That single status was written into law as a precaution that the child would be recognized as a fully 'kosher' Jew by the rabbinical establishment because a child born to a married woman and fathered by a married man who is not that woman's husband is considered a bastard under Jewish law."

Dr. Teman told me that what came out very strongly in her interviews was that carriers were not ashamed to admit that, at least initially, they were doing it for the cash. The women were all raising their children, some with deadbeat husbands, but mostly single moms. "They needed money, and they wanted their kids to have a good Bar Mitzvah and they became surrogates to pay for that," she said. "And they all said, 'I did it for the money but also for the mitzvah,' which is, like, the good deed. It wasn't like there were two separate spheres; getting money didn't make mitzvah—the good deed—not be there." However, like their American counterparts, a number of carriers said that it later became more than just about the money. The desire and accomplishment of delivering a healthy baby had taken precedence over making extra money.

In 2013 Israel changed its laws around surrogacy, in part, because fewer unmarried women were willing to become surrogates. Plus, the country's chief rabbi wrote a letter supporting the change. While there were some similarities between the two cohorts, this second group of (mostly) married gestational carriers including Orit—who at the time of our interviews in 2020 was doing her doctorate focused on surrogacy—were in a higher socioeconomic category than the previous group of women and surrogacy was no longer seen as something odd.[102] "When they allowed married surrogates, they were not women who needed the money, they were women who wanted to do something for society," Dr. Teman said.

This reminded me of a Jewish friend telling me there is deep-rooted feeling in many Jewish communities across the globe that you should have one more child than your parents did to make up for the murder of six million Jews during the Holocaust. Maybe this was a subconscious societal reason as well for why Israeli women wanted to do surrogacy. "Women are saying 'how can I do something that can make the world a better place?' or 'how can I do something that will make me feel like I have been here, I have done something important?'," Dr. Teman told me. "A lot of these women [use] surrogacy as a model to teaching their children to stay involved in society."

This new cohort described their surrogacy experience as a "journey" (just like US surrogates did) and they downplayed the role of payment as a motivation.[103] Orit told me that there is something of a basement and a ceiling in terms of compensation and she even knew a surrogate who asked for less than what the IPs had offered her because she didn't need the money. "I saw the money not as a salary but as compensation," Orit said, adding she used her payment not only for a long-awaited family trip to South Africa but also to help finance her doctorate. "The amount is not an amount that will change your life. It's not like you are winning the lottery, right? You can't build a house with that money."

Conversely, however, in places like India and Russia, that oftentimes was precisely the case. "[Surrogacy] really helped a lot of families where they had this shift of living in a *kutcha* [mud] house to having a duplex house, which is concrete," said Ms. Goswami. "They would say, 'We can live on the ground floor and the second floor we can rent this out' so that is ongoing income." The demographics of women in India who become surrogates are very often those from lower middle-class and poor backgrounds, and many are not well-educated.

According to Dr. Amrita Pande, a Cape Town–based anthropologist, this has led to some in the international arena not bothering to confer with them when it comes to discussing and debating the complexities of surrogacy in India. "I get [from people] 'there is no point in consulting these women in India, there might be some point in consulting surrogates in Israel or a point to those in the US,'" said Dr. Pande, who has created and toured a multi-media theatre production *Made in India: Notes from a Baby Farm* that is based on her ethnographic work on surrogacy. "But somehow women in the Global South fall through the cracks because they are assumed to be uneducated [and] that someone else needs to speak on their behalf."

Many Indian surrogates faced a high degree of stigmatization, keeping their surrogacies a secret from their communities and families. Some even chose—or were greatly coerced by their clinics—to live in surrogate hostels for some or all of their pregnancies. "If all things were fine, if it was not a stigmatized occupation, if there was insurance, if there was health care for these women in their villages they would not have to stay in these places," said Dr. Pande. She added that while hostels were not the norm—of the 2,000 or so clinics in India only about three or four surrogacy doctors had hostels in place—and many women could not wait to leave them, they also became informal spaces for sharing collective grievances and camaraderie with other surrogates. A few women who met in surrogacy hostels even went into business together afterwards. "The [women] are quite cognizant of the fact that if they were at home, they would have to do all of the housework and have sex with their husbands and not be able to take care of their bodies the way they want to," she said. "So they make the best out of the hostels."

There have been situations in China too. Though commercial surrogacy has been illegal since 2001 there are reported to be up to 10,000 surrogate births annually in the country plus about 1,000 Chinese surro-babies born in the US each year.[104] Some Chinese gestational carriers were contractually obligated to reside in surrogate dorms. They were governed by rules including having to be asleep by 9:30 p.m. and not being allowed to tell family and friends their whereabouts.[105]

For many Russian surrogates, during the later stages of pregnancy they lived away from home as well, sometimes either with their IPs or in apartments nearby to "monitor and control them."[106] In Russia—where surrogacy became legal in 1995 and international surrogacy ended in 2022—many women do surrogacy in order to buy their own flat. Dr. Christina Weis, a British-based sociologist who has done research on surrogacy in St. Petersburg, said that is in part a hangover from the Soviet days where apartments were collective properties. "Having a flat that nobody can increase the rent or take away from you means a lot," she told me.

One of the nurses who worked in a surrogacy clinic told Dr. Weis that these days it would take two pregnancies for a surrogate—who can expect to receive compensation between $10,000 and $20,000[107]—to afford to buy a home. However, in the early 2000s when surrogacy was more of a rarity, women could "literally swap a pregnancy for an apartment."

Russian surrogates, as well as a number of Ukrainian and Belorussian women who traveled to St. Petersburg to be carriers, tended to be almost an even fifty/fifty split between single mothers and those either in a relationship or married.[108] They were quite well-educated, with many having good schooling and a degree, but they struggled to earn a decent wage in a post-Soviet economy.[109] While Dr. Weis found that they were definitely not the poorest women "they are not middle class like Americans." Russian agencies tended to have bad opinions of women who are surrogates. "They view them as uneducated, stupid women, and have very misogynistic ways of talking about them," said Dr. Weis, who wrote *Surrogacy in Russia: An Ethnography of Reproductive Labour, Stratification and Migration*. "I have horrible quotes about how these women are 'made to give birth in the woods and in the fields and we need stupid, sturdy women that breed.'" She said the agencies, which in turn pass this philosophy down to IPs, believe that "the dumber the better" because they likely wouldn't question the rules.

Most Russian agencies would only accept women who are financially motivated and weren't keen to have altruism as a reason why gestational carriers want to do surrogacy. That Western cultural framing of surrogacy being a gift, or a "labor of love" is generally absent in Russia (as well as Ukraine) and it was seen as a purely economic exchange. That's in part because surrogates who appeared too selflessly motivated, who have emotional involvement and a good relationship with IPs could spoil the outcome. Agencies wanted their surrogates to be financially focused. "They ground their policies and rhetoric on the notion that money-oriented women make better workers," wrote Dr. Weis in an essay, "as they will do whatever is necessary to maximize their profit."[110]

Jay Nault, a California-based father who chronicled he and his wife's Ukrainian surrogacy journey in the blog flipflops inkiev.com, said that was the impression he got from their surrogate. The woman, whose name he was never told during their entire surrogacy journey, reached out to him about six months after their twin boys were born in Kyiv. "I get a Facebook direct message [from] a name I did not recognize and it's her and she [writes], 'just so you know, if you need any more kids, you can contact me directly,'" Jay told me. "I think for her this was entirely a business arrangement. I think she got about $15,000 or $20,000 [for the surrogacy] so remember that was the equivalent of three and a half years of the average women's income in Ukraine." He said he'd been told she was remodeling her entire house with the money she received for the surrogacy.

Like in the US and Israel, Russian surrogates also have turned to the internet to seek support. In large part that's because being a gestational carrier in Russia—where it's estimated there are between 400 and 500 surrogacy births a year[111]—is stigmatized not only by the wider Russian public but often by surrogates' families and friends as well. Researchers in Israel who looked at one Russian-language platform found that the stigmatization fell into four categories: bad mothers (because they are seen to give away "their" children), bad wives (women humiliating their husbands by carrying someone else's baby), pathetic losers (taking part in "indecent and physically revolting" practices), and greedy women who get large sums of money for something that is seen as an easy job.[112] "Russian surrogates," the researchers wrote, "often cloak themselves in silence over their work, fully aware that others might reject them on moral grounds."[113]

Another country that had, for a short time, a thriving surrogacy sector was Mexico. According to April Hovav, a California-based academic who did research on Mexican surrogates, most women were not the poorest of the poor. "Within Mexico there are really extreme levels of poverty and I think there was an assumption [on my part] before I went that women would be the kind of most extreme poor and they weren't," she told me. "But it's all relative because I was told that if you have flooring instead of dirt you are not seen as super poor. [It] was more lower-middle-class women [who] had limited employment options."

While most Mexican surrogates did understand the health risks, many of them actually didn't grasp the medical nuances of a surrogate pregnancy—namely, how the babies got into them in the first place. If they had a husband or a partner, the man sometimes assumed that she had a sexual relationship with the intended father. Because the IVF procedure is so technical, it is not well explained to them and there might be an insecurity to ask. "So they just say 'yeah, something happened and then after I got pregnant and I think it wasn't my ovaries, but I am not sure,'" said Isabel Fulda Graue from GIRE. "There is a general lack of understanding the idea that they are doing an arrangement to carry the child of someone else."

This Mexican scenario reinforced to me the huge difference between surrogacies and how in many developing countries surrogates seemed to lack voice and agency over their decisions and experiences. Personally, I would never have been comfortable not knowing my surrogate and not being able to communicate with her. While Julie and I both openly acknowledged that we would never end up being bosom buddies, I wanted to get to know her out of respect to her, plus probably there was some control-based reasons for me in terms of being able to reach out to her directly whenever I wanted.

Sadly, in a number of cross-border surrogacy experiences, it's not an unusual story for both IPs and surrogates to never get to meet and know each other either before or during the pregnancy. This is in part because, agencies claim, it could create tricky situations. "I think it was genuinely just complex, the whole scenario," Lakshmi Little[114], a British-born Indian-based mother through surrogacy, told me in terms of meeting a potential Indian surrogate. "It's definitely partly financial, especially with foreigners, like [surrogates deciding] 'I want more money.'"

According to Mariam Kukunashvili, a doctor who is the Georgian co-founder of the IVF, egg donation, and surrogacy agency New Life that over the years has set up—and sometimes later closed—business in countries including Mexico, Kenya, Thailand, and Ukraine, this has been the case with some of her surrogates as well. "Not every surrogate has the same character," she told me. "Sometimes if parents have a close relationship with them, they start [telling tales]. We have had such situations and parents get very nervous." A mother herself through surrogacy, she told me that while her surrogate lived at Dr. Kukunashvili's mother's house while she was pregnant with Dr. Kukunashvili's triplets, some IPs want to have a more formal relationship. "Some parents do not want to have direct contact," she told me. "If parents want to have communication, it's okay and if they don't want to, we cannot force anyone."[115]

What I found telling—and troubling—from this conversation was that many relationships are led by what the intended parents (the paying clients) want; that oftentimes the surrogates seem to have no say in the matter. Dr. Jadva said she discovered this during a conference where the contrasts between the US and Indian surrogacy struck her as very stark. The idea of switching to a different surrogate on the day of implantation—which happened with some frequency in India and Thailand—was shocking to Americans. "But the Indians were saying 'yeah, but if a different surrogate is going to have a better success rate than, surely, we should go for that surrogate,'" she said. "It was just very different attitudes to who they saw as their patient and what they thought was important."

Lakshmi was never allowed to meet her Indian surrogate throughout the entire pregnancy and didn't even get a chance to thank her in person after the gestational carrier gave birth to their daughter. When I asked Lakshmi's gynecologist, Anahita Pandole, why she was not able to meet her carrier, I was told that the situation in India is completely different to Western countries where surrogacy is legal. It was, she felt, equally important to take into consideration how the surrogate felt. "Sometimes the surrogates are not comfortable," she told me, flipping Mariam's point about Georgian and Ukrainian surrogates. "And you have to respect both sides." However, Dr. Jadva's research in India revealed that while several surrogates she spoke to did want to meet their IPs, the new parents didn't want to meet them so agencies followed what the IPs wanted. "They didn't really consider the surrogates' own views," she said. "We published our findings that actually the [surrogates] would benefit from this, and they would like to have some sort of information about the child and a photo as a little memento."

Interestingly, this mindset has started to carry over a bit to the US where many Chinese, Indian, and Asian IPs show little interest in getting to know potential surrogates. Julie told me she turned down one Chinese couple because it felt to her like it was a business transaction. "They were like, 'yes we want you to give us this kid, but we don't want to talk to you and we don't want to know anything about you,'" she said. Over the years Wendie Wilson-Miller, who runs two West Coast surrogacy agencies and is former president of the US's Society for Ethics for Egg Donation and Surrogacy (SEEDS), has made a point to educate a number of foreign couples who came to her with a similar take.

Initially, she said, they're confused as to why they need to have a relationship with a surrogate if she is getting compensation. "There is just this sort of cultural divide in the way that they view it," she said, adding that open communication between IPs and surrogates has become one of SEEDS ethical standards. "What we are trying to do is bring babies into this world where from the very beginning, it's something that is more connected, more human. [So] if somebody comes to me and says, 'I don't want a relationship, I just want a carrier,' I am not the right agency for them."

When I returned to London from Kenya, my husband and I sat down to talk. It was yet another heart-to-heart that related to having a baby. Though we had asked Circle back in the summer about looking at working with a potential egg donor in case our embryos didn't work out, it had been more of a pie-in-the-sky conversation. I hadn't had to really think about what that process would look like because we still had some hope. But we were now all out of that, so we had some serious soul searching to do.

Chapter Five

Don't Spoil the Eggs

Few people on the planet can make me laugh like Ben and Offir.

I'd first met them through one of my closest friends, Bari Shaffran, in London. Ben was Bari's cousin who lived in Tel Aviv, and he and his partner, Offir, had come for one of her son's Bar Mitzvahs. We hit it off right away, in part because I was drawn to how smart, savvy, and salacious they were. Ben ran a photography gallery while Offir was a choreographer, and they could spin a yarn that could keep me rapt with attention for seemingly hours at a time. They had a talent for turning even the most banal or solemn of topics into something witty and thought-provoking.

Way back in the early days when my husband and I were still trying IVF, Ben and Offir were in London on another visit, and they told us that they wanted to have a baby via a surrogate. While Israel was the first country in the world to regulate surrogacy by legislation, during the time of our conversation the law in Israel was that only heterosexual married couples and single women could use a surrogate.[116] That meant that their only option was to find a surrogate abroad and since most countries that allowed compensated surrogacy—which at the time included

Russia, Georgia, and Ukraine—were only available to heterosexual couples, the US was the easiest, if priciest, option. They found a lawyer who then connected them with a clinic to find both an egg donor and a surrogate.

As we sat in Bari's garden one summer evening during their visit, we contemplated how the whole process would happen, and who their ideal egg donor and surrogate would be. They said while the most important thing about a surrogate was making sure they got along with her, they also joked that they hoped she'd be from a more "fun" state that they could explore before the baby (or babies) arrived. I asked them how they picked their egg donor, and they teasingly told me that they viewed it like looking through a J.Crew catalogue, finding physical attributes that they liked in terms of skin tone, body shape, and eye color.

Ben's family were Ashkenazi Jews from Hungary and the Czech Republic while Offir's were Sephardic Jews from Morocco. They put those aspects into consideration as they were hoping for twins, one would be genetically related to Ben and the other to Offir. When I pontificated that if I were ever in that situation, I would want someone who had a good level of education they laughed at me. "Why is that?" Ben asked me quizzically. I liked that they often challenged my throwaway comments on things, forcing me to have to articulate my thought process. "I guess I would want a smart kid," I said, laughing.

Offir then asked me something that I thought a lot about later. "Why would it matter how smart she is on paper or how much schooling she had? Look, we will educate our kids, give them life experiences, and make sure they get a great education," he said. "Sure, there's a whole nature point to all this, but they will have half my genes or half Ben's. Plus, we also believe a lot in nurture and knowing us, they are going to be fascinating, cool kids." I laughed at his assuredness and comedic touch. However, knowing them, I didn't doubt that would be the case anyway.

About two years after that initial conversation, while their West Coast-based surrogate was pregnant with their boy and girl twins, I called them up. "I need to talk to you guys," I said as I pulled into a parking space at a local John Lewis department store to run the most mundane of errands, buying a new toaster. I reminded them of our deep-into-the-night conversation from a few years back and filled them in on what had happened while I was in Tanzania. I then told them that while my head was moving ahead, my heart was still stuck over the fact that I wasn't going to have a genetic child. "Ginanne, come on now. Look, our cats aren't related to us and yet we love them like they are our own," Ben said, making me chortle (he and his two siblings were obsessed with cats and at one point they had something like a dozen between them). "And your dogs, Betsie and Mila, you love them unconditionally, right? They are like your furry children. You didn't give birth to them, and they obviously aren't related to you. But that doesn't matter does it?"

I agreed but argued that dogs and cats aren't the same as kids. "Well, obviously but the point is, you love something so much but aren't related to it, so what is blood?" Offir said, which we joked was funny considering that in order to be considered Jewish, it's about being born from the womb of a Jewish woman. "Who cares? Your baby will be your baby, you spent way more time thinking about and planning for this baby than your friends who get pregnant after a night out clubbing in Soho. Plus, who knows, maybe your kid will be better looking than if it was your genetic child." Their droll banter helped on this most heady of conversations. As I stared out into the suburban parking lot with moms pushing prams with screaming kids having tantrums, something in my heart started to shift. It seemed incredibly odd, ethically ambiguous, and yet also kind of intriguing to be able to pick out qualities like hair thickness and height. We did indeed live in astonishing times.

After a quick update on how their surrogate's pregnancy was progressing, I hung up and headed in for my toaster. As I walked through John Lewis, stopping to look at some tea towels and a toilet bowl brush, I thought about what Ben and Offir had said. For me, coming to terms with the realization that I wasn't going to pass on my genes was yet another deep loss that I had to endure on this IVF and surrogacy journey. Was I that much of a Dorian Gray narcissist that I needed a child to come from me? And what did it mean to be a mother—how do you define what that actually means? Someone born from your body? Someone related to you? With the donor do we become family to each other? Whose family is whose?

Renate Klein, an Australian women's health researcher and anti-surrogacy activist, examined egg donation in her rather outlandish (and sometimes inaccurate) book *Surrogacy: A Human Rights Violation*. She wrote that "some women feel resentful about the baby they know is not their own, and bitter because they remain infertile" yet they feel they aren't allowed to talk about it in public.[117] She goes on to say that selecting an egg by "looking at porn-like photos of young beautiful women on the internet" and choosing the provider of half the genes of a baby that will become the intending mother's child could release anguished emotions, which then lead to serious woe and even trauma.

These were concerns that I certainly had with donor conception, which according to *The Economist*, brings new kinds of relationships into the world "just as it brings new babies and new sadnesses."[118] Dr. Teman found in her research in Israel that many women concealed the fact that they used donor eggs. This is something that is consistent in Western popular media that depicts "the miraculous births of twins to postmenopausal celebrities without ever mentioning" the use of donor eggs. That's consistent with anthropological studies of secrecy among families who use donations of sperm or eggs.[119] "There's so much pressure on women to bloody procreate, spawn a child and become a mother," said Michael Johnson-Ellis, a gay father-of-two through surrogacy who runs the British-based My Surrogacy Journey consultancy, when I asked him the difference in how gay men and infertile women view egg donation. "Women are almost shamed into thinking, 'well, I do not fit the norm, so I am just going to keep my mouth shut.' And that really makes me sad [that] many women fear outing themselves."

Back in the later 1990s when I was young and lived in Washington, DC, a friend of mine told me she was thinking of donating her eggs to get some extra cash. We worked together at CNN, and we got meager paychecks for long stressful days running around the newsroom being yelled at and sometimes bullied by producers, editors, and on-air talent. On one hand I totally got that it was a struggle to pay her bills but, as I argued with her, egg donation wasn't the same as donating blood or plasma. "Eggs are your DNA; you have no control over how they are used or by whom and do you really want your genetic child out there in the world that you aren't raising? And that's not even considering how all those hormones could impact your health," I said to her as we strolled around Union Station's food court deciding between getting a salad or a burger.

I continued to deride her idea, saying she'd feel very weird if one day a random person (or even a couple of them) showed up at her house saying she was their genetic mother. She, of course, had a different take, saying she thought it would be cool to help people who couldn't have a child. Plus, she simply didn't view her eggs the way I did; they were something that she had that were little more than cells in her body that she shed each month. "I don't need those eggs right now and it's either that or I just lose one egg at a time with each period, which to someone who wants to start a family feels wasteful," she said. I took her point, but it still was something that made me uncomfortable. "You know what, to each their own," I said, attempting to defuse the conversation as I was getting more animated than I would have expected. "Do what you think makes the most sense to you." In the end she didn't do it, likely because our crazy and stressful work schedules would have proved an even more fraught experience pumped up with all sorts of hormones.

However, that conversation—and my hard and fast opinions on egg donation—had stuck with me for all those years. The fact that this now was the way we were likely going to have a child therefore felt slightly disingenuous to my old, vaguely constructed set of beliefs. For weeks I wrestled back and forth with the idea. I internalized so many questions: How did I know I could trust the donor in terms of the information she gave on mental and physical health history? What if my kids wanted to meet her one day, how would I handle that? How would it feel when people would say, "Oh she looks just like you?" Would I feel the desire to correct them? Would it be something that was always just a tinge of concern in the back of my mind, that I was not my child's "real" mother?

My husband and I talked—and argued—a lot about it all. He didn't really want to be involved in choosing a donor, saying it was up to me and my decision, though he did say he wanted the donor to be on the taller side. I think part of that was since I was the one who wouldn't be genetically related to the child, he felt I should choose what characteristics I was looking for since I now had a choice—and maybe some control—in the matter. But in hindsight, I understand that it was hard for him too. One time, when I was tearful about what to do—should we, shouldn't we?—he said with raw emotion, "You don't think that it makes me sad and hurts me too that we won't have a genetic child together? That we can't have your child? You never ask me what I feel, it's only about you." To be honest, he was completely right. I had never thought about it that way before. I was so caught up in how this was affecting me that I never did take the time to ask or understand his feelings. And I think this is one of the reasons that IVF can be so tough for a couple—that the infertile person becomes so consumed and obsessed in their own pain and heartache that they often don't have the capacity to contemplate how their partner feels. Guilty as charged.

Once we had finally made the decision to go ahead, I sent out an email to Circle, asking them about working with one of their egg donors. I didn't have the energy or interest to go to egg donor websites who worked with Ivy League-educated or model/actress egg donors. I was cognizant also that all this was affecting Julie's life, that we were essentially asking her to put her life on hold while we figured things out. To have to go through dozens of websites to find "the one" was going to be a time-consuming (and wasting) process. Really what we wanted was someone who was healthy, intelligent, kind and, for my husband, preferably over five feet four inches.

So much about infertility is the gaining and losing of control, which for someone like me was incredibly difficult. I had no control of my body in terms of getting pregnant naturally, so I took control by deciding to freeze my eggs and try IVF. But I lost my control with IVF because even though there is the misconception (pun intended) that if you can't get pregnant naturally, you can easily get pregnant with a little help from a doctor (who controls your doses) and syringes (that control your life in terms of when you have to take the shots); you can't control if what looks like a perfectly healthy bunch of cells in a test tube don't blast into an embryo. If you can't get pregnant because you have an inhospitable womb (can't control that!) you can take charge by deciding to go the route of surrogacy and selecting your surrogate.

But then you have to cede power to your surrogate in terms of her taking charge and making the best decisions for the baby while it's growing inside of her. With choosing an egg donor, I gained back (or so I thought) some control over the situation again because even though the child or children would not be genetically mine, I could cherry pick certain qualities and characteristics that I liked. While in a sense it felt like ultimate control, it also felt like a really intense game of Russian roulette because you really didn't know what you were going to get, and I realized I just had absolutely no power over any of it. All I could do was to keep moving the process along.

Once we had emailed Circle, Callie got back to us right away:

As you are looking at donor profiles, you should not only consider your preference for physical characteristics, but also her lifestyle, family medical history, and whether she would like to be a known or anonymous donor. You may also see the donor's requested fee on her profile. This fee is usually based upon whether or not she has donated before. Some donors will have the words, "On hold" or "Currently in Cycle" on their profiles. This means that they are currently matched/matching with another set of Intended

Parents. In your case, you want to find someone who does not have these words on their profile or whose availability date is within the next few months in order to keep your journey timeline on track.

Age, it seems, really does matter when it comes to egg donation, something my general practitioner had told me all those years ago when I froze my eggs before I turned the big 4-0. (According to *The Economist* currently less than 1 percent of births are from frozen eggs but it's estimated that number could rise to 10 percent, which could considerably increase the size of the global IVF market.)[120] The CDC has found that women of nearly any age can get pregnant as long as they use young, freshly donated eggs from women under the age of thirty.[121] That Julie was in her early 30s didn't matter if we could find a young egg donor. And there seemed to be a plethora to choose from. In the past several years there has been a sharp increase in the demand for donor eggs across the globe, in large part because many women (like me) wait to have their families until they are in their late thirties or forties. Unfortunately, by that time, their own eggs have deteriorated, and their supply is depleted.

Every year in the US, nearly 20,000 donor eggs are used to create IVF and surrogate babies and a woman can be paid between $5,000 and $10,000 and even more depending on things like where she went to college or her skin coloring and ethnicity.[122] Asian donors, for example, are rarer and therefore get paid more. In Spain, donors receive between €800 and €1,300 per donation while in Britain it's a different story.[123] There, all donors receive the same compensation of £750 per donation.[124] Emily Galpern, a consultant with the US's Center for Genetics and Society, said they should be called "egg providers" not donors because "they are paid." You can even choose what religion the donor is as, for example, to some Jewish couples that's important. In the US (as well as some other countries that actively participate in the global egg market), "aggressive heavily drug-dependent approaches that yield eggs in greater numbers" is the norm.[125] In Europe and other countries, meanwhile, where the sale of eggs is tightly regulated, and in some cases prohibited, health concerns have led to an increasing use of a natural cycle and minimum IVF stimulation.

I would assume that for anyone who has had to poke themselves with needles to insert synthetic liquid hormones into their body, there's at least a passing question or two over the potential health risks of what they're doing. For me, that was certainly the case, and I did have some moral quandaries about asking another woman to jack herself up on estrogen and other hormones to produce a large number of eggs for my benefit. Donors have to be on hormones for three weeks, must continually go to doctor appointments where they have blood work done and ultrasounds to see how the eggs are developing and how many are there. It's a grueling process and one not taken lightly unlike sperm donation, which is an easy process that usually doesn't take more than 15 minutes.[126] Like in any IVF procedure, eggs are removed surgically using an ultrasound probe connected to a needle that is pushed up through the vagina and into the ovary. Sometimes this procedure can puncture the ureter or an artery, causing abdominal bleeding or other internal injuries.[127] Ovaries that are hyper-stimulated to produce maturing eggs can sometimes swell up so much that they twist around other ligaments and cut off blood supply. As well as being very painful (and supposedly quite rare) it can also lead to an ovary having to be removed.[128]

The greatest risk, though, are the drugs themselves that are used to affect the number of eggs that will develop. And as any woman going through IVF (or working with an egg donor) will tell you, the more the merrier as it becomes a numbers game. More eggs mean, of course, more chances for creating more embryos. And that means better chances for pregnancy. But to get more eggs, women have to be pumped up to accelerate the process of multiple egg maturation. And that can lead to Ovarian Hyperstimulation Syndrome (OHSS), an exaggerated response to the drugs that can include symptoms like weight gain, nausea, and vomiting. (I knew one woman who was going through IVF and ended up in the hospital for about a week with OHSS.)

For women who have severe cases, blood vessels can become leaky with fluids gathering in the peritoneal cavity.[129] That can lead to everything from thrombosis to kidney and other organ failure, and, in some cases, death. All this coupled with the fact that there has not been a huge body of work examining the down-the-road health risks of IVF can be something of a scary prospect. Can fertility treatments lead to a greater risk of getting ovarian or breast cancer? And, for egg donors, how could it affect their future fertility? According to Debora Spar in *The Baby Business*, the "long term implications of egg donation are unknown."[130]

According to Liz Scheier from We Are Egg Donors, a US women's health and support forum, there has also never been a single long-term longitudinal health study on donors. "The words that every single donor has heard in this order are 'there are no known health risks to egg donation,'" she told me, adding she had donated three times when she was younger. "And that is true [because] no one has ever bothered to find out. Well, what we know anecdotally is that a lot of us are sick." The Center for Bioethics and Culture, a California-based conservative evangelical Christian think tank, has stated that fertility treatments are a "reckless endangerment" to women and babies. Its founder, Jennifer Lahl, a former pediatric nurse who also founded the Stop Surrogacy Now campaign, has been vocal that the assisted reproduction industry has a "dirty little secret," claiming that women who express an interest in egg donation are heavily pressured by clinics.[131]

Part of the problem, some say, is that advertisements meant to entice young women to donate oversimplify the process and downplay the risks.[132] That is in part because the fertility industry is worth billions and the need for donor eggs is a key component to the process. They need that supply because the demand keeps growing. "We need really good studies to follow these women for a long, long time because these breast cancers don't show up early," Ms. Lahl told me. "Two of my colleagues and I published a case report ["Long-term Breast Cancer Risks Following Ovarian Stimulation in Young Egg Donors" in Reproductive Biomedicine Online] of five otherwise healthy women who were not BRCA [breast cancer] gene carriers. Why did they get breast cancer? It usually does not strike women young. Shouldn't we investigate that? And it was absolute hell in the peer review process to get it published."

That's possibly because members of the fertility community are said to often dismiss research suggesting the risks of cancer and other health issues. They argue that—at least in the case of infertile women—these examples are likely not caused by the drugs themselves but by the women's underlying infertility.[133] An egg donor herself, Wendie Wilson-Miller told me that fertility issues like endometriosis and polycystic ovarian syndrome (PCOS), often don't show up in women until they are in their mid- to late-twenties. That's the age range that also happens to coincide with when women start donating. "One of the things we say [to potential egg donors] is 'if anybody in your immediate family—your mom, your aunts, your grandmothers—had endometriosis or if you have ever been told you may have it,' we say, 'do not do this, do not,'" she said. "We don't necessarily know if the donation might be exacerbating an issue that is already there."

However, many in the fertility industry emphasize that the increases in risk are small.[134] "We have very good robust data that shows no increase in breast cancer, no increase in ovarian cancer," Dr. Sara Matthews, my gynecologist who has some of the broadest experience in Britain in fertility medicine, told me in a video interview in 2021. "You are talking about a short stimulation phase, even if it is an egg donor or if you go through IVF yourself. As an egg donor you are not putting your life or your health at risk." But as Ms. Lahl told me, follow-up studies are lacking and as drug protocols continue to change, researchers who investigate some of these issues rarely have information on specific drugs used.

In a rare moment of agreement, Barbara Collura, the president of the US's RESOLVE: The National Infertility Association, said that on one hand Ms. Lahl was correct in terms of there being no long-term data and no registry of egg donors. But she added, "At the same time, egg donors don't take different medication than any woman who is doing IVF," she told me. "Millions of women who have done IVF over the last thirty-plus years have taken the same medication and I think we would have seen [this] if there was some horrible adverse outcome. So part of it is sifting through the drama—and I am not trying to take away that these women have had adverse outcomes—but I did IVF, I was overstimulated [and] that is an adverse outcome to a tiny number of women. It is part of the risk." It's a controversial topic, to say the least.

Women who are doing their own IVF tend to be from a specific age demographic or as Ms. Scheier told me "rather a collection of cohorts of demographic groups" meaning that it's completely different from younger egg donors who, because of their age, have larger and generally healthier egg reserves. "You cannot," she said, "extrapolate the results from one to the other." In general, women who are going through IVF for themselves aim to get between ten and twenty eggs. But according to Ms. Scheier, with egg donors it's not unlikely for them to be producing between sixty and eighty eggs. She added that "clearly there is something very different" about the way they are treated during a hormone cycle. Emily Galpern, who helped create the Center for Genetics and Society's Surrogacy 360 project, which looks at the practice through the lens of reproductive justice, agreed, saying the safety of hormonal stimulation for egg retrieval still has yet to be established. "And mostly [the donors] are told that it's safe," she said, "as opposed to being told, 'we don't have information on long-term health consequences, because we haven't done hardly any research on egg donors.'"

Many in the field in the US fervently believe that there needs to be some kind of national database that tracks health issues that arise from egg donation. "That is every single agency and every single clinic because it is our responsibility and we have not done a very good job of it in my opinion," Ms. Wilson-Miller told me. "I have donors who write to me and say 'Hey, I have had x and y happen' and I immediately put her in touch with the doctor. I will say 'whatever research you are gathering, make sure you add this.'" One of the other issues with tracking is that most donors aren't seeing their normal doctors when they're doing their donation cycle. "When they walk away after retrieval," Ms. Wilson-Miller said, "the clinic never sees them again and has no follow-up." The vast majority of women who later have any kind of side effects end up going to their own doctors, so things go unreported. We Are Egg Donors are one of the few places that are tracking some of these issues and trying to connect the donation dots.

One of the things I was quite keen about was that Circle offered IPs known, semi-known or anonymous egg donation options. Semi-known meant that we could share some information with each other and could choose to meet over video call or not at all. It was really up to our comfort level. Or we could be totally known where everything, like names, were in legal contracts. As I was a curious person in general but also, I was extremely concerned about health issues (when I was younger, I suffered from panic attacks and so mental health was always something that was forefront in my mind), I wanted to speak with the donor myself. After all my years of interviewing people, I felt like I could put these skills to good use. Therefore, we decided to go with the known option. Many who work in the field of egg donation strongly feel that ethically known or open donation is the best way to go.

I asked Ms. Wilson-Miller, who for years worked for an egg donation clinic, why that was the case when many people I knew had decided to go the anonymous route. "We see that the vast, vast majority of donor-conceived children are curious about their biological connections, and this isn't about intended parents, this is about the children's future and it's their story," she told me. "It would be a disservice to keep it anonymous in my opinion."

Anecdotally, there are some cultural differences when it comes to choosing between known or open, semi-open, or anonymous. Many Asian and Indian couples, for example, are inclined to want to keep the donations anonymous. That had tended to be the case in Europe as well, though in recent years countries like Austria, Britain, and Germany have passed legislation ensuring that children born through donation can access the identity of the donor once they turn eighteen. These trends might be reflecting the "assumption that a child born of IVF using a donor egg" will demand access to their biological origins.[135]

Meanwhile the Czech Republic has emerged as one of the top European destinations for reproductive tourism because, unlike most countries, as of 2024 it still offers anonymous egg donation. For those who live or travel to Spain for egg donation, while clinics try to match the egg donor's looks to the mother's, IPs are told nothing about distinctive characteristics and are provided no information about the donor. According to *The Economist*, "That devotion to donor privacy means that" unlike children in places like Britain or Austria that have a right to learn about the donor's identity when they reach eighteen "the Spanish process does not."[136] "It is a cultural divide," said Ms. Wilson-Miller, "even upon education, although when I educate, I would say everybody understands it or just feels a lot stronger about it [not being anonymous]."

There are a growing number of egg donors who are eager to do semi-open or open donations. That's because even though they're not expecting any kind of deep relationship with the child, there is often a general sense of curiosity. About 85 percent of egg donors surveyed on the We Are Egg Donors site said they'd be willing to or would like to be known to any future children.[137] "With egg donors what usually gets them thinking about it is when I say, 'What if you found out today that you were donor conceived? Would you be curious about the biological connection?'" said Ms. Wilson-Miller. "And if your answer is yes, then it really truly is the way you need to go into it emotionally."

On the East Coast of the US, however, many agencies still tend to support anonymous donations and only show childhood photos of the donor to the IPs. (This had also been the case when

I used the sperm donor clinic in Denmark.) That's probably because that's how it's always been done. "And you talk to lawyers who say, 'Well the more you make it anonymous, the less legal ramifications could come out of it,'" said Ms. Wilson-Miller. "They have this old school way of thinking without really considering the fact that it's the children's story." Some agencies often tell donors that it's either not possible or actively damaging for children to know who their donors are. "What we know from donor-conceived spaces," Ms. Scheier said, "is that the exact opposite is true."

The secrecy around donor conception in the US at least could all be changing. In the past several years, thanks to easily accessible DNA technology that people can do from home, that guarantee of anonymity has ended for donors. According to the *New York Times*, "as a result, major sperm banks in the United States are requiring donors to agree to disclose their medical histories up front and reveal their identities when a child turns 18."[138] The recently formed U.S. Donor Conceived Council, which wants the US to have a total ban on anonymous donation, has so far successfully lobbied Colorado to be the first state to mandate that sperm and egg donation banks disclose the identities of donors to children who ask for the information when they turn eighteen.[139] A bill was introduced at the end of 2023 in New York state that would mandate similar obligations as well as give parents of children born through donor conception access to a donor's information at birth.[140]

Circle, who I was later told have a good reputation in the egg donor community, sent along several brochures for us to read to understand a bit more about not only the process but how they chose egg donors:

Prospective egg donors apply by [completing] an online application that consists of roughly 100 questions regarding her physical profile, biographical information, health and family genetic history, as well as education and career path. Applicants must meet our strict requirements in order to move forward. Our staff reviews egg donor applications according to current requirements of the American Society of Reproductive Medicine (ASRM) and IVF clinics as well as our own standards. On an average month, only 5% of applicants are accepted. [We] start the matching process when an intended parent expresses interest in working with an egg donor. Matching at Circle is a reciprocal process. We believe that intended parents should choose their egg donors, and egg donors should decide whom they want to help. Once you find an egg donor whom you believe will be a good match, we send her your redacted profile. This allows you and your potential donor to learn more about each other.

Our company employs licensed social workers who do thorough assessments on all egg donors upon matching. We require all egg donors to have a psychosocial assessment, which evaluates some of the egg donor's motivations and verifies that she understands the risks and commitments involved. All egg donors are required to take the MMPI or PAI, which are two of the most frequently used personality tests in the mental health field. These assessments were designed to identify any illnesses, emotional problems, or personality disorders and are administered by an independent psychologist.

[To] get an idea of what we go through, the majority of the applications received by Circle Egg Donation on a

monthly basis are automatically screened out. In order to move forward, prospective egg donors must meet the following qualifications:

- Between 20 and 29 years of age (up to 31 for experienced donors)
- Body Mass Index (BMI) lower than 28
- No more than one occurrence of the same cancer in family history (except non-genetic cancers, such as leukemia and lung)
- No heart disease under age 55 in family history
- No psychiatric hospitalizations
- Be a U.S. citizen
- Minimum of high school degree (college degree preferred)
- Applicants of all ethnic and racial backgrounds are encouraged to apply
- Must be comfortable with giving yourself daily injections
- Must answer all detailed family health history questions thoroughly

Even with all the aforementioned restrictions that permit only a small percentage of applicants to move forward, even more will be rejected because of psychological testing, medical genetic screening, or by their own actions. Keep in mind that donors are young women whose adult lives are just beginning. Despite wanting to move forward when they first sign up, vacation opportunities, jobs, and the reality of what they are doing can cause them to change their minds.

I read this with much interest, especially in terms of the psychological and health screenings. As much as any of this was a gamble, it felt like a lot of emphasis had been placed in making sure the donor had gone through a lot of evaluations before Circle would even sign them up. That, I assumed, implied also that the women were informed about some of the health risks in egg donation. Since our egg donor was going to be known to us, I made sure this was something I would discuss with her when we spoke. I also appreciated the acknowledgment that for some accepted egg donors, even once they got that far down the line, they still might decide the process was not for them. That would be heartbreaking but considering what we had gone through already, it was just another par for the course.

We soon got back to Circle's egg donation coordinator saying we were ready to move forward. She gave us the password for the site. And off we went. I started combing through the site with a forensic eye. It was overwhelming with page upon page of donor profiles. In order to weed out many of them I plugged in a few criteria: Caucasian, over five feet, four inches tall (a nod to my husband's wishes), northern European ancestry (my family were a mix of British, Dutch, French, and German so that made sense to me for some reason), and some level of higher education. Dr. Teman found in Israel that intended mothers who were working with anonymous donors were interested in obtaining information about them "that could help them imagine" their future baby. Some of the women she interviewed chose donors whose coloring resembled their own. Those choices illuminated "the importance of being able to identify a reflection of one's self in the egg" and of cultivating a connection to their future child on the basis of resemblance.[141]

While for me that helped narrow down the choices a bit, there were seemingly still tons of donors to choose from, so I just kept whittling and whittling. Finally, I sent a list of six donor ID numbers (there were no names listed) to check what their avail-abilities were going to be to coordinate with both Julie and our schedules. Two of our choices fit our timeframe, and in the end, we chose a woman called Wanda.[142] On paper, Wanda seemed like she was our ideal egg donor: she had done both her under-graduate and graduate degrees in communications, she loved to travel, and adored musical theatre. This was surely a woman after my own heart! She was also attractive and slender, some-thing I had longed to be my entire life and what I hoped could genetically pass along to my children. I didn't want my possible future daughter to have the hang-ups I did, my thick waist and "big bones" passed down from one generation to the next.

We had a video call with her, and she was, in a word, lovely. Wanda came across as thoughtful and bubbly, and during our conversation, I could tell that she had really thought a lot about what she was doing. She had never donated before and I told her that while the shots were no fun, what she was willing to do for us hopefully outweighed all of that. After speaking for about for-ty-five minutes (we talked travel, our favorite musicals, and what her future plans were including that she wanted to use the money to pay for a possible doctoral program), my husband and I were smitten.

I immediately emailed Circle to say we really wanted and hoped that she would be keen to be our donor. I was elated when a few hours later our coordinator got back to us and said Wanda felt the same. She had to do part two of her psych evaluation, then we would be off and running in terms of signing contracts and getting her ready to go out to PFC for an examination. I mes-saged Julie to tell her the good news and she said that she would be good to go for January. It seemed things had fallen into place quite well considering all the hemming and hawing I had done over the decision. But then, of course, things didn't go to plan.

Her examination had been fine, she had taken well to the hormones and when they did the egg retrieval, they got seventeen. Of those, eleven were mature and seven of those had been normally fertilized. It seemed like things were heading in the right direction. Dr. Sahakian's assistant even sent us a calendar for Julie and asked us what sexes we wanted, as the plan was to put in two embryos. "A boy and girl please," was my response. We had requested that there be genetic testing done on the embryos to make sure that things were okay and healthy. After everything we had been through, we wanted to make sure the embryo(s) would be as robust as possible.

And then the email came through saying, "you have one normal female embryo." Dr. Sahakian's assistant sent the report stating that the other embryos had chromosomal issues. Dr. Sahakian was also concerned about the low quality of the one normal embryo and so he wanted to speak with us about our options. One of the things that had first struck us about Dr. Sahakian was that he did not suffer fools. He was a straight shooter and once you get in on the fertility game, you realize that's what you need. We didn't want hand holding, we wanted results. On our call he went right in with his reservations.

While our donor looked heathy, there was a concern that if we asked her for another donation, the situation might prove to be the same with chromosomal problems. It was, he said, an expensive gamble. Plus, it might not be her eggs that were the problem, maybe it was my husband's sperm that was the issue. That comment felt something like a hard slap to the face. (In about 20 percent of infertility cases, the problem is male infertility and low sperm count is a contributing factor in a further 30 percent to 40 percent of cases.)[143] All this time we had thought the "problem" had been me and my eggs. "The only way we will really know that is the case is if you used another donor and the same problems arose," he told us. "That would imply that his sperm is where the problems are coming from."

He then recommended that what we should do was find another donor, someone who had donated before who had a proven track record of healthy eggs. It would cost more, but that elevated price also came with some peace of mind. He said to get back in touch with Circle and once we had found a few donors we were keen on, to reach back out again. He would look at their previous donations and see which ones he thought might give us the greatest chance of success. "I really like you both and I know you have had a long rough journey so far," he said, for the first time giving us something that came from his heart. "Let's get this right and make you parents finally."

Looking back with hindsight over our journey, I'm surprised that we didn't just give up at some point. We kept getting knocked for a loop but we kept barreling ahead, spiraling through this crazy abyss that at times felt both pointless and endless. But knowing my kids, both of whom have very strong, strident personalities that simply don't take no for an answer, I think their spirits were already in the ether, desperate to be born. So we just kept marching forward. We told our coordinator what Dr. Sahakian said, and she sent us two previous donors who were ready to be matched right away. At this point, we were over the whole J.Crew catalogue process that Ben and Offir had jokingly suggested. We just needed someone with a proven egg record.

Dr. Sahakian was sent the files of both women and as it turned out, he had worked with Dani[144] before. He said she had been great to work with and, more importantly, had produced a number of healthy eggs for another couple. The other potential donor seemed fine on paper, but she wanted $10,000 more, in part because she had a master's degree. Dr. Sahakian's advice: get over your education bias and let's get a move on. We spoke with Dani twice over video call. While she wasn't warm and fuzzy like Wanda had been, she came across as exceptionally practical and having gone through donation before, she knew what it all entailed. She had a few children of her own and she seemed smart, scrappy, and driven. Plus, she had grown up along the shores of my beloved Lake Michigan.

Surely that had to be a sign.

Chapter Six

My Body, Your Choice?

In the last year of the last decade of the last century I got a tattoo.

I had moved to London a few months previously for graduate school and had come back to the US for several weeks on my spring break. While visiting my parents in Michigan, I decided to head over to Chicago for a few days to see some friends from CNN who were now living in the city. On one of the afternoons after a tipsy brunch in Wrigleyville, we happened upon a tattoo parlor, and decided to go in for laughs. Once inside, one of my friends figured that this was the perfect time to fix up a tattoo she had but hated. The rest of us decided that since she was going to do it, we might get tattoos as well. It was an idea forged in friendship and sealed by too many Bloody Marys.

While one friend picked out a delicate flower and another decided to get a cute tiny blue elephant, I, of course, had to be different. I wanted something that had personal significance to me. While I was thinking what to get, I kept moving my hands up to my necklace, playing with the silver charm around my neck. My college friend, Annie Walsh, had gotten the charm for me (and similar ones for two of our other friends from school) in Gabon where she was teaching. On a whim, I decided I'd have the tattoo artist copy the charm and have the simple figure inked on my inner right ankle. It would be a permanent reminder of how profound and seminal my recent trip to southern Africa had been for me.

I had spent almost three weeks in South Africa and Zimbabwe with Annie. It had been my first trip to Africa, a complex, wonderous quilt of a continent I had yearned to visit since I was a young teenager. One of the reasons we had decided on South Africa was that I was writing my graduate dissertation about the internment camps of the Boer War, so it seemed like a great excuse to mix my research with a holiday. The trip was meaningful for me on many fronts but most of all because it kick-started what would become my lifelong interest and love for sub-Saharan Africa. I was fascinated not only by both the colonial history and the independence movements that had taken place across the continent, but it was also my first experience spending time in the developing world. After that trip I even briefly flirted with the idea of refocusing my career to work in either international development or diplomacy.

The charm Annie had given me was an *Akua'ba*, a female fertility figure of the Ashanti people (who are part of the Akan ethnic group), in what is now modern-day Ghana. The disk-headed figure is one of the most recognizable forms in African tribal art. Though it's used in a number of contexts, it's known mostly for being carried by women who are hoping to conceive a baby. The flat head is an exaggerated standard of the Akan ideal of beauty, including a flattened oval forehead while the rings on the neck are meant to represent rolls of fat, a sign of beauty, health, and wealth in Akan culture.[145] The small mouth is set low on the face and the tube-shaped torso has very simplistic depictions of breasts.

The name of the figurine is derived from an Akan legend. Akua was a woman who had such trouble getting pregnant that she went to a priest for advice. He instructed her to commission a carver to make a small wooden child and for her to care for that surrogate baby as though it was her own. Though she was mocked by her community, who dubbed the figurine *Akua'ba* (Akua's child), she soon conceived her much-desired baby. Not long after, those who had been so cruel took to carrying around similar wooden figures to overcome their own infertility. To this day, families often either return the *Akua'ba* to shrines as offerings to the spirits who responded to their appeals for a baby or keep it as a family heirloom.[146]

When I got the tattoo, which the artist made a little crooked and people to this day still mistake it for an alien, I did it as a symbol and reminder of that momentous first trip to southern Africa. I had no idea that it would also prove to be an ironic permanent symbol of my infertility. Forever etched into my skin, my outward hopes for my unfruitful womb never answered. Years later in January 2017, I was in Ghana for a reporting trip, and I popped by a curio shop on the outskirts of Accra. Lined up in one of the back rooms were rows and rows of dusty *Akua'ba* carved figurines in a variety of sizes and shapes. I bought one in part because I wanted to once and for all show my husband what exactly my tattoo was supposed to look like. But there was also a little hope that maybe this one might bring me better luck. Three months later, Julie was pregnant with twins.

Back in Chicago, eighteen years after I had originally gotten my tattoo, to anyone who might have been paying any attention to us—and really why would they?—we probably looked like two couples on a double date taking off work to catch an afternoon of baseball at Wrigley Field. But for our foursome, it certainly wasn't your average day at the ballpark. It was July 2017, and my husband and I had gotten up early that morning at my family's home in Michigan to drive the five hours down to the Windy City. It was the first time we were going to be meeting Julie and Chad in person.

As we wound our way down the cerulean blue Lake Michigan coast, we pontificated about what kind of day it was going to be. I was fretful about how the game and the dinner at an Italian restaurant afterwards was going to go: What would we talk about? Would there be awkward silences? Would my husband's smoking and colorful language offend them? Did we have to stay the whole game? He, meanwhile, wasn't worried at all, taking it all, at least to me, annoyingly in stride. I had purposely chosen the activity of a baseball game to give us something to focus on that was not pregnancy related. If conversation was faltering, at least we could have the excuse of watching the game to fall back on.

Dani had proven to be a successful egg donor and we got six male and nine female embryos, all of which were strong, and which had ruled out that my husband's sperm had been the issue. We asked that the best scoring female and the best scoring male be transferred and several weeks later we got the great news that she was pregnant with twins. By the time we were meeting up with Julie and Chad that summer she was already almost twelve weeks pregnant. We had tempered our hopes over this pregnancy but as we edged closer to the end of the first trimester, a glimmer of possibility had snuggled up into my heart.

It was a gorgeous day in Chicago, a slight breeze and not a cloud in the sky. Both my husband and I were wearing royal blue Chicago Cubs hats, not because we were super huge Cubby fans, but to keep the sun our of our eyes. I couldn't relax, bouncing my leg up and down in my seat. My husband was also slightly nervous at this point, asking me a bit about how baseball was played. Luckily my older brother had been obsessed with the Detroit Tigers growing up so I not only knew a lot about baseball but had been dragged to numerous games throughout my childhood so I could answer his questions with a certain level of authority. I figured it was only in this state of heightened stress that my husband, the world's biggest sports fan, would ever deign to ask me about how a game was played.

And then I turned around and saw her. Even though she wasn't even three months pregnant, she had that pregnancy waddle as she came down the sticky cement steps to her seat. I was deluged by a number of emotions including being sad that I wasn't the one who got to waddle around with my babies inside my belly but also, after so much sorrow, in awe that this was really happening. Chad followed down after her, giving off this compassionate and good vibe as we shook hands, which sort of seemed very formal and stiff considering the fact his wife was carrying our babies. They took their seats, Julie next to me and my husband next to Chad. Turns out, we did in the end have a lot to talk about that was not baby related, which we saved for our dinner later that evening. While Chad and my husband discussed the finer nuances of baseball, Julie and I chatted about her kids and her career. And then she asked me about the fire.

Three months earlier in April, right before the embryo transfer, my husband and I went to a friend's for a barbeque in their backyard in north London. It was the first truly warm and sunny day of spring, so we decided, last minute, to also take our dogs with us. Right before we left our house, my husband had turned the dimmer switch on and off in the spare bedroom, which was already somewhat decorated as a nursery with bright butterfly wallpaper in blues, greens, purples, and pinks. I'd originally bought the house when I was still single, and my plan had been this would be my forever home. Once we got married and got two dogs, the house was feeling a bit cramped, but we still loved it even though we hoped to move before we had kids. I'd flung a towel over the door of the bathroom and some laundry in a woven basket under the sink. After setting the alarm, we headed out.

A few hours later, as I was grazing over the picnic table for seconds, I noticed my phone had a ton of missed calls from a number I didn't recognize. There was also a text message from the same number. I opened it.

Hi, it's your neighbour from number 83, I have tried calling you but cannot reach you. Your house is on fire.

I reread the message and then screamed out, dropping the phone. My husband ran over, and I told him what had happened. I was way too shaky to drive and so our friend's boyfriend offered to drive us back to the house while the dogs stayed with her. We sped down the road and I tried calling our neighbor back. He finally picked up and said that he had called the fire department and they had kicked down our mint green Art Deco door. They were controlling the blaze, but it didn't look good. By the time we got to our street there were three fire trucks putting out the blaze. Black and gray angry smoke was still billowing out of the top two floors, and I just stood in the street, surrounded by neighbors, staring open-mouthed at my house.

I had that reaction that so many people seem to have when in shock: half your mind is on the ground taking in the scene and half your mind is floating above, looking down with a bird's-eye view. I kept saying, "What are we going to do? Where are we going to live? What about all our stuff?" One of my neighbors, who was a member of the Salvation Army's clergy, gave me a hug. "It's just stuff," she said, "you are safe, your dogs are safe and that is all that matters." She was right, of course, but it certainly was a bitter burning pill to swallow. When we were finally let into the house, it felt ruinous inside. The towel I had haphazardly flung on the back of the bathroom door was now ash, the straw basket from Senegal, toast. It felt like my house had tried to commit suicide.

We couldn't move back in for months, and we spent the next several weeks going from one friend's house to another. Finally, we rented a place a few miles away and started to slowly put the literal and proverbial things back in place in our lives. We were battling it out with the insurance company, who made the incredulous claim that the sun that day, as it shone through the window, reflected and refracted sunbeams through the glass doorknob onto the wall, causing the blaze. An independent investigator (and several people from the fire department) laughed at that assessment, saying it was very likely a fault with the dimmer switch. But the insurance company could potentially get money from the manufacturer of the door handle and likely why they were pursuing that line.

While all this smoky drama was happening in London, meanwhile in central Illinois, Julie had her bloods drawn and found out she was pregnant. While this was fantastic news, I didn't quite have the bandwidth yet to deal with an entire rebuild of our house, plus stress about a pregnancy I had no control over. We had had so many false hopes before and because the fire and its aftermath were proving to be an incredibly traumatic event for both my husband and me, our focus was elsewhere.

That meant that we weren't very stressed about the pregnancy, which probably took the pressure off Julie. And, in a sense, I think that suited her well too, not having me constantly texting to check in or asking about her next appointments, like I had done with the previous pregnancy. As balls cracked on bats and the crowd cheered on the Cubs, I thanked her for taking the lead during that first trimester. "I'm not really good at letting go of control," I said, likely telling her something she already knew. "But I've learned a lot of things in the last few months and sometimes, like Elsa sings, you just have to 'let it go.' I trust you and your decisiveness." It was a super lame *Frozen* joke, and she sort of smirked, pushed her glasses back up onto her nose and smiled. Since our journey with her had been going on already for such a long time—at that point almost two years—we were confident that Julie had the intelligence, proactiveness, and sense of agency to take the lead during those vital early days.

It's the concept of a surrogate having agency and choice over her decision that is just one of the intensely debated issues that surrounds surrogacy. There is a plethora of other ethical dilemmas that surrogacy throws up including everything from the perceived financial discrepancies between IPs and their surrogates to issues that range from religious beliefs, legality, technology, exploitation, parentage, human rights, informed consent, and reproductive rights. According to Judith Daar, author of *The New Eugenics: Selective Breeding in an Era of Reproductive Technologies,* those conundrums and debates have long been attached to assisted reproduction with "an initial negative reaction" of fear, concern, and often imagining worse case scenarios. "Typically, as experience has shown us," she told me, "gradually those reactions do soften particularly as those [ARTs] prove to be very useful and very helpful to have families come about in the ways they wouldn't otherwise."

That was the case for both sperm donation and for IVF. Louise Brown's parents for years received hate mail and it wasn't until the early 1990s that opinion firmly changed on fertility treatments. Surrogacy just joined that parade. "There is more acceptance of it obviously, you see the legal landscape in the United States shifting and that is a sign that the normalization is well under way," Ms. Daar told me. "I do not look at surrogacy and the perceptions and attitudes in isolation. I think you have to look at them overall in the whole basket of reproductive technologies that have emerged in the last 100 years."

Feminist academic Emma Maniere has written that, not surprisingly, "feminist scholars do not share a single position on the growing practice of commercial surrogacy."[147] She pinpoints three main camps of ethical thought: libertarians (of which Ms. Daar is placed), reformists, and abolitionists. The libertarian view, which tends to be a less common one, centers around a belief that a free market enables reproductive choice in important ways.[148] In other words, women should have the freedom to contract for labor, be it working in a factory or bearing a child.[149] This perspective stands in contrast to "the majority of feminist scholars who view federal or international regulations" of assisted reproductions and surrogacy as needed urgently.[150]

That's the overall opinion held by reformists who, though troubled over some of the aspects of compensated surrogacy, take the view that while it does need regulation, it should not be abolished. They feel that prohibition of surrogacy would be detrimental because it would create underground and unsafe markets, though of course there have been a number of horrific situations that have taken place in jurisdictions where there are already strict ART regulations.

One of the most appalling cases happened in the US in 2011

when Theresa Erickson, a prominent San Diego attorney in the fertility field, pled guilty to federal fraud charges to what amounted to an international baby-selling ring. An FBI investigation found that she and her two co-conspirators got American women to travel abroad where they were implanted with embryos. When the surrogates reached the second trimester, the trio recruited prospective parents who were lied to, being told that other couples had backed out now that their carriers were pregnant. These couples would then pay Theresa upwards of $150,000, and she would then submit false documents to the local San Diego court seeking a pre-birth order to allow the "substitute" parents to be put on the baby's birth certificate. One suspicious surrogate grew concerned that there seemed to be no IPs, so she contacted a lawyer who "quickly sized up the situation" and then notified authorities.[151] Ms. Erickson and her co-conspirators all were given jail time and fines.

Reformists also argue that while there are ethical quandaries, if compensated surrogacy were to be properly regulated by state or international bodies, it could be beneficial for the IPs, surrogates, and children born through surrogacy. "Organizations like mine and other women's rights, reproductive justice and human rights organizations are becoming less and less afraid of talking about surrogacy," said Karla Torres who is the Center for Reproductive Rights' senior human rights counsel. She added that there is a move of now "thinking about the reproductive rights that are implicated in surrogacy and trying to incorporate these [rights] into legislation [so you can] identify, promote and protect the rights of all parties." Reformists also tend to feel that by restricting a woman from entering into a surrogacy contract, it denies both her reproductive and democratic freedoms. This view sees surrogacy as no different from any other wage labor contract.[152]

Dr. Amrita Pande, the author of *Wombs in Labor: Transnational Commercial Surrogacy in India*, has written extensively on this aspect. She has stated that compensated surrogacy should be seen as a form of work subject to labor laws and protections, including highly regulated contracts and health care follow-ups post-birth.[153] By gestational carriers demanding better working and health conditions, as well as better financial compensation, it can lead to surrogates feeling empowered.[154] Dr. Pande, like a number of other feminist scholars, has compared surrogacy to how sex workers in some countries across the globe have been able to get their governments to view their work as labor practice.

Most surrogates, however, aren't very keen to be compared to sex workers. "The parallels of sex work and surrogacy, if you look at it quite analytically at least, is quite revealing because [that battle to be seen as labor] is exactly how it was for sex work," Dr. Pande told me. It took years for conversations around prostitution to move from that of victimhood to sex work, and the feminist camp is still as divided about sex work as it was in the 1950s. While most reformists advocate for making surrogacy legal, they also endorse regulating the practice.[155]

And then there are the abolitionists who believe that surrogacy should be banned altogether. They argue that surrogacy is the commodification of women and that it reinforces gender and racial hierarchies. Renate Klein, the Australian women's health researcher, has argued that surrogacy is a violation of human rights for the surrogate, the egg donor, and the child.[156] "Pared down to the cold hard facts," she has written, "surrogacy is the commissioning/buying/renting of a woman into whose womb an embryo is inserted and who thus becomes a 'breeder' for a third party." She went on to argue—using words like "reproductive slavery" and "bondage"—that those who speak of choice often don't take into account the social context within which a woman makes a decision to become a surrogate. Those against surrogacy often also compare it to prostitution, where someone pays for the use of a woman's body.

Swedish feminists Kajsa Ekis Ekman, Linn Hellerstrom, and the Swedish Women's Lobby argued in an essay that surrogacy has nothing to do with empowering women or surrogates' self-determination. "In reality," they wrote, "it comes down to reproducing the patriarchal view that women and women's bodies exist for the pleasure and benefit of others."[157] For some abolitionists, surrogacy also reflects class exploitation where they believe that wealthy couples (both hetero and gay) or even single IPs take advantage of women who have less means. They argue that as it becomes more feasible for a woman to carry a fetus that is not genetically hers, more poor women of color and those in the developing world will be sought as surrogates.[158]

These ethical debates date back to the early 1980s when surrogacy first began to take hold in the US. Critics at the time were concerned that the "baby business" had gone too far with radical feminist writers like Gena Corea referring to surrogates as "breeder women" who were part of the opening of a "reproductive supermarket."[159] According to Professor Sital Kalantry, radical or second-wave feminists—who by and large fall into the abolitionist camp—have views on surrogacy that were informed from their experiences in the 1970s. During that time there were different gender inequalities and she said, "when there was no knowledge about what surrogacy would be." There was a worry that this was yet another way to exploit African American women and poor women. As per previous chapters, this has turned out to not be the case in the United States at least.

Though the calls for the banning of surrogacy were more

common in the 1980s and 1990s, they do still exist and movements like Stop Surrogacy Now serves as an international umbrella campaign for both radical feminists and staunch conservatives who are against everything from birth control to fertility health care. Both argue that women's rights should not include the right to contract procreative services. Religious organizations, in particular the Catholic Church, have historically opposed surrogacy of any form and in the past have taken an active role in shaping US policy. Many pro-surrogacy lawmakers over the years have blamed the Church for being instrumental in their bills not being passed.[160] A 1987 document from the Vatican set out the church's objections to surrogacy:

> *Surrogate motherhood represents an objective failure to meet the obligations of maternal love, of conjugal fidelity and of responsible motherhood; it offends the dignity and the right of the child to be conceived, carried in the womb, brought into the world and brought up by his own parents; it sets up, to the detriment of families, a division between the physical, psychological and moral elements which constitute those families.*

In early 2024, Pope Francis got into the mix as well. Likely egged on by a conservative Italian government that in 2023 introduced a bill that would make international surrogacy illegal for Italians, with potential fines of up to €1 million and jail terms of up to two years for those who break that law, the Pope called surrogacy "despicable." In a speech from the Vatican, the pope stated that surrogacy was a "grave violation" on the dignity of women and that the international community should "prohibit this practice universally." In October 2024, the Italian Parliament voted 84-58 to ban international surrogacy for its citizens. That effectively now means infertile couples and gay men will no longer be able to go abroad to pursue having a family. It is the West's most restrictive law against cross-border surrogacy.

Domestic surrogacy has already been banned in the majority Catholic country, as it is in other European countries, including Germany and France. But this new law goes even further, classifying it as, according to the *Washington Post*, "a rare universal crime that transcends borders, like terrorism or genocide."

Nicola Procaccini, an Italian member of European Parliament from the ruling ultra-nationalist populist Brothers of Italy party, wrote in an email to me:

> *Surrogacy is forbidden by law, and someone avoids the ban by going outside of Italy, using surrogacy in a country where it is not forbidden, and coming back to Italy with a child. This is only a way to escape the law, but the problem remains. [This] is blackmail. The buyers use the children like human shields [to] force the legislators to accept something that is not acceptable. They want to defend their right to buy the life of someone else. This is why we don't accept this blackmail.*

In Europe—where compensated surrogacy is either unregulated like in Poland or is banned like in France, Italy, and Spain—a coalition against surrogacy between conservative Catholics and radical feminists has been growing for a number of years.[161]

They are seemingly strange bedfellows, especially as radical feminists—like Gloria Steinem—have long held the "My body, my choice" view as their guiding principle when it comes to reproductive choices around abortion, and yet they don't feel women should have the right to choose to be a surrogate if she wants. Jennifer Lahl, the founder of Stop Surrogacy Now, not surprisingly, disagreed with me on this. "I think it is a thin retort, 'that is my choice,'" said Ms. Lahl, who is the mother of three daughters. "It is utter bullshit because I can't sell my kidney. It's my body, my kidney, my choice and I want to put my kidney on Craig's List to the highest bidder. You cannot do that."[162]

That conservative Ms. Lahl—who in 2021 penned an essay that she was part of the "super straight" movement that demands the same respect as marginalized sexual identities but is really just blatant transphobia—and feminist icon Ms. Steinem can meet in agreement on surrogacy is truly an odd juxtaposition to me. Sean Tipton from the American Society for Reproductive Medicine (ASRM) chuckled when I told him that I found Ms. Steinem's views on surrogacy to be inconsistent with her views on reproductive rights overall. "Of course you can't align with that, because it is logically nonsensical," he said. "This concept that women need to have agency to make their own determinations about pregnancy, but they can't use that same agency to make their determination on what to do with their gametes or their uterus, it's just ridiculous."

Ms. Steinem got in some hot water when she penned a letter in 2019 to then New York Governor Andrew Cuomo, arguing against proposed state legislation to legalize surrogacy. Several of her arguments were either out of date or simply no longer true about surrogacy. The co-founder of *Ms.* magazine—who I have written for—penned in her letter that women who would serve as surrogates were "poor" and "disenfranchised women" and had few or no economic alternatives. In a retort to her letter, RESOLVE—after stating that Ms. Steinem was a personal hero of theirs and how she has been an inspiration for women across the globe—fact checked her arguments. They disagreed with her sentiments about US surrogates, stating that most gestational carriers today were from moderate-income families and while compensation for surrogacy could be somewhat beneficial, the amount was "merely supplemental" and could not be seen as essential for the surrogate's survival.

Ms. Steinem also, wrongly, stated that the bill would allow for women from anywhere in the world to be brought to New York "in order to carry a commercialized surrogacy." Meanwhile, the bill required that surrogates must be US citizens and New York residents, and that surrogates legally had to be fully informed about all the health risks that could be associated with being a gestational carrier. To Ms. Steinem's intimation that surrogacy undermined women's control over their bodies and "jeopardizes women's reproductive rights" RESOLVE's letter argued that the choice to have a child "must be treated with the same respect we give to women as the choice NOT to have a child" and that "those who seek to prevent women from making their own life-giving choices are the ones undermining women's control over their bodies" and were "impeding their reproductive rights." (When I reached out to Ms. Steinem's office for a comment in 2021, I was told she was behind on a book deadline and so did not have time to speak with me.)

New York state Assemblywoman Amy Paulin, who first began work in 2006 on getting the state to change its laws on surrogacy and introduced the first version of legislation in 2012, told me that she was disappointed with Ms. Steinem, someone who was a hero of hers. "I had to come to grips with how I felt about that," she told me. "She was perfect for her time, but times change and so therefore if you want to help women now, you have to be open-minded and she was not open-minded." She also told me that she got some pushback from other feminists as well, ones that she had worked with for years on bills. "It was a particular nightmare for me because I was always aligned with them, I was their chief ally for all their bills on sex trafficking, choice and all this," she said, adding that she understood it when surrogates said they enjoyed pregnancy because she had as well. "So they became my worst nightmare and we had to overcome them."

Others who opposed the New York bill included anti-trafficking non-governmental organizations and conservative Catholic organizations, who disingenuously compared surrogacy in India to how it could be in New York. "When a practice is thought to contravene women's equality in one country, that same practice is considered to have the same consequences in another country," Prof. Kalantry said at a conference on surrogacy at University of Cambridge in June 2019, adding that those groups argued that New York surrogates would be subject to the same abuse as gestational carriers in India: "Radical feminists' perspectives opposed surrogacy from an ideological perspective but shroud their views in empirical predictions based on empirical realities in other countries."

She told me later in an interview that while liberal feminists are guided around notions of freedom of choice and body autonomy, those feminists might also be more supportive of the rights of surrogates. However, just as Assemblywoman Paulin had said, they weren't speaking out. "Those who have spoken out in favor of the right to choose," Prof. Kalantry said, "they do not speak out much in favor of surrogacy."

After much back-and-forth discussion on the legislation a Surrogates' Bill of Rights was added, ensuring that carriers would have unrestricted rights to make their own health care decisions, even if that meant termination. The Child Parent Security Act did pass and went into effect on February 15, 2021.

Meanwhile, back at our Chicago dinner on that balmy July evening at Mia Francesca, a popular Italian restaurant a baseball's throw from Wrigley Field, we didn't directly broach any of the ethical debates and views around surrogacy. But we did talk a bit about how our families and friends viewed surrogacy now that the four of us were in the midst of a pregnancy. While my family was very supportive and knew a bit about surrogacy, it was something foreign and odd for my husband's family. Surrogacy is illegal in Serbia, so they didn't know anyone personally who had done it. But they also were deeply saddened by our fertility struggles and understood our deep primal desire to have children.

For Julie and Chad, there was mixed reaction in their family. In terms of their children, the older ones who were teens weren't particularly interested while their younger children asked a lot of questions, which they both encouraged. Meanwhile, both of their parents and siblings found it disconcerting that Julie had signed up to be a surrogate and, rightly so, were concerned about her health now that she was pregnant. We all agreed as we dug into our pizzas and pastas that, at least initially, it did seem an odd and ambiguous practice, and that took a lot of time to wrap our heads around.

Like Julie and Chad's family, for many people surrogacy is just plain old confusing. Karla Torres, from the Center for Reproductive Rights, told me that a lot of the work they do is about demystifying and destigmatizing surrogacy. Oftentimes people don't know what surrogacy is—one friend of my mother's even had a funny way of pronouncing "surr-OHHHH-gate"—or have preconceived ideas about it. "Someone might think, 'oh, that person had sexual intercourse with the person who intends to parent and then they give up their baby,'" said Ms. Torres. "[So] then you have to take a step back and say, 'Well, there is this form of assisted reproduction known as IVF and here is what that looks like.' And then there are preconceptions about what that is. To say just 'surrogacy' is asking a lot of a lot of people."

She added that once you "parse it out" and explain to people what it actually entails, that can be very helpful. Dr. Jacobson agreed, telling me that when she interviewed surrogates for her book, they discussed how they needed to do a lot of educating people, including their families. "The place they needed to begin was basic reproduction like, 'there is an egg and there is sperm' and they had to bring them around to understanding IVF," she said. "There is a very basic level of knowledge that some people have just even about the human body. I guess it shouldn't be surprising that for some people [infertility] itself is still a curse from God." (When I wrote a story for the *Financial Times Magazine* in 2021 entitled "Surrogacy, America and Me," I was flabbergasted by some of the comments on the story and how little people understood about infertility. One commentator wrote that I was obviously not infertile because I had produced eggs. It took a lot of willpower not to write back a snarky retort.) When Julie and I talked for this book, she told me that to this day her mother-in-law still insists that Julie's children are siblings of Ransom and Lexie. "How are their brother and sister in England?" is often the question Julie gets from her, and she says she has given up trying to explain it.

We ended up lingering over dinner longer than expected which I felt slightly bad about because I knew they had a long drive back to Peoria ahead of them. Sitting in a back corner of the exposed brick restaurant, we stayed for coffees and dessert before a gentle jousting back and forth over who was going to pay the bill. Out on the sidewalk we said our goodbyes and while I didn't ask to put my hand on her belly—I always found that annoying when I saw people do that with pregnant women—I wanted to somehow reach out to my babies and tell them I was near.

Evan Ryan, who along with her husband, Antony Blinken, have two children through surrogacy, told me how difficult it was seeing her surrogate in person when she was pregnant. "The really hard thing was leaving lunch and watching her walk away to the car," she said, of which I completely understood. "It dawned on me that I had been totally fine up [until] then, talking to her on the phone and over text. [But] it was that moment of seeing her in person and walking away where I wasn't. It was easier for me with both surrogacies not to be nearby." While I didn't give Julie a super prolonged hug that evening, I did hold on to her a beat or two longer than was natural for two people who had just met face to face.

As they headed off toward their car, I turned to my husband with a mixture of happy and sad tears in my eyes and said, "There go our babies."

Chapter Seven

I Want to (But Can't) Have Your Babies

Dusk had already taken a firm foothold as Mom and I meandered down the backcountry roads near Stratford, Ontario.

We were on our way to our hotel there—the city is known for its annual theatre festival—and we kept passing a number of well-kept farmhouses that had sprawling side extensions on one or both sides. Many of the houses also had lit white candles in the front windows, their tiny flames dancing and wavering in the blue-inky gloaming. We were completely enthralled and perplexed by all of this, spending much of the drive pontificating why the houses had been built in that way—"the extensions must have come later but why that style?"—and what the candles signified. We came up with all sorts of possibilities as to why and we were pretty spot on, when later during dinner, our waitress confirmed that there was a large Mennonite community in the region. Turns out the candles were a way to signal a friendly home to other Mennonites who might be travelling through the area.

The extensions, meanwhile, were because sons, once they were married would, instead of building a separate home, just add extensions onto their parents' houses. The more extensions, the more married sons they had. This was one of our favorite things to do together: mentally chewing and verbally turning over ponderings and quirks that we came across in both our day-to-day lives as well as when we traveled. Over the years my brothers, my dad, and my husband had learned to tune us out as we would, ad nauseam, discuss a profusion of topics. We were a mother-daughter team of two investigative journalists taking in information, processing, and analyzing. Oftentimes we were wrong in our hypotheses, but as the old adage goes, getting there is half the fun.

My mom is bar none my favorite travel companion. When I was still single, we tracked tigers on the back of an elephant in Nepal, watched the Wagah flag ceremony on the border between India and Pakistan, got our jeep stuck in a deep muddy ditch in Botswana's Okavango Delta, spent New Year's Eve amid the magnificent glaciers of New Zealand's South Island, and visited by dugout canoe tiny settlements along the Ucayali River in Peru. My mother thought it was hilarious when a local tribal chief, in all seriousness, asked her if she would let me marry him as he needed a third wife to help with the cooking. "Don't say no one ever proposed to you," she said, chortling.

Once I got married—not to the tribal chief!—we did not travel as much, in part because of all my fertility struggles. But since I knew I'd have to be back in the US again in October 2017 for Julie's twenty-two-week scan in Peoria, we decided to plan a much less exotic but equally fun last hurrah before the twins were born. One of the closest and most intriguing options we came up with was to explore Western Ontario. I had always been told the coast of

Lake Huron was spectacular (we were underwhelmed) and that Georgian Bay and Lake Muskoka were stunning (they were). So off we headed by car, crossing the border from Michigan to Canada, another adventure awaiting us.

One of the reasons I always wanted to be a mom is because my mother and I have such a wonderful relationship. I wasn't the easiest of teenagers but, like so many other women I know, as I became an adult, I grew to appreciate her not only as my mom but as my dear pal. The comedienne Joan Rivers once famously said, "I gave birth to my best friend," and I always flipped that quote around. There is something quite extraordinary, if you are lucky, in getting to be best friends with both your mother and your daughter. As it turns out, my innate desire and need to be a mom came in part because of my upbringing.

It wasn't until the 1980s that sociologists even started to investigate why women wanted to be mothers. Before then the "mother mandate" (so dubbed by American sociologist Nancy F. Russo) was just assumed; being a mother was not a choice or a calling because womanhood equaled motherhood.[163] Nancy Chodorow concluded in her *The Reproduction of Mothering* that fundamental characteristics of motherhood—including nurturing and protecting—developed in a woman's personality as a result of her attachment to and identification with her own mother. And women pursued motherhood, "to enact and to regain those feelings that have become a part of them."[164]

Interestingly, research has found that poorer women tend to want to become moms because of perceived individual advantages they will gain from having a child. Therefore, their motivations are focused on the effects of having a child. However, women from higher socioeconomic backgrounds want to be moms because of the mothering role itself versus what the child will bring them. These women have adopted conventional ideas around motherhood, "and attaining those social norms motivates their desire to mother."[165] Women from higher socioeconomic backgrounds feel that you should become a mother after achieving adulthood while women who come from lower socioeconomic backgrounds hope that having a baby will bring about that maturity. "Answers to the question of why women want to mother," wrote Ann V. Bell, "reveal the complexity of motherhood and expose how motherhood intersects with race and class."

My mother and her mother, who I was partially named after, were also very close. My mom was utterly devastated when Grandma died from cancer when I was almost four. I remember my grandmother from snippets of memories: playing with pots and pans in her farmhouse, sitting with her at a diner while she ate French fries and drank coffee, and how she just exuded a certain *joie de vivre* that was infectious. Maybe it was selfish, but I wanted the same for myself in terms of having a daughter: best friends who were passed down over the generations, bridging a link between my grandmother and my daughter. During our Ontario trip, we talked a lot about that and also how special it was being a mother to sons as well. I have two brothers and we to this day tease each other over who is my mother's favorite. Obviously, I am. Maybe.

On one of our pit stops on the road trip, we parked at an access point to view the wild waters of Georgian Bay. As we walked along, the autumnal breeze whipping our hair in our faces, I shared with her a lot of the angst I had about the pregnancy and the giving over of control to Julie. I felt in many ways quite sad that I wouldn't get to physically give birth to my best friends and I wasn't getting a chance to bond with them while they were in utero. Julie was, which was a gift, but I also had more than a tinge of jealousy, which I felt very guilty about. Here was this woman giving her body over for my twins to grow, such a selfless act, and while I was certainly grateful, the green monster did rear its ugly head at times. I learned later that these are all very normal thoughts that intended mothers have when it comes to surrogacy and negotiating the very complicated yet incredible connection to their surrogates.

A lot of Dr. Teman's research has looked into feelings of angst and jealousy and she found that it's about navigating an entirely new kind of relationship that creates intimate links between people who might not otherwise interact. The balance is intricate and delicate, which at times can be riddled with risks and miscommunications. "An intended mother faces the reality that another woman is carrying her baby; this other woman potentially has the privileged claim to social recognition as the baby's mother," Dr. Teman wrote. "Both women straddle a delicate position vis-à-vis one another in terms of control: each has reason to feel loss of control during the process, just as each has reason to blame the other for misusing her power."[166]

According to Zara Griswold in *Surrogacy Was the Way: Twenty Intended Mothers Tell Their Stories*, a number of intended mothers, worrying about the pregnancy—being cautious, anxious, afraid of disappointment and being careful to not jinx their good fortune—is a way to connect with the process. This thinking, trying to deal with this lack of control by worrying, was something I innately understood, and it all stemmed from a cartoon I saw as a child on *Sesame Street*. It depicted a little girl, Linda, who has a red balloon. She sees her friend Donald who is on a skateboard and holding his dog by his lead. She wonders what would happen if she popped the balloon and it scares the dog who will then take off with Donald trailing behind him. It's entitled "What would happen if..." and it imagines the consequences of her actions. For my whole life, worrying about things and thinking about the possibilities of what could happen has given me a perverse sense of control.

I spoke with a number of (former) intended mothers and this was very much a common thread. Evan Ryan told me, "This is a journey of control or letting go of control because once I made the leap—and I really had to be pulled into it and grieved that I wouldn't be carrying [my child]—I was then insistent that the surrogates be right near me, so I could run over every day and feel [their] belly or something," she said. "And in both cases that did not happen [but] in a very strange way it ended up being wonderful."

Letting go can be a hard ask but ultimately, it's something that intended mothers—like myself—have had to negotiate and get our heads around. We are all little girls desperately holding on to red balloons for some semblance of control. Dr. Jacobson has written about this, stating that a number of surrogacy professionals told her that because many IPs have had such long battles with infertility, that can translate into an inability to trust the surrogacy process and constantly expect failure. This can be confusing for surrogates who can interpret IPs having a cold distance, like being emotionally unavailable after a miscarriage.[167] "People who have really struggled through the trauma [of infertility], they have trouble letting go and being part of the surrogacy process," said Jennifer White, who co-hosts with her sister, Ellen Trachman, the podcast *I Want to Put a Baby in You.* "Especially the women, they don't want to be a part of coming to ultrasounds because it's like, 'hey every time I have a loss or bad news it's always in the ultrasound room' so they won't allow themselves to be a part or trust that it is actually going to happen."

Some intended mothers also have found it hard to engage with their surrogate because they are scarred from their IVF cycles. "They feel it is awful to give up control of their reproduction to someone else and they find it impossible to have a relationship with their surrogates in the early months," Sam Everingham, who is the founder of Australian-based Growing Families, told me. "They don't dare to think that this particular journey might work when fifteen others with their [own] bodies have failed in the years gone past. [So] they can treat the surrogates abysmally and it makes a pretty tough journey for the surrogates as a result."

While this may be true for a minority of intended mothers, Anna Buxton, for one, has yet to come across that scenario. The British mother of three children—her daughter was born via surrogate in India when cross-border surrogacy was still legal while her boy and girl twins were born via a California surrogate—is now a coordinator with the British consultancy My Surrogacy Journey. "I don't have people who are having problems bonding with [their surrogates]," she told me in a phone call one night once her children—and mine—were in bed. "If you want a child, if you have ever contemplated or looked at the possibility of childlessness as your future, as your reality, it is so daunting and hideous that once you get to the point of finding a surrogate, you're just so grateful that everything else just seems a little bit small [and] unimportant."

Those conversations in Canada with my mother were cathartic for me and I shared things with her that I hadn't even told my husband. I was afraid of how motherhood was going to change my life, my marriage, and maybe even the relationship between Mom and me. We were so close and did so much together, and that was likely going to be different now as well. All of these concerns are normal ones for any soon-to-be mother but mine felt more amplified because of the surrogacy. I also told her I was scared.

I had wanted to be a mom for so long but now that it looked like it was going to happen, I was terrified. I wasn't sure I would be a good mom because I was selfish, spontaneous, and spirited. The responsibility for another human's life—let alone two—was enormous and it felt overwhelming. At one point during our trip, she reminded me of a story that she had told in the past, but one I had forgotten.

My mom and my aunt—her sister-in-law—had had their first babies within two months of each other. Aunt Becky, who was a jovial and charismatic music teacher, took to motherhood with aplomb. My mom, meanwhile, struggled. In part, it was because she admitted she was not very good with little babies, and she also missed having a career and being independent. That all sounded incredibly familiar! She spoke with Grandma about her concerns. "Look," my grandmother told my mom one day when she watched as my mom was trying to cope with my newborn brother. "Becky is a natural mother and that is marvelous. You aren't a natural with babies. But boy do you ever try, and in the end that's what is important." I interpreted that to mean that there was something about the effort that made it almost more valiant. "And I think it might be the same for you," my mom said as we pulled into a parking space outside several shops in Stratford the day after we had come across those Mennonite farmhouses. "You may also not be a natural mother, but you will try your damnedest."

As we browsed through the stores, I saw a canvas bag in one place we stopped with the phrase *Let That Shitake Go* written in bold black letters. My mom and I chuckled as I hemmed and hawed over buying it. I decided not to but as we nosed around doing more shopping and then had lunch, I kept thinking about the bag. It seemed so fitting for my life at the moment: we had gone through so much crap with infertility and I had no control over the pregnancy, I had to just shrug things off and hope for the best. Plus, I would be dealing with a lot of *shitake* diapers in a few months. I doubled back to the shop and bought it, thinking it might be a rather funny diaper bag.

A few days later with my new bag slung over my shoulder, I landed in Peoria.

There were just three things I knew about Peoria when I arrived at the airport: It was the home of tractor company Caterpillar; I had a third (and a half) cousin who lived there that I've never met but whose number my mom insisted I have; and that there is a famous expression "Will it play in Peoria?" in the American vernacular. Peoria—smack dab in central Illinois in the middle of cornfields—over the years has been considered to be representative of the "typical" American opinion, away from the pressures of big cities and state capitals. And it's also supposedly a tough place to get a laugh. So, if an act or play received a good reception in Peoria, it was assumed it would play well anywhere. After I dropped my bags off at my downtown hotel—called the Mark Twain, it was close to the Caterpillar Visitors Center and was where we planned to stay as we waited for the twins to be born—I called Julie to arrange to meet her for dinner.

Then I headed off to the OSF St. Francis Medical Center, where I had organized to have a tour of the maternity ward. This was something that Circle had recommended so that I would not be coming into the hospital completely clueless right before the babies were born. I was a bit nervous because I was not sure how well surrogacy played in Peoria, but my mind was quickly put at ease by the very friendly hospital administrator who met me at reception. Midwesterners—of which I am proudly one—are said to be the friendliest of Americans but even I was taken aback, in a good way, by how kind and sweet the hospital staff were to me as we walked around. She introduced me to a number of the nurses on the ward, telling them that my surro-babies were due in early February. They all smiled and said they looked forward to seeing me in a few months. One or two even squeezed my hands in congratulations. Turns out, they had had other surrogate pregnancies before, so it didn't faze them, and they knew all the protocols.

One of the main ways for intended mothers (IMs) to advance their claiming practices for their children is through participating in the surrogate's prenatal care. Dr. Teman found that IMs eagerly participated in the medical management of their surrogates' treatment and medical care. By taking over some of the medical responsibilities, it was a way for intended mothers to help carry some of the weight and lighten the load for their surrogates. "In a new take on their carrying roles," she wrote, "surrogates carried the baby, while intended mothers 'carried' the documentation, artifacts, time-management responsibilities, and identity-generating potential of the pregnancy."[168] While I don't think I did this consciously per se, I did feel that getting a tour of the hospital and later driving out to Julie's obstetrician's office to introduce myself to her nurse and receptionist (the doctor was not able to meet in person that day), was a way to establish myself more in the pregnancy. I was not some faceless woman who was swooping in once my children were born to whisk them away across the pond, but a concerned future mother who wanted to make sure that Julie—and my children—were getting the best care.

Since I had not lived in the US for twenty years, I wasn't fully versed on things like the Health Insurance Portability and Accountability Act (HIPAA), which along with modernizing the flow of health care information, also controls data protection. That therefore meant that because Julie was the patient there was only so much information I could get about the pregnancy from her doctor. But my thought was that since her obstetrician knew it was a surrogate pregnancy, though I didn't want to break any HIPAA confidences, she needed to be aware that I expected to be as well-versed as I could be on the twins' progress with phone calls and paperwork.

Health care in the US is not only a confusing myriad of laws and regulations, but it also is known worldwide as being exorbitantly expensive. Having a baby in the US is seen by insurance companies, the government, and the military as an elective which means infertility treatments are not included in most health care packages.[169] (However, there are several big tech companies in Silicon Valley that are now including this in their packages. Facebook, for example, covers up to four IVF cycles, including genetic testing, with no preapproval required.)[170]

According to the *Harvard Business Review*, 80 percent of Americans have little to no insurance coverage for their fertility treatments and that only 12 percent of more than 1,000 respondents to their survey said they receive fertility and family-forming benefits from their employer.[171] Unfortunately, as of 2024 only twenty-one states in the US currently mandate insurance coverage for infertility. That for me is pretty shocking considering that up to one in six of the world's population have suffered at some point from infertility, something the World Health Organization (WHO) has declared as a disease. The WHO definition of infertility is "a disease of the male or female reproductive system defined by the failure to achieve a pregnancy after twelve months or more of regular unprotected sexual intercourse." In the US that translates to millions of Americans not being able to get pregnant without assistance.[172] That number, of course, does not reflect women who are cancer survivors, have diabetes, congenital heart issues, diseases like lupus, and a myriad of other health issues that mean they cannot safely carry a pregnancy to term. Nor does that number consider LGBTQ couples, who physically cannot achieve pregnancy with a same-sex partner and is categorized as social infertility.

According to the CDC, a woman has roughly the same chance of being infertile as she does of getting breast cancer at some point in her life. And like breast cancer, infertility strikes randomly. Doctors consider it to be a physical disease in the same vein as they do other diseases like diabetes. But it isn't just the physical turmoil that infertility plays on the body, it's also the psychological and social turmoil that can feel just as damaging. I learned firsthand that involuntary childlessness—as some people call infertility—can lead to depression, anger, distress, loss of control, and stigmatization. I certainly felt all of those emotions.

But instead of internalizing my pain, I became incredibly open and, probably sometimes even a bit in-your-face aggressive about it. But, of course, not all people react the same and that can be especially true between different ethnic, racial, and socioeconomic communities. The way infertile women (and likely men) see themselves is also related to the social and cultural contexts that they live in with "self-identity among minorities who experience infertility" inextricably linked to their identity as a member of their minority community.[173]

Interestingly—and sadly—women of color experience medical infertility at a higher rate than white women, with Black women twice as likely to experience infertility. Research published in the British medical journal *The Lancet* in April 2021, found that miscarriage rates are 43 percent higher in Black women. According to the CDC's 2002 National Survey of Family Growth, infertility is higher among married couples when the woman is non-white, with the incidence of infertility highest among Black women at

20 percent, followed by Hispanic women at 18 percent and then white women at 7 percent.

Researchers found this was likely in part because of environmental factors (including living in more concentrated urban settings that can lead to more exposure to things like air pollution and toxic waste).[174] But lifestyle aspects were also likely to play a part. Black women, for example, are more commonly affected by fibroids, which are non-cancerous tumors in or around the uterus that can be part of the reason a woman cannot have a baby. Obstruction of the fallopian tubes, also known as "tubal factor infertility," is also more prevalent in Black and Hispanic women.

According to Ann V. Bell, in her book *Misconception: Social Class and Infertility in America*, over the years women from minority communities have often suppressed their infertility, in part because their stories have been muzzled by social misconceptions about race, class, reproduction, and fertility.[175] For example, social and cultural factors may play a role in accessing fertility care in the Asian population, and Asian-American women in general have lower pregnancy rates after IVF versus white women.[176] Couples and women of East Asian descent often wait substantially longer before they consult a physician about fertility.

Dr. Victor Fujimoto, the director of the IVF program at the University of California, San Francisco, told NBC News that they are much less likely to seek early intervention when they are having problems getting pregnant.[177] "When we looked at our population of Asian patients," he said, citing a report he co-authored in 2007, "40 percent or more were delayed in speaking for at least two years after their problem began." Dr. Pragya Agarwal, a behavioral psychologist and author of *(M)otherhood: On the choices of being a woman*, wrote to me that, "we don't hear many stories from Brown and Black women about infertility." She went on to add that in "a pro-natalist patriarchal culture like in India, where fertility has been celebrated with rites and rituals, and childfree women shunned and stigmatised, it has taken a long time to overcome the shame associated with infertility."

It is typically white professional-class women whose stories get told, with still almost no research on working class and poor women's experiences with infertility. However, slowly the myth of what Anna V. Bell writes is the "hyper-fertile [B]lack or [B]rown woman" has been transitioning from "a hushed reference" to being more openly acknowledged.[178] That's not only thanks to public figures from Michelle Obama and Angela Bassett to Priyanka Chopra and Gabrielle Union talking about their struggles with their infertility but also blogs like *The Broken Brown Egg* and support organizations like Fertility for Colored Girls (FFCG) and Michigan-headquartered Mothering Justice.

Reverend Stacey Edwards-Dunn, the Chicago-based founder of FFCG, who herself suffered from infertility, agreed that there are a lot of "myths and misconceptions of what it means to be a strong Black woman" and how that plays into fertility struggles. "We all grieve," she said about infertility in general but, "there are some things attached to our grieving that other communities do not have to experience." She went on to tell me that for many Black women that she counsels, it's hard enough to have to explain to family and friends that they have to use a surrogate to have a baby. "What is more challenging is if you had to use a donor to get to that point as well," she said. "I just spoke to a woman who is going to work with a gestational carrier that I set up and that is her challenge. She was like, 'it is one thing that I'm not going to be able to carry the baby, but how am I going to explain that I had to work with a donor?'"

Part of that might stem from the argument that perceptions

around the inability to conceive are not just internalized, but also come from external forces too. There has been research that suggests that there is a lot of distrust in the US health care system by men and women of color because of a "long history of racism and discrimination in the delivery of reproductive health care in general."[179] Some of that dates all the way back to the nineteenth-century experiments by J. Marion Sims, who is considered to be both the "father of modern gynecology" and a controversial figure who operated on enslaved Black women both without anesthesia or their consent. "At the root of the gynecological practice, testing and research is the racist experimentation on Black women," said Dr. Edwards-Dunn. "Dr. Sims embodied white supremacy and racism, which I think in turn is woven through medical education and people are very unconscious of that."

There has been an inclination by doctors to diagnose white middle-class women who are having trouble conceiving with having endometriosis, which can be treated by IVF. Black women, meanwhile, who are in the same situation are often diagnosed with having pelvic inflammatory disease, something often treated by a hysterectomy. There are also lower referral rates of minority patients to infertility specialists though "[on] the other hand, physicians report that minority women, particularly African American women" are much less likely to seek out treatment.[180] That can then exacerbate any biological reasons. "Waiting to seek a diagnosis and treatment for infertility," wrote Judith Daar, "means that the woman experiences reproductive aging in the interim."[181]

Over the years, there have been arguments that women who cannot conceive may be partially to blame for reasons like being over or underweight, putting off the exploration of their infertility or waiting to have children until later in life. As Leslie Morgan

Steiner argued in her book, this "does not lessen her suffering any more than a smoker stricken with emphysema or a diabetic whose obesity has worsened the disease."[182] When I asked her to expand more about this in a phone interview, she told me that what "breaks her heart" is what our culture does to women who find out they are infertile.

Historically, it was assumed that infertility was the woman's fault but over time most of the world has come to recognize that this is far from the case. "So many women told me that they thought they could not have a baby [because it] meant that God hated them or that the universe hated them, and they did not deserve to have a baby," Ms. Morgan Steiner said. As the mother of three children, she had loved being pregnant as well as being a mom. "And it made it sad for me that many women would not have that experience or even if they did [become mothers through surrogacy] they would feel that they were not the real mother or good enough or deserving enough," she said. Surrogacy, she added, "should be legal, covered by insurance and much easier to access."

Back in Peoria, Julie ended up having to skip dinner because one of her children had afterschool activities that ran late, so after my pit stop at the OBGYN's office I got to explore Peoria a bit more. I did a little bit of window shopping and had a pretty decent Mexican dinner before meeting up with her. When she toddled into the hotel later that evening, I caught my breath a little bit. Though she was twenty-two weeks, she looked a lot further along.

I said something like, "Wow, you're big," and then fumbled a weird apology, explaining that though I obviously knew she was carrying twins I didn't expect her belly to be protruding so much already.

Sitting in a booth in the hotel's exposed wooden beam-and-brick bar/restaurant, we talked about how the pregnancy was progressing. Julie said she was more tired this time than she had been for her pregnancies with her kids. She chalked most of it up to them being twins and also that she was now in her mid-thirties, almost a decade from her last pregnancy.

I asked her if she was craving anything and she said cinnamon rolls, so throughout the rest of the pregnancy I would sporadically send gooey ones direct from Zingerman's, my favorite deli in Michigan. "And though I am not a big drinker, I really cannot wait to have a glass of Moscato in the hospital room once the kids are born," she told me with a wry smile. I made a note to see if I could smuggle a bottle into the hospital for her. She also said that she was having a bit of back pain from a pinched nerve. I asked her to tell me the name of her favorite local spa so I could get her a gift certificate for a series of massages. All these being little things that I thought could be of help and some small way to show my gratefulness to her.

After a quick catch up on what was going on with their kids, we decided to go through the birth plan that we needed to send back to Circle. Along with some of the more mundane questions like who would cut the cord, and would we want our son circumcised, was the question of who would be with Julie when the babies were born. Since we already knew that she would have to have a C-section (all three of her kids were born by Caesarean), the hospital administrator had told me earlier that day that only one person was allowed to be in the room with her. Obviously, Julie wanted Chad and I totally respected that. But I was a bit sad that I wouldn't be able to see my twins being born and taking in their first gulps of air.

Another question was, "If you can't stay overnight in the hospital, will the baby(ies) sleep in the nursery?" Earlier that day the hospital administrator had asked me that same question and I had looked at her blankly. I told her I didn't know but assumed we would stay in a hotel room until the babies were released from the hospital. I honestly hadn't made the mental leap that once they were born, we as their parents were the ones in charge and would need to be with them. So, on the birth plan form I wrote:

> *The hospital administrator said if they have a spare room on the ward, they will set up a room [for my husband] and me. I am unclear if this is to stay or just to use when we are at the hospital. I suspect we would stay with the kids until closing hours and then go back to the hotel and come back the next day. We are trying to figure out how long the babies will be in the hospital (depending on the birth) and also how long the paperwork will take . . . we will likely just stay in a hotel while we are in Peoria.*

As if foreshadowing, I would later unfortunately learn along with my brother and husband, that Peoria also has a rather booming convention industry in January, and visitors were hard pressed to find any last-minute accommodation. But because I thought I was so on top of everything, after Julie left the hotel to go back home, I went to the hospital's reception desk to pre-book rooms for early February. Here I was in a classic case of trying to be organized and on top of the situation. I smiled smugly as I walked away from the reception desk. Little did I know that parenthood, like life, often doesn't go ahead as planned.

Back in August Julie had emailed to tell me along with my coordinator at Circle what her scan schedule looked like:

Upcoming Appointments:

September 18th with Maternal Fetal at 8:00 am
September 22nd with my OB at 10:15 am
October 13th with Maternal Fetal–Anatomy Scan and Cardio Scan at 9:30 am

According to my OB, the "20 week Anatomy scan" happens sometime between the 20 week and the 24 week mark, depending on when they are able to make an appointment. My OB is deferring to Maternal Fetal for these scans. She is in agreement with the 22 week point for the anatomy scan. In addition to the anatomy scan, there will be a cardio scan. Maternal Fetal stated that there was a higher risk for heart defects in IVF babies, and it is their policy to do a cardio scan in all IVF babies they see. Additionally, at 35, I am now at an "advanced fertility age," therefore there could be other risk factors, thus the cardio scan. I was told to anticipate about 2-3 hours for the cardio appointment and 2-3 hours for the anatomy scan appointment—which will all take place on Friday October 13th.

It finally was feeling so real. Up to that point, I had not bought anything for the babies, in part because we were still living in a rented flat as our house was being redone after the fire. But I also didn't want to jinx it after so much pain and heartache.

And I was not the only intended mother who felt this way. Anna Buxton told me she and her husband didn't talk openly with anyone about their surrogacy pregnancy in India until around week twenty eight. "I couldn't let myself believe that we were going to have a child once and for all," she told me over the phone after describing her harrowing infertility journey that included several miscarriages and surgeries. "I felt really conspicuous during our whole pregnancy, and I remember looking at prams at John Lewis and then running away when someone asked, 'what are you doing?' I didn't do any [prenatal] classes and I thought people might think, 'oh, she can't be bothered to have a baby?' So from that point of view, it was tricky."

After tossing and turning most of the night, I decided to get out of bed, go for a run along the Illinois River to clear my head, and get the endorphins pumping. Following breakfast, I headed to meet with Julie at the hospital complex for the anatomy scan. We chatted in the waiting room, talking quite a bit about how Chad's family, in particular, were having a hard time getting their heads around the pregnancy. Julie was then called in for the scan and this started off a chain of rather bizarre—and sometimes funny—explanations of who I was and why I was there. Julie was obviously the patient but the little people she was carrying were mine. "These routine acknowledgments of the surrogate's absent pregnancy and the intended mother's experiential pregnancy led women to engage in a game," wrote Dr. Teman, "in which they challenged those around them to identify who was who, ritually validating their interchangeability."

One common area for this kind of identification is the ultrasound exam and this certainly came up for Julie and me several times during that day. The doctors and nurses at times didn't know who to look at when talking about how Baby A and Baby B were growing. I remember that during the first scan they referred to Julie as the mother, to which I sort of jumped down the sonographer's throat—in a nice way—saying I was actually the mother. It was this very visceral reaction that the correct terms needed to be used. Julie needed to know how her health was, but I needed to know how the babies' health was. (The term "surrogate mother" rankles many intended parents, including myself, and I have been known to send fiery letters to journalists who use this term in their reporting on surrogacy. Surrogates also get annoyed by this term, arguing, rightly, that they are not the mothers of the children they are carrying.)

And yet, it was all interchangeable, one and the same. Dr. Teman found that "each time similar scenarios are enacted the intended mother is made to recognize the differences and similarities between herself and the surrogate." One intended mother in Israel described to Dr. Teman a situation where the doctors didn't know whose name should go on the ultrasound report, the surrogate or the intended mother. "We are always encountering that kind of thing and we laugh about it. Because on the other hand, the pregnancy is here . . . so we do it once under her name and once under mine. Or whatever we feel like . . . It is her pregnancy but my test."[183]

And that was sort of how Julie and I both felt. I had this need to take ownership over the pregnancy and while I didn't develop physical signs of pregnancy (something that Dr. Teman wrote about including two intended mothers who spontaneously had breast milk by the time their babies were born[184]), I certainly felt the need for the doctors, nurses, and staff to acknowledge that these were my babies and some of the decisions were ones that I needed to make. "Ultrasound played a significant role in the women's attempts to grasp the 'realness' of their expected child," wrote Dr. Teman.[185] "Once regular ultrasound scans had commenced, the intended mother was able to access material (photos) representing her future child. She also had the opportunity during scans to position herself within the narrative of the child's development." This was, it seemed, very much what I was doing.

Standing next to Julie, her tummy slick with conductive gel

for her ultrasound, my hands started to sweat as the sonographer started the scan. Julie had sent ultrasound photos from time to time, but I now was about to hear their heartbeats for the first time. And it was amazing to watch them kick and move. Ransom (Twin A) even kicked his foot out and I made a joke about how he was going to be a soccer player. And I got a peek of Lexie's cute button nose as she moved around in the amniotic fluid. Julie didn't seem embarrassed by me being in the room and she was good-natured when I asked if I could take a photo of her belly. "I have already had three kids so that kind of stuff does not embarrass me," she said with a laugh. I also took photos of the scan of each baby and sent them to my husband, marking up Lexie in pink and Ransom in orange.

As we moved on to the cardio scan, Julie and I discussed how odd our relationship was. This really intimate thing, getting a scan, with someone who was, while not a complete stranger, not a family member or a good friend. What were we? How would we describe our relationship? Years later, when talking to Julie for this book, I asked her again how she felt about our relationship as I had read that many intended mothers and surrogates had awkward moments of negotiating their relationship. "I viewed it as you guys cared about Chad and I [sic] because of your children," she told me. "And that didn't hurt my feelings. I wasn't offended because without children involved, clearly, we would not have had any reason to meet or communicate. But it goes back to me being okay in my headspace for a number of years to be a surrogate before I jumped in and did it." While I agreed that we likely wouldn't have met under normal circumstances, there certainly was now a bond that we shared though it wasn't something that could easily be put into words or defined. There was forever a connection.

Inge Sorensen, a Danish woman I had gotten to know through my Circle intended mother's support group, told me that there isn't an adept word to describe the relationship between a surrogate and intended mother.[186] "I would describe it like she is one of my very good friends," Inge told me in a video call. "And it is something between friends and family. We will always be connected. She is not my friend. She is not my sister. She is something in between." Orit Chorowicz Bar-Am, the Israeli surrogate who Dr. Teman introduced to me through email, agreed, telling me there is no such word in Hebrew to describe what the relationship is. "It is a unique kind of relationship," she told me. "You can't compare it to anything else."

It was during the cardio scan that I had my first hint of mother bear instincts for my children. As they were scanning over Ransom's heart, the sonographer thought she saw something wrong, a potential heart issue. It looked like either a shadow or some kind of possible murmur and they told us they were not sure if it would develop into something. My heart dropped and I started a rat-a-tat line of questioning of what this would mean, what we could do, and how this could have happened. The doctor reassured me that it might turn out to be nothing but with IVF babies, as Julie had written in her email several months back, sometimes there can be heart issues.

The doctor said Julie would now need to come back every few weeks to have it looked at in case they needed to do something in utero. "We will monitor it and chances are, it will be nothing, but we just need to make sure," the doctor said, leading us out to reception to schedule her for her next scan. As Julie and I said our goodbyes in the parking lot—this was becoming something of a habit—I gave her a big hug and told her I had emailed her the gift certificate for the massage. We joked that after that long day and the potentially scary news about Ransom, we both needed massages. As I climbed into my rental car to head to Chicago to catch my flight the next day back to London, I called the hotel to ask them to book me in for one that evening.

Driving along through the central Illinois landscape, I called my mom and my husband to tell them the news. They both flipped out, but I reassured them that Julie was on top of it, as she always seemed to be, and we would just have to be patient to see how the next scan went. After my massage that evening, my friend Suzanne, who I had known all my life, met me for dinner at my hotel. We had grown up together along the shores of Lake Michigan and being like a sister to me, I was comforted to have someone I could talk with in person about my incredible day. I whipped out my phone to show her the ultrasound photos.

I wasn't the only intended parent who had done this, of course, as Dr. Teman found that intended mothers consider these photos from the ultrasounds to be something they carry with them, "keep in their homes, and symbolically retain close to their bodies and selves." After years of hearing and listening to my friends talk about their children and showing off photos of them—which as my infertility progressed became almost physically painful for me to have to endure—finally it was my turn to be able to show off my impending children. Suzanne, who has two kids, asked tons of questions, and said she couldn't wait for our kids to all grow up together. After she gave me a hug goodbye she said, as she enthusiastically high-fived me, "So, I guess I'll see you next at the baby shower!"

That sounded spectacular to me . . . but it never ended up happening.

Chapter Eight

You'll Blow Us All Away

With dawn barely a promise along the horizon, I hit repeat for the umpteenth time on my car's CD player.

As the opening strains of "Dear Theodosia" from the *Hamilton* soundtrack played, I took a deep breath in, ready to belt out the song at the top of my lungs along a lonesome patch of mid-Michigan highway. The song is a duet between Aaron Burr (Leslie Odom Jr.) and Alexander Hamilton (Lin-Manuel Miranda) about the birth of their children, Theodosia and Philip. "Dear Theodosia, what to say to you/You have my eyes/You have your mother's name/When you came into the world you cried and it broke my heart," purrs Burr in a soliloquy to his daughter. Then after a few cascading notes on the violin, Hamilton croons in: "Oh Philip, when you smile I am undone/My son, look at my son/Pride is not the word I'm looking for/There is so much more inside me now."

I had listened to that song so many times before and had always been tearfully touched. But now as I was on the cusp of motherhood, the lyrics had a deeper and richer resonance, detailing in musical theater form all the conflicting and swirling emotions that I had felt for the past nine months. My kids would never have my eyes, but they would have my name. I sobbed as I sang my way through the song over and over again because even though I was nervous, excited, and fearful, singing has always had a way of bringing me great comfort.

I'd gotten up at 4:30 a.m. to leave my mother's house to drive the six-plus hours to get to central Illinois. This had not been a part of the birth plan that Julie and I had concocted those three months earlier back at the hotel bar in Peoria. Julie had been scheduled for the C-section in early February 2018, but I had decided to fly home to Michigan on January 15. It was in part to get my mom's house ready for the twins as she'd generously agreed to let us stay for a few months while we got them vaccinated and waited for their passports. But I also wanted to get home because several of my Chicago-based friends were throwing me the baby shower on January 27. The adorable invitations—resplendent with hot air balloons that closely matched the wallpaper in our newly decorated post-fire nursery back in London—read "Up Up and Away, A Sweet Baby Girl and Boy Are On Their Way."

However, once I was home, the C-section kept getting moved up. Things were fine with the babies; in the end what the sonographer had seen in October was actually just a shadow on Ransom's heart. But Julie's doctors were concerned she may have a blood clot in her leg. She also had developed a bad case of acid reflux that had been making both her hands and the insides of her feet itch. "When I described that to the nurse practitioner she was like, 'Yeah, let's run some tests,'" Julie told me. "It was bile from my liver that I was burping up and that was probably the worst part of being pregnant. I couldn't lay down until they started getting medicine for that."

Turns out, she was suffering from obstetric cholestasis, which is a liver disorder that occurs during pregnancy and is more common in multiple pregnancies. It reduces the flow of bile down the bile ducts in the liver, leading to leakage into the bloodstream. This was one of just a number of health issues—including anemia, gestational diabetes, blood clots, and high blood pressure—that can occur when there is a multiple pregnancy. There are also concerns for premature births and low birth weights, and twins are five times more likely to die within the first month than singletons.[187] And while Julie did not suffer from gestational hypertension, gestational diabetes, or preeclampsia, there has been some limited research on the long-term outcomes of pregnancies with third-party eggs.

Jennifer Lahl from Stop Surrogacy Now told me that a woman, "pregnant with foreign eggs, donor embryos" can be at a higher risk to contract these problems and, "that is compounded if she is carrying twins or triplets." There is a suggestion that there can be increased complications possibly because, "she is exposed to complex immunologic interactions unlike those that occur when her own egg is used."[188] However, the jury is still out on a verdict. Dr. Wulf Utian, who for decades worked on issues related to infertility and menopause, said that while there has long been fascination on this, every pregnancy has foreign DNA because of the sperm. "It's a very intriguing question," he told me but, "I think the issue is moot and don't think it carries any water."

Overall, research has demonstrated that pregnancy outcomes in the context of surrogacy are similar or better than non-surrogacy IVF pregnancies. Both surrogacy and IVF use the same embryo transfer process. There is not a higher risk in pregnancy for surrogacy.[189] Pregnancy outcomes for surrogates versus other patients who conceived through IVF were similar.

Since my babies had reached the pivotal thirty-six-week stage, Julie texted me a few days after I arrived in Michigan to tell me that the doctors wanted to move the C-section up again to January 22. She told me that between the twins pushing up on her lungs and having a bad sinus infection, she had trouble breathing. She felt huge and couldn't find a comfortable position to sit and sleep. "Probably what [my] kids remember most is me being a turtle," Julie told me in a video call a few years later, laughing as she pushed her wire-rimmed glasses up on her nose. "We have this chair that reclines in our living room and that was where I would sit quite a bit because I could kind of lay back. But I couldn't get up by myself toward the end. So, I'd be like 'Help, help—turtle stuck!' and the kids would come and pull me up."

All these changes in plans were starting to freak me out. Just when I would make a new reservation at the hotel in Chicago for the shower, a new reservation for the hotel in Peoria, and new flights for my older brother to come from Washington, DC, and my husband from London (he was finishing up some work on our house after the fire), they shifted the date again. And while I was really worried about Julie and frustrated for her, I would be lying if I said that I was fine about having to cancel the baby shower. I even contemplated seeing if we could still hold it on January 27 and just bring the newborn twins with me. That idea was instantly shot down by everyone who I mentioned it to.

Sociologists have written about how intended mothers who have gone through years of infertility like to have their "now it's my turn" moment after suffering for years through friends' and families' baby showers and kids' birthday extravaganzas. That was totally me. I dearly wanted to play the stupid games that I used to roll my eyes at during other showers. And to "ooh" and "aah" as I opened perfectly wrapped plush pink and blue presents, even though throughout much of the pregnancy I told everyone I wasn't going to gender my kids with corresponding colors associated with girls and boys.

Of course, my friends who were hosting the baby shower—all moms themselves—were cool about having to cancel, and in the end, they gave me a cute scrapbook with words of wisdom from many of my pals who had been invited. One friend wrote: "If you sometimes find yourself wishing you could send your kids away it does not make you a bad person. 99% of parents have these moments. Kids make you crazy, but you love them anyway." In hindsight, having to cancel that much longed-for afternoon soiree was a great introduction to putting my kids' needs over my own, something every new parent has to learn pretty damn quickly.

So instead, we scrambled to make plans for my husband to fly into Chicago on January 20 and I'd meet him there. We'd then see some friends—the same ones who were going to host the now-cancelled shower—for dinner that evening. The next morning, we'd pick my brother up at the airport and make our way leisurely down to Peoria on the 21st to be ready for the birth the next day. However, like almost our entire surrogacy journey, things didn't go according to plan.

On Friday, January 19, Mom and I had driven out to a town near her house to have the fire department assist us with fitting the car seats so we'd be sure they were installed safely. But in the midst of one of the firemen helping us—the three of us completely befuddled over how to hook the seats into place because of the convoluted directions—he had to leave to put out a five-alarm fire. "I doubt this will take long, as sounds like there's nothing to save," he said, "so come back in an hour or so and we will keep trying to get these in." Having recently suffered through the trauma of our fire, I shuddered.

With time to kill we decided to grab lunch at a local greasy spoon. Just as we sat down, my phone buzzed in my coat pocket. It was a message from Julie. *"Can you get to Peoria tomorrow by noon? They want to do the C-section then."* I looked up from my phone, stared at my mom, and said, "Oh shit!!!!" I called Julie to say yes, I called my husband to see if we could get him on an earlier flight (we couldn't) and I called my older brother who was nonplussed about the change in plans, again. Luckily, my mom and I are a great team in crisis mode so by the end of the lunch—I wolfed down nachos that I barely tasted—Peoria hotel rooms had been rebooked, and my brother's flight had been moved to that evening. I arranged for a Serbian friend of my husband's to pick him up at Chicago O'Hare Airport and our dinner with friends was cancelled. I looked out the window as we were paying the bill and saw that the firefighters were back. I had no control over the birth but at least I had some control over the car seats.

Early the next morning after giving my mom a massive hug and us both crying about how the next time we saw each other I would be a mom and she would be a grandmother—again, as my younger brother had two boys—I headed off. About ninety minutes into the drive (I had given Lin-Manuel and Leslie a well-deserved respite so I could listen to the news on National Public Radio), I pulled into the McDonald's in Albion, Michigan. Aside from needing a bathroom break and an Egg McMuffin to curb my nervous hunger, it was also something of a calculated nostalgia stop. While the McDonald's itself was not particularly special to me, it was in the town where I had gone to college. Just a few miles up the road from the idyllic bricked campus quad, we had had countless hungover breakfasts here after sorority formals and late-night binges when we were pulling all-nighters on papers. Plus, I have a fleeting memory of eating there with my mom when she came to pick me up in November of my freshman year after my paternal grandmother died. I remember sitting there crying while my mom told me about the plans for the funeral. I'm not sure why that seems to stick out except that it was the first time I had, as an adult, dealt with a death in the family so it somehow etched itself in my cerebral recesses.

Over twenty-five years later as I got back in my car with my steaming latte and breakfast, I thought about how as a co-ed not in a million years would I have imagined that I'd be back here at this McDonald's in Albion getting breakfast on the morning my children were going to be born. I certainly never consciously thought about becoming a mom when I was in college, which was not surprising since I hadn't thought much about what kind of career I wanted to have either. And I can pretty much guarantee that as a student the concepts of infertility and surrogacy never crossed my mind. I just assumed, as I did with so much back then, that things would just fall into place.

As I got back on the freeway, passing by a number of other locales we used to frequent as students, I got to thinking how different my undergraduate experience must have been from Julie's. She had been married young and had her first child, a boy, by the time she was twenty-one. She had to grow up quickly. Meanwhile when I was twenty-one, I got excited to go to the local grocery store and slap down money to buy my first legal six-pack of beer. I chuckled out loud at the apparent difference between us at that age. With a long drive ahead of me, I let my mind wander, thinking about a few of the ladies in my surrogacy support group, including Inge, who were also about to become moms around the same time as me.

What had been one of the biggest eye openers during our surrogacy journey was that unlike the stereotype that intended parents were all either super wealthy, well-connected, or famous, I discovered that a vast majority I had come across were average, middle-class couples. A lot were like my friends Ben and Offir and Nir and Or, scrimping and saving to fund their surrogacy. Gay intended fathers and women like Inge—a cancer survivor—who have had long-term health or reproductive issues, have known for years that they physically would be unable to carry a pregnancy. "These are people who have saved up for a long time because they found out when they were younger that they couldn't have kids," Paul Morgan-Bentley, who wrote about he and his husband's surrogacy journey in the *London Times'* Saturday magazine in 2021, told me. "They couldn't carry kids naturally and they have kind of come to terms with this, that the only way they are going to have kids is to save that money for IVF and save up for surrogacy."

While the US by far leads the world in being the most expensive place for surrogacy, it doesn't mean that those who seek out surrogacy in America are wealthy.[190] Lisa Schuster, a former gestational carrier who at the time of the interview in 2020 was the gay parenting assistance program director of the non-profit Men Having Babies Foundation, told me that it is definitely an outsider's stereotype. "When I was first going through it, I was like, 'Is it only for rich people [because] I don't want to if it's for an elite [group] of people,'" she told me. "And, shocker, they are just regular everyday people, but that was my preconceived notion as well. I think this is a very common view." She said that opinion has diminished a lot in the past number of years in the gay community because surrogacy is much more widely known and talked about.

Yet even with that knowledge—and a lot of financial

planning—surrogacy still remains scarcely affordable to the middle class in most countries. Israel is an exception to the rule, where the country's national health insurance offsets the costs of fertility treatments. Surrogacy in Israel, of course, still is not cheap, with gestational carriers receiving around $25,000 in compensation, as of 2021. Other expenses can include the extra outlays required by the state-supported approvals committee that screen both surrogates and IPs (at around $9,000 it's refunded if not used) and $1,800 for psychological testing. However, writes Dr. Teman, as a result, instead of "being reserved for the economically privileged" commercial surrogacy is more "readily available to Israel's middle class."

Compare that to the US, where according to Richard Vaughan, a family formation lawyer based in California, "Insurance companies don't want to cover it, they think it is an elective." He told me that if surrogacy were not so expensive on the medical side, "more people could afford to do it." It's little surprise that researchers from the University of California in San Francisco found that nearly 50 percent of couples seeking fertility treatments used some of their savings or withdrew money from their retirement funds to cover the costs.[191] Only about 3 percent of Americans have an annual household income that exceeds $125,000 per person and even some of the wealthiest Americans have trouble devoting upwards of $100,000 to afford the surrogacy process.[192] Anderson Cooper, one of CNN's best-known broadcasters, who is gay and the son of New York society doyenne Gloria Vanderbilt, complained to *People* magazine in 2020 how "incredibly expensive" the surrogacy process was. He has two sons born through gestational surrogacy.

Couples who have either pursued surrogacy in the US or in other countries—where it can be cheaper but with tricky ethical questions—have downsized to smaller houses in order to offset the costs or used money inherited from relatives. Inge, for example, told me that not only did she save for years, having found out in her early 20s that she would have considerable trouble carrying a pregnancy, but she had also inherited some money from her father when he died. Sadly, this was the same case with us as well. My father had left me money when he died in 2004, which I had put into savings and investments. So that was in large part how we had been funding our surrogacy. "It's unfortunate that a death in the family," said Jennifer White, "can be what can help somebody grow their family."

Potential future grandparents, aunts, uncles, in-laws, and godparents have also helped loan money to couples who are desperate to use surrogacy while other couples have also been known to get equity by refinancing their homes. "One of the ways I try to encourage people to do it is in manageable chunks," said Ms. White, who herself suffered for years from infertility (she now has a teenage child). "People think it has to be all done at once, especially if you need an egg donor. Like 'I must do it all in one continuous line or else we can't get there.'" She has told clients that if all they can afford at the time is to make and freeze embryos, to do that first. Then wait until they are financially ready to take the next step.

Of course, there is a massive realization by agencies and clinics that surrogacy is expensive and, for a majority of couples, it is a difficult reach. Some agencies will offer discounts for what Ms. White called "pet projects"—she, for example, is married to a career serviceman so her agency offers discounts for active-duty military families while others might do the same for, say, cancer survivors or gay couples. "There are of course advantages and disadvantages to each of these though," she warned, "so if you use a discount provider, then sometimes you get locked into services or parts you don't want." Some agencies try to help IPs offset costs by recommending fertility clinics with different price points. Circle, for example, had given us a list of several and once we looked into it, PFC had not only a great reputation but was a lot less than some of the other clinics they had told us about.

Ms. White said sometimes the highest cost clinics in an area can be three times the price of the least expensive. "My fear," she said, is that people often, "don't realize the extent of how big those numbers can get and are not appropriately educated on them." Some agencies, clinics, and law firms have even done some questionable marketing to entice clients looking to save money. Miranda Davies, who edited the book *Babies for Sale?*, told me that she used to attend the Alternative Parents Show in London, which for a number of years was an annual event. "In that third year, things really changed," she said. "The commercialization was really evident as most of the stands were lawyers who were giving away things like champagne, cupcakes, and balloons. One stand, which blew me away, had a raffle and the prize was a batch of frozen eggs."

As I zoomed across the border into Indiana, I thought about my two times at the same London event. For me, it had been quite an odd experience: childless gay and heterosexual couples and singletons walking around being approached by overly familiar representatives from adoption agencies, sperm and egg clinics, family formation lawyers, and even foster care organizations pitching you their "product." They would hand you glossy brochures that had pricing plans and payment packages, and while I was intrigued by the business of babydom, I was also completely overwhelmed. It seemed like fake smiles, free chocolates, and fizzy drinks belied the reason why everyone was there—they wanted to have a family and they couldn't without help. Instead of being excited and full of hope when I left, both times it felt like it was something quite out of reach for so many people, including myself.

Now in the bowels of Indiana, I decided to stop somewhere along I-94 to get another coffee and fill up the tank. As I pulled into the service station and parked, I saw that they were charging $2.89 per gallon. This made me chuckle for two reasons. One is that it feels like many Midwestern Americans love to talk about the price per gallon of gas. Like, all the time. I love shocking my family and friends when they complain how pricey gas is by telling them that when I fill up my car in London it costs something like £110 (about $155). Meanwhile, here in Indiana it would only set me back by $30. The other reason I was inwardly cackling was that as a child I remember on one occasion where my father drove away from a gas station—though we were practically driving on fumes—because they wanted to charge him $1 per gallon. "I will NEVER pay a dollar for a gallon for gas," he said angrily as he sped away.

That exemplified my dad, who in many ways was very conservative with money. He would tell my brothers and me over and over throughout our childhood that "money is so damn hard to make and so damn easy to lose." As I walked into the service station to pay, I shook my head as my dad's words seared through my brain and I shuddered. We had taken a beating over the last year not only with the fire taking a large chunk out of our savings (our insurance finally paid us back a year later) but also all the big and little costs that seemed to add up with the surrogacy. I was already stressing about how the hospital bill was going to be a killer and all the not-so-seemingly miniscule costs like my brother and husband having to change their flights. And the costs of the hotel rooms. And even here just filling up the gas tank. Cha-ching, cha-ching.

But we were the lucky ones. Like adoption, which can run upwards in the range of $60,000, for families in lower income brackets, assisted reproduction can feel completely out of reach. "It is an expensive proposition," admitted Assemblywoman Amy Paulin, who said when they were lobbying to change the surrogacy laws in New York they did bring "regular" people to talk about surrogacy but the perception of who had access to it was hard to change. "People have to have some ability to get money. It is not a poor person's endeavor. It is going to be for poor people who have rich parents, poor people who can leverage everything in their life to do this." She added that she hoped one day it would become more affordable. One of the things they argued in the bill debates was that not forcing New York residents to have to go out of state to do surrogacy would help to make it less expensive.

Most US states do not cover infertility treatments to their poorest citizens who might be on things like Medicaid, which is medical coverage for people on a limited income. These policies therefore "withhold the choice for poor women" who suffer from infertility and reinforce a stratified system "by providing the option of reproduction for some groups and not to others."[193] According to Dr. Bell, in a recent National Survey of Family Growth, of women experiencing reproductive problems, only five percent with less than a college education received access to ART, compared to nearly twenty percent of those who had at least a bachelor's degree. Or as Judith Daar put it more succinctly to me, "clearly the big barrier to accessing reproductive technology, which disparately impacts minority women, is class."

She went on to add that "forced childlessness is a feature of American life for many people." The intersectionality of infertility and class, along with issues of race, means that there is little chance that many Americans can afford surrogacy as conception, gestation, and the birth of a surrogate baby can cost almost as much as what they would spend in a child's lifetime (rough estimates are about $200,000) to raise them.[194] "Whether one is discussing access to abortion, contraception, or IVF fertility therapies," wrote University of California at Santa Barbara sociologist France Winddance Twine, "services related to the reproductive functions of women are highly stratified along racial, ethnic, class, and religious lines."

The paradox is that lower income Americans will travel to places like Ukraine and Mexico to work with gestational surrogates because they are priced out of being able to afford surrogacy in the US, which attracts an international clientele. "You have people coming from outside the US who are driving up the cost because you have a gestational carrier who will find someone to pay $20,000 more," said Barbara Collura from RESOLVE. "There has to be something that makes it more accessible and does not make it about supply and demand." Meanwhile the "impoverished and infertile" from places like Ukraine are unable to access those services in their own countries.[195]

There are several reasons why intended parents are driven to go abroad for surrogacy. Number one, of course, being the obvious cost. Karla Torres from the Center for Reproductive Rights told me that some of the things her organization has advocated for in terms of their surrogacy document *Baseline Guiding Human Rights-Based Principles On Compensated Gestational Surrogacy In The United States* are things that increase the cost of surrogacy. Those include life and health insurance as well as legal counsel. That means that intended parents end up footing the bill for a surrogate's lawyer, which, for example, is one of the stipulations in the new New York law. "On the one hand, we're trying to make infertility care more equitably accessible, looking at finances and discrimination against folks," she said. "And then on the other we are trying to make surrogacy as levelled a playing field as possible and then that raises the price for certain parties." It's understandable how that could drive some people to either do informal surrogacy arrangements in their own country or to go abroad.

Jay Nault and his wife, for example, chose to go to Ukraine because he speculates it was 80% cheaper than if they had done surrogacy in their home state of California. And that was inclusive of the cost of several international flights and accommodation in Kyiv. While certainly efforts to lower the cost of surrogacy by going abroad to some countries can be attractive to intended parents, dodgy caveats or workarounds that are sometimes attached can be hugely problematic for all involved. "A lot of times people say, 'Oh, it's totally possible for gay men to do surrogacy in Ukraine, you just have one partner [go] and he has to marry the surrogate but it's only on paper,'" warned Ms. Schuster. "Once you start having these deceptions, that really opens you up to a lot of risk."

Another reason intended parents decide to go abroad for surrogacy is that for many couples, surrogacy is either illegal in their country full stop, or if they are a gay couple, it might be that surrogacy is legal where they live but because of discrimination it's not available to them. For example, with surrogacy already illegal in Italy, IVF is only available for heterosexual couples.[196] This has led to cross-border surrogacy travel, which has been dubbed by some as "procreative tourism."[197] However looking to save money, warned the Center for Genetics and Society's Executive Director Marcy Darnovsky, often ends up with very sketchy companies, agencies, and clinics doing shortcuts that really harm surrogates and egg donors. "There have been too many scandals over the years," she said, "to think that's not a problem."

Gordon "Bud" Lake, an American, and Manuel Santos, his Spanish husband, found this out the hard way. The Spanish-based couple were not only priced out of doing surrogacy in the US but it's also illegal to do surrogacy in Spain. So, the couple went to India to have their son, Alvaro, who was born right around the time cross-border surrogacy became illegal there. In order to have a sibling for Alvaro, they then decided to do surrogacy in Thailand. Bud told me in an interview in 2020 that at first everything seemed straightforward when they signed a contract with New Life, the Georgian-owned agency run by Dr. Mariam Kukunashvili, which had a Bangkok outpost. But things quickly turned sour. "It was like being in some sort of Twilight Zone for a year and a half," he told me in a Zoom. "It was fucking crazy."

It all started when their original surrogate—who the couple had spent time with—was switched out at the last minute for new surrogate, Patidta Kusolsang, who they had not met. After she became pregnant with their daughter, Carmen, working with a donor egg and Bud's sperm, the 2014 Thai coup d'etat happened, which threw everything into a tailspin. "Surrogates were afraid for their lives, people stopped going to their appointments," Bud said. "New Life told us they had to burn all the records because they did not want the surrogates to be identified." He said that they had limited contact with the agency—and none with Ms. Kusolsang—and at one point they even offered to bring her to Spain before things finally calmed down politically.

But things were just heating up for the couple. Soon after Carmen was born in January 2015 and was released from the hospital, Ms. Kusolsang refused to sign the paperwork that was needed for Bud and Manuel to take her back to Spain. She claimed that she was never told they were a gay couple, and she didn't think two dads could be parents.[198] "It was so weird because even though Carmen was given [US] citizenship because of my biological claim, because I did not have a legal parental claim [in Thailand] they would not let me sign for her passport," Bud told me. To this day he suspects that Ms. Kusolsang was being used as a political pawn by people within the country who were against cross-border surrogacy.[199] It was made illegal in July 2015 through the Protection of Children Act but in March 2024 it was reported in *Voice of America*, the head of Public Health Ministry's health service support department announced plans "for draft legislation to legalize commercial surrogacy for both local and foreign couples, among a package of reforms aimed at reversing the country's falling birth rate."[200] "In the beginning we were living in fear, scared shitless that they were going to come for her at any minute," Bud told me over video, just as Carmen and Alvaro came into his office to show him their Halloween costumes. After having to crowdfund for the $36,000 to cover their legal fees, the Thai courts ruled in Bud and Manuel's favor. They brought their daughter back to Spain in the late spring of 2016 and only in the end of 2020 did Carmen finally get her Spanish citizenship.

For many gay couples like Bud and Manuel, the cost of surrogacy in the US has proved to be prohibitive. This was something that Ron Poole-Dayan, an Israeli-born New York-based gay dad of twins born via gestational carrier, noticed whenever he would give talks about surrogacy within the gay community. "These men were really being priced out of parenthood in a lot of ways," said Lisa Schuster, who spoke with me about why Mr. Poole-Dayan set up Men Having Babies' Gay Parenting Assistance Program (GPAP). "He kept waiting for a provider, a surrogacy agency, a clinic to offer some sort of program and then he realized, 'it's gotta be me.'" The program—which has two tiers—helps to lower the financial barriers for men interested in surrogacy. It's open to men in the US, Canada, most of Europe, Taiwan, and Israel. For couples who qualify for Stage I support, they get access to 10 percent to 50 percent discounts on professional services and they navigate their journey on their own. Those who are accepted for Stage II are matched with donated services and GPAP work with them throughout their entire journey. As of 2020, sixty babies had been born to couples who took part in the Stage II as well as fifty participants who were somewhere in the process from just getting started to the imminent birth of their baby.

GPAP is one of almost three dozen US-based programs that have focused their efforts on helping couples afford assisted reproduction and surrogacy. Fertility for Colored Girls (FFCG), first launched in 2013, each year gives grants of up to $10,000 for couples in need as well as grants toward medications. According to founder Reverend Stacy Edwards-Dunn, as of 2020 FFCG has helped over 200 women become parents, either directly through grant money or local chapters that offer support and counselling. Meanwhile, the Cade Foundation was founded in 2005 by Camille and Jason Hammond, two doctors who as a couple struggled for five years with infertility. Camille's mother, Dr. Tinia Cade, who was fifty-five at the time, ended up being their gestational carrier and gave birth to their triplets in 2004. "We were grateful when we had our children after so many years of infertility," Dr. Camille Hammond told me, "and we knew at some point we wanted to give back and support others who are still struggling." Cade offers fertility treatment and medication grants, which as of March 2024, have led to 189 grants funded and 110 babies adopted or born.

Meanwhile, by the time I finally reached the hospital where my babies were about to be born, I was so jazzed up on show tunes and caffeine that I could barely contain myself. Luckily, since I had done the hospital tour back in October, I knew where I needed to head once I parked my car. My brother had arrived about ten minutes before me and so once I checked in on the maternity ward—where I was greeted by very enthusiastic and friendly staff at the front desk—I sped down the hallway. When I found my brother, he hit me with some troubling news: "So Peoria is like the convention capital of the Midwest in January because when I checked in at our hotel"—it was not the Mark Twain because we couldn't get rooms there and now I was starting to understand why—"they say we can only have our rooms for the night and then we need to leave." I gave him a frustrated stare, my head about to explode. "Say what? I can't deal with this right now, just let me take a breath and figure this all out," I told him. Just then Susan LeBlanc, the nurse who had been assigned to our case, came to introduce herself to me and take me down to see Julie and Chad.

As we walked down the hall, I told her about my long drive to get to the hospital and she began to walk me through what the current situation was with Julie. The doctors were slightly concerned because whenever they tried to tip Julie backwards in the bed to examine her, she had trouble breathing because of her cold, and her sinuses kept draining. "They are going to come again in about a half an hour and reassess the situation then," Susan said kindly, probably seeing my blood pressure go up exponentially. "These babies might not be coming today after all." I wanted to stomp my feet and scream and shout, me never great at things not going according to plan. But instead, I just smiled, fake as the day is long, trying to contain my rage and emotion. We then stepped into the room where Chad was sitting at the side of the bed with Julie.

I don't remember this but Julie claims that I had a Wendy's cup in my hand when I came in to see her. She had not been allowed to eat anything since the day before and hadn't been allowed to drink anything that morning. So me breezing in with an iced tea was too much for her. She surreptitiously told Chad to pull me out of the room and tell me to throw my cup away. I did remember that she seemed pretty on edge—which I understood—and I guess when Chad asked me to throw it away, I immediately did. A few years later when I was confirming some of the delivery day procedures with her, we had funny back-and-forth banter about the cup. "Sorry about that, I was pretty moody," she wrote in a text, sending emojis of two babies and an exasperated woman with her hands up in the air.

I stayed in the room with them and made pained small talk—I could tell even talking to me was a struggle because of her cold—while I also texted my travel agent to see if they could scramble to find rooms for us for the next night. Julie's OBGYN, who I had never met but had spoken to on the phone after my October trip, then came in. She said they were going to take Julie into the operating room and see if they could get the bed in a position that would feel comfortable for her. The doctor then told us that she was not sure if these births were going to happen today, but she was going to try. Julie said something like, "Well, I think I would rather suffer through not breathing and get these babies out than have to wait another day or two."

On one hand I totally agreed with her; I was so excited to meet these babies and I had sped precariously down the highways of three Great Lake states to get here so I didn't want that to be for naught. But I also really wanted my husband to be with me when our babies came into this world. As it stood, his flight from London wasn't going to be arriving for a few hours, meaning he wouldn't get to Peoria until early evening. Plus, I wouldn't mind for the babies to stay in a little longer, as they were going to be slightly on the premature side coming out a few weeks earlier than expected. Cooking a day or two more didn't sound so bad. But I shut my mouth, just smiled, and said, "Whatever you advise, doctor, and whatever is best for Julie and the babies."

I finally had accepted that I had no control---and to be honest, it was quite liberating.

Chapter Nine

Birthing the Mother

With an Arby's roast beef sandwich on my lap—doused with way too much horseradish sauce—I looked out over the bleak terrain of a Peoria strip mall parking lot and sobbed.

It had been four days since Ransom and Lexie had been born and I was a wreck. When they had wheeled Julie out of her hospital room ninety-six hours earlier, I had shouted after her, "Good luck," unclear if the next time I saw her my babies would be out here in the world or still in her belly. I had known that I wouldn't be able to be in the delivery room, but it really killed me watching her be wheeled down the hallway, Chad at her side. I found it excruciatingly sad that I wouldn't be able to describe to my kids what it was like the moment they were born.

Some surrogates and intended mothers have chronicled those very intense last moments leading up to the birth. Dr. Teman writes how many of the surrogates in Israel that she spoke with did such rituals as putting their bellies together to give each other strength or for those lucky enough to be in the delivery room, gestational carriers would squeeze intended mothers' hands with each contraction. Some intended/impending mothers even claimed they felt the contractions as their gestational carriers were in labor. When Israeli surrogate Orit Chorowicz Bar-Am went into labor with her surro-baby, her husband filmed the actual birth because he knew that his wife would likely not remember.

When she watched the tape back again—Orit on all fours, eyes closed, her hair in a messy bun and wrenching around on the bed —the intended mother was doing the same next to her. "When I gave birth to the baby, the actual moment, I was completely quiet, breathing and quiet, and she was screaming," Orit recalled to me. "She was screaming, 'I can't, I can't believe it,' like she was hurting. It was like yin and yang, symbiotic. And after the baby came out, she came over and hugged me, she came to me before she went to the baby. She was holding me, and my husband is telling her at some point, 'go to your baby, he's yours.'"

Orit sent the video to me, and it's incredibly powerful to see both Orit so serene, in pain but peaceful, and the intended mother screaming, sobbing, and wailing like she too was feeling intense physical agony. Dr. Teman describes this concept as "birthing a mother."[201] While doulas and midwives nurture and guide women through the childbearing process, surrogates help infertile women (or those who for other reasons cannot bear children) give birth to themselves as mothers. "Most of the surrogates I spoke with," wrote Dr. Teman, "saw themselves as having achieved three significant things: they have helped produce children, contributing to the continuation of 'life'; they have made childless couples 'families'; and they have made infertile women into 'mothers.'"[202]

In the end Julie did have the babies that afternoon of January 20, 2018—remember the panini?—and gave birth not just to my children but also to me as a mother.

By early evening, my husband had arrived at the hospital and after meeting the babies, he requested that my brother and I go to the hospital's parking garage for a Serbian ritual. He took off his shirt and put on a not so nice old T-shirt he had specially brought. A Serbian friend from his hometown, now a chauffeur in Chicago, joined us for the ritual. He proceeded to rip at the T-shirt being worn by my husband with some violence. My husband then asked my brother to also rip at the shirt. My brother shot me a look like, "What in the hell?" but he good-naturedly took part too. After they all did a shot of plum brandy, I was told this is an old ritual that likely comes from the days when women gave birth in their homes, in the fields, or forests. As the newborn needed to be wrapped up in something, the mother would rip the shirt from the father to swaddle the baby. I have no idea what happened to that T-shirt but I wish we had kept it for the kids to have someday.

While I appreciated the ritual, I was dead tired at this point and needed to go check on Julie. She had been recovering in her room on the maternity ward and I wanted to make sure she was okay before we headed back to the hotel. Since everything had been so last minute with the twins' birth, it was too late to arrange a room on the same floor that evening in the hospital. The babies would be spending the night in the nursery, which was fine but I was a little worried about the nurses' shift change. That was in large part because my children had birth tags on their wrists that read "Baby Boy" and "Baby Girl" followed by Julie's last name. I asked if they could switch the tags to read with my last name and my husband's last name (we had decided to double barrel the children's surnames).

However, we were told that since Julie was the registered patient and we were not, it might cause some administrative confusion. I got that, but my claiming practice as a mother was also really important to me. These were my kids, not Julie's, and while I was forever grateful to her, I needed recognition that I was their mom. Plus, if there was some kind of health issue, my husband and I were now the ones to be making those decisions. The lovely maternity nurse Susan—who I'm still in touch with over Facebook—reassured me that everyone had been briefed that it had been a surrogacy birth, and they were just disappointed for us that we couldn't stay there with the twins. In the end, that evening we were lucky to get a good night's sleep at our Holiday Inn right off the freeway because those next several nights, there was no room at that Inn...or any other lodging in Peoria.

The next morning, after a quick buffet breakfast, we zipped back to the hospital and, in between feeds, we found a room for my brother for two nights at another hotel in downtown Peoria. The hospital said we could stay the night in a room so that the twins could sleep with us in their plastic carts, which we could wheel around the ward and over to visit Julie. That was a huge relief to be able to be in the room with them, though I was not sure if I was completely ready for middle of the night feeds just yet. Though, let's be honest, I don't think any parent ever really is.

Susan and another lovely nurse both repeatedly showed me how to swaddle the babies, yet it was something I just couldn't master. Frustrated and still slightly freaked out about handling newborns, I turned to the maternity nurse with tears in my eyes and said, "I have two master's degrees, yet I can't swaddle my babies, what is wrong with me?" She laughed and said, "Honey, I have taught fifteen-year-old girls who are meth heads how to swaddle their babies so I have every belief I can teach you too." In the end, after posting my frustration on Facebook, a friend wrote back to me: "It's like wrapping a burrito—the swaddle is the tortilla, and you want to fold it up tight so that none of the ingredients fall out." The food analogy worked and soon I was swaddling like a pro and, to be honest, craving Mexican food to boot.

In the later afternoon, after the hospital photographer came by and took sweet but cheesily posed photos of the twins, one of the hospital administrators came by to input information for the birth certificates. Because we had already filled out the Illinois Surrogate Parentage Statement several months' back, our names automatically went on the birth certificates. "Illinois is even ahead of pre-birth orders because what they have is an administrative statute that allows you to get parentage solely based on the fact that you complied with the law," Circle's Dean Hutchison told me in an interview a few years after their birth. "You fill out those affidavits, you file them with the hospital and the Department of Public Health, and you do not even need a court order. [So] they went the extra step to make it easier for the parent." All we had to do was pick up the birth certificates in a few days' time from Peoria's County Health Department.

On the second day after the twins were born, things started to go a bit off the rails. Not only did we realize that my car was not going to be big enough to fit the twins, my brother, my husband, me, and all our suitcases but also Ransom got a big fat fail on his first ever test. It's standard practice in the US that babies who are born before thirty-seven weeks need to take what is called a "tolerance test," also known as a car seat test. We had to bring one of the car seats into the maternity nursery and they sat each baby in it for ninety minutes while their heart rate, breathing, and oxygen levels were monitored. Lexie passed with flying colors, but not so Ransom.

The nurses referred to him as a "wimpy white boy," which at first kind of offended me but they explained it's American medical slang for infant boys who don't hit their milestones as quickly as others. Because of him not passing—and knowing we had a six-plus-hour car ride ahead of us—we needed to stay another night in the hospital to do the test again. My brother picked up an SUV rental and we hoped to hit the road the next day because as I called around, there were still no hotel rooms available. That evening, increasingly stressed out, we wheeled the babies in to see Julie, who was scheduled to check out the next day. Several of her convivial children were in her room and they all took turns holding the babies. We laughed and had a chance to bond with family, them telling us some of the funnier anecdotes of a pregnant Julie.

The next day Ransom not only failed again, but they decided they needed to move him to the neonatal intensive care unit (NICU) because during the test they noted he had pauses in breathing, which is a symptom of infant sleep apnea. Looking back, this was my first real test as a mother. The panic and feeling of protectiveness (and, of course, loss of control) that my baby had to be hooked up to wires in another part of the hospital away from me was almost unbearable. Plus, they had already checked Lexie out of the hospital, so we had no place to stay let alone a place where she could sleep. That's how I found myself sobbing in the parking lot of Arby's.

The previous week in Michigan I had gotten a gel manicure, which meant that the polish would not only stay on my nails longer—no chipping!—but also, I'd have to get it removed in a nail salon because only a special kind of acetone could take gel polish off. When we had checked Ransom into the NICU, I was told that I either had to get my nail polish removed or I'd have to wear awkward latex gloves the whole time I was in the unit, even when I held my baby. Rather hysterical, I called Julie and asked her where I could get gel polish removed. After conferring with friends, she said Walmart had a nail salon that could do it without an appointment.

The next morning—after the wonderful maternity ward staff let Lexie and me be squatters in our hospital room the previous night (while my husband slept in a chair in Ransom's room in the NICU) "as long as no one else comes in to give birth and needs it"—I got ready to drop Lexie off with my brother at his hotel. As I gave Susan a hug goodbye and told her I had no idea where we'd be sleeping that night, she mentioned Family House. It was a health care hospitality facility not far away that was for family members whose relatives were being treated in one of Peoria's four hospitals. I called to see if we could get a room and they said they'd add us to their list. Since people didn't check out until noon, they wouldn't know if they had a room available (once you had a room you could stay as long as you needed). The kindly receptionist told me they didn't have any kind of crib for babies.

So, my trip to Walmart, in gray sweatpants that were too short which I had incongruously coupled with Ugg boots, would kill two birds. I got my nail polish scraped off, leaving my nailbeds weak and splintered. Then I had a huge drama with my credit card not working and the owner of the nail spa getting more and more agitated with me. Finally, I was able to get cash out from the ATM to pay him, but I was now quite on edge. I found a "pack and play" down one of the aisles that could serve as Lexie's crib, plus bought some diapers and bottles. As I headed out into the cold parking lot disheartened by the whole experience, the wind nipped at my partially uncovered legs like a vicious, relentless dog.

Starving, as I hadn't eaten all morning, I eyed the horizon for a Wendy's, my go-to fast food fix. But all I saw was an Arby's, which had never been a favorite of mine. While I was Googling where to find the closest Wendy's—it was something to bring my mood up—my brother called me panicked that Lexie was screaming. Then my husband phoned, agitated, to ask when I was getting back to the hospital. Meanwhile, now after noon, I had Family House's number on speed dial but the calls kept going unanswered. Coming to the end of my tether, I decided Arby's would have to do. As I ordered at the drive-thru window, I was already shaking with sobs. "Please," I said between warm, fat, ugly tears, "can I have some extra horsey sauce?"

I drove to the pick-up window, blubbering, picked up my sandwich and parked. I wolfed down my food while I screamed and cried over my frustration. This was supposed to be this beautiful time of new motherhood where my babies gurgled and cooed and I coaxed them to drink their bottles, my longed-for infants finally here. Yet instead, it was incredibly stressful. I had no idea what I was doing with them, and I was stuck, indefinitely, in central Illinois. With no place to stay. And my little boy was hooked up to monitors, seemingly so fragile.

Luckily a few hours after my parking lot meltdown, I got a call that Family House had a room for us. By the next day, Ransom was improving by leaps and bounds so the NICU doctor told us we could likely check out the following morning. (In a telling comment, one of the nurses said she was amazed how big and strong Ransom was because the babies they saw in NICU were quite sickly, underweight, and very premature because so many were born from mothers addicted to either opioids or crystal meth.) Julie and Chad came by the NICU to say goodbye to us, and it was all rather awkward because they had to sign in and we had to explain to the nurses, who were very strict on guests, who they were. Dr. Teman has dubbed this "the glass wall," that hospital staff often "did not always know what to do with" surrogates after the birth. Meanwhile for surrogates, who for nine months are charged with the absolute and ultimate care for their surro-babies, they are, "suddenly required to ask the [mother] for permission to see the baby" and the surrogate is "dismissed from her intermediatory role."[203]

A number of surrogates I spoke with—including Julie—all said this was quite an odd experience. Briana Mohler, the Minnesota-based mother of two who three times has been the carrier for Nir and Or, said that as a surrogate you're placed on a pedestal. "Then of a sudden, they have the baby, and now you're no longer this trophy [and] you have to realize they are parenting," she told me over a video call, one of her daughters doing homework in the background. "I hear the baby crying and I want to go to her and feed her but she's not my baby. I am in the room with them but essentially now I am just a friend that's witnessing my friends caring for a baby. And that was a strange dynamic."

Six days after the twins' birth, and after having to go through a ton of paperwork for Ransom's breathing monitor that he'd end up having to wear for the next month, we were finally checked out and on our way to my mom's house. It was a long drive, though I had silence in my car because my husband and brother were driving the twins in the SUV rental. We had to stop every ninety minutes to get the twins out of their car seats for five minutes and pull over to feed them every three hours. We didn't get back to my mother's until almost midnight; a journey that should have taken about five hours took over nine.

The next few months, while I waited for their Social Security cards and then later their passports, were not only a bonding time between the twins and me (my husband had gone back to London after ten days to finish up the house) but also with my mom. She helped with the feeds. She changed countless diapers. We together took them to doctor appointments, including Ransom finally getting the all clear on his sleep apnea. She helped me entertain a number of family and friends who arrived from London; New York; Washington, DC; Las Vegas; and Chicago, as well as from all across Michigan, who came to meet the babies. But smartly, she didn't do nights.

One of my enduring memories of those early months was doing a feed one morning at 3 a.m. Bleary-eyed, I changed and fed Lexie; I never quite managed to feed them at the same time. And before picking up Ransom, the cords from his monitor always making me have to do a careful dance, I thought, "Oh man, I am only 50 percent done." (I have little time or sympathy for parents of singletons who complain about night feeds.) As I rocked Ransom, I saw my mom's motion light go off in her back-yard. Startled, I looked out to see sitting in the deep snow in the bright spotlight, a gray bunny. Other than gently twitching its nose, it sat there like a noble statue, pristine and still in the serene whiteness of the landscape. I took a deep breath, staring out for a few moments. With my child safely snuggled in my arms feeding I thought, "there is peace in my kingdom, and I got this."

A few months later, after a London-based friend flew back with the twins and me to London on Easter Sunday, safely ensconced back in our renovated house in London, we had our first meeting with our British family law solicitor. While all the paperwork in the US was finished—save a few hospital bills that periodically kept showing up in my mother's mailbox—it was now time to start the long process of getting our kids' British citizenship.[204] Getting US citizenship for the twins was no issue because not only are children born in the US automatically American citizens but also, as their mom, they also would get it from me. However, in Britain they still adhered to the *mater semper certa est* principle. That meant under British law Julie and Chad, Americans who lived in Illinois, were the legal parents of our kids who were with us in London.

In order for them to become British citizens, we'd have to get them British birth certificates. But we could only get those once we got a parental order. That's a legal mechanism that transfers parenthood from the surrogate and her partner to the intended parents—one of whom had to be biologically related to the child—thereby terminating the surrogate's legal parenthood.[205] A parental order can't be applied for until after a child is born, so therefore it was paperwork we couldn't do beforehand. And the court can't make a parental order less than six weeks after the birth, as a surrogate's consent can only validly be given after that timeframe ends.

That meant that not only would Julie and Chad have to sign documents relinquishing their rights to parent our children, but we'd also have to go—twice—in front of a family court judge at the High Courts of Justice in London.[206] Julie and I, texting each other back and forth, laughed a lot about how it all felt very Monty Pythonesque. They couldn't legally move to Britain without visas. And if for some reason Julie and Chad didn't sign the documents and they decided they wanted to parent our kids back to the US, once Ransom and Lexie hit US shores, they would again be seen as the children of my husband and me. I asked our British solicitor why we had to do this whole process as their US birth certificates listed us as parents, and no one would be the wiser. She told me that while, yes, no one would ever necessarily know that the kids were born via surrogacy, legally as a British citizen, it was something I needed to apply for up to six months after their birth. Also, in case we ever got a divorce in Britain—which in the end we did a few years later—it could prove to be a sticking point when it came to custody as the children were genetically related to my husband but not to me.

Britain's antiquated surrogacy laws date back to 1984 when the Warnock Report stated that, "it is inconsistent with human dignity that a woman should use her uterus for financial profit and treat it as an incubator for someone else's child."[207] The next year the British government, one of the first jurisdictions in the world to introduce legislation, outlawed commercial surrogacy, ensuring that private agencies could not financially benefit from an agreement.[208] This was in large part related to the 1985 case of "Baby Cotton," Britain's first surrogate baby born via a commercial arrangement. Kim Cotton, the 28-year-old traditional surrogate, decided to become a carrier after watching a television program about an American surrogate agency that was opening in Britain. Ms. Cotton's thought was that she could earn some money—in the end she received £6,500 in compensation—while she stayed home raising her two young children. The idea of helping a couple who could not have babies also appealed to her, and when she became pregnant after IVF, no one outside her social circle knew.

But then the surrogacy agency that Ms. Cotton was working with publicly announced rather mysteriously that a British woman was pregnant, and the (wo)manhunt to find the surrogate began. Wanting to control the narrative and figuring the likelihood of remaining anonymous was slim, she took the advice of a neighbor who had contacts with the media. She sold her story to a tabloid for £15,000, in part because they promised to protect her once the baby was born.[209] While there was a media circus outside the hospital when she went into labor, inside the delivery room Ms. Cotton was asked "a barrage of questions" from social workers. They wanted to know not only the identity of the baby's parents but also about the US agency that had brokered the arrangement.[210] "It was a nightmare," she told me over a video call in 2020. "I had social services interrogating me and I actually got out of bed and shut myself in the toilet to get away from them. They were shocking, they knew I was going to give birth around that time, but they waited until I was in labor to bring all this stuff up."

She kept telling the social workers that she knew nothing about the couple, who were from another European country. Ms. Cotton told me that in the midst of labor "they made the baby a ward of the state." As all this was happening, the US agency abandoned both her and the IPs. "They dropped the couple with no legal backup," she said, "and I think it cost thousands of pounds in court fees to get custody of Baby Cotton and leave the country." To this day, Ms. Cotton doesn't know the name of the couple or whatever happened to the baby girl. "It was anonymous," she told me, "which is disgusting to me now." According to Dr. Teman, the 1985 law exhibited the "opposition of British national values to American capitalist culture and the perceived threat of commercial surrogacy to British national identity."[211]

Another reason for not allowing surrogacy contracts to be enforced was the strong opposition from the Warnock Committee that women should not be made by legal sanction to part with "their" child. There was also a reluctance in English law for child-bearing to become part of a commercial sphere and under the scope of contract law.[212] When I asked one British family law barrister (who requested not to be named) who works on international surrogacy cases why Britain was so uncomfortable with commercial surrogacy contracts, she told me, "I don't know, it's kind of a British thing." She then used the example of California, saying that the process works well, there is a system of registering all the documents in court and it's very straightforward. "Maybe," she pontificated, "we do need to catch up a little bit with the times."

In fact, that catching up is already starting to happen. In 2018 the Law Commission of England and Wales and the Scottish Law Commission began a more than eighteen-month consultation process to reform British surrogacy laws. That included public forums on surrogacy held across the country and meetings with stakeholders on all sides of the surrogacy debate. Prof. Nicholas Hopkins, a commissioner on the English and Wales Law Commission, told me in 2020 they expected to publish their proposals in the first half of 2022 along with draft legislation. (This was before COVID-19, so with everything else backed up, it finally came out in March 2023.) "It is then over to Government to decide whether to accept our recommendations," he told me, jokingly describing it as an "oven-ready" deal. "And, if so, to introduce the bill into Parliament in order for it to become law."

When the law commissions first floated the idea of making law reforms on surrogacy, they received one of their biggest responses ever to a project. "I think, in essence, it is a case where the legislation we have no longer reflects social and political attitudes to surrogacy," Prof. Hopkins told me. The number of parents applying for parental orders has quadrupled over the last decade, from 117 in 2011 to 413 in 2020.[213] International surrogacy has become so mainstream in Britain that there's a specific category for it on British passport applications.[214] That's something he credits to both increased awareness and acceptance of surrogacy and also with same-sex marriage being legalized in 2013; many gay couples have used surrogacy as a way to expand their families.

This all comes on the heels of years of lobbying from those who work in fertility and family law. Natalie Gamble told me that as far back as 2008 when she worked on a case where, because of a legal loophole, a British couple struggled to bring back their twins who were born via a Ukrainian surrogate. She and others began stressing that the laws needed to be re-examined. "We have been involved in a lot of cases where High Court judges have criticized the law [saying] 'We have to bend and stretch the law to make this work for the child' or 'it's not really fit for purpose, it should be reviewed' so there has been pressure building on that front," she told me. "This Law Commission [project] is the first time there has been a proper review of surrogacy."

A top issue that the law commissions have been keen to explore is what constitutes "reasonable expenses." That's not only in terms of granting a parental order in domestic surrogacy cases but also reviewing those expenses in an international surrogacy arrangement, where the costs can be much higher. One of the initial things we had to do was to prepare for the courts a fairly general calculation of the costs paid to Julie, including everything from providing money for maternity clothing to paying for her to have a house cleaner the last few months of the pregnancy. Plus, we had to list the amounts of reimbursements she received each month that were, according to her contract, "a portion of her living expenses." (It also strongly stated in the contract that "it is expressly understood that these expense reimbursements in no way constitute payment for child, or payment for relinquishment of parental rights to any child and custody to intended parents.")

I remember being slightly concerned about how the court would interpret our "reasonable expenses" because they would be seen likely as much higher than they would be for a British surrogacy. In the end I shouldn't have worried because it was, like so much of the parental order process for us, just another hoop to jump through in order to tick the legal boxes. "The truth is, really, the whole thing is a bit of a legal fiction," said the family law barrister who spoke to me on condition of anonymity. "Because ultimately, unless the court makes the order, the [foreign born] child effectively doesn't have legal parents in this jurisdiction." Despite payments ranging from upwards of $50,000 in the US to £3,000 in India and £8,800 in Russia, no application for a parental order has been refused on the grounds of payments in Britain.[215] The lawyer did add however that, "the court really has to strain to find those expenses reasonable."

In the end, the draft legislation does not allow for commercial surrogacy. And that could be in part because a number of surrogates and not-for-profit agencies told the law commissions that they were not keen for it to go in that direction. Sarah Jones from SurrogacyUK said that commercialization comes with things attached. "Are you now an employee because you are being paid to provide a service?" she asked me rhetorically. "Do you have a contract and now you have to stick to that contract? Surrogates genuinely felt that while they wanted parents to be recognized, they did not want to be dictated to about choices they wanted to make through the pregnancy." She told me that overwhelmingly the surrogates she works with told the law commissioners that if surrogacy became compensated in Britain "they wouldn't choose to do it."

That was in large part because it would go against the "friendship first" model that has developed in the country over the past few decades with some surrogacy agencies. SurrogacyUK, for example, holds open houses—which from what I've seen seems more like speed dating events—where IPs and surrogates meet. Intended parents have to "pitch" themselves to the surrogates, who then decide if they want to be matched with the couple. Once matched, over time they work together on the "intention document" that covers a number of issues. Because contracts are not legally enforceable in Britain, all the protections that IPs have (and it certainly seems to me that surrogates in Britain do get the upper hand on a number of things), are these documents that are usually looked over by lawyers.

Interestingly, Kim Cotton, who now runs Cots Surrogacy UK, said she was against lawyers getting involved whatsoever saying, "Why do you need to see a lawyer? Half the lawyers in the country don't know anything about surrogacy. It seems to me that because the government works so much with lawyers, it's just another parasite to add to the expense." While I understood her frustration that lawyers add to the cost, as the daughter, granddaughter, sister, and friend of lawyers, her comments made me wince. So too did a comment that Michael Johnson-Ellis of My Surrogacy Journey told me. "We advise that you get your lawyer to send [the intention documents] to all parties," he told me. "It's common sense and a lawyer said to me recently if your surrogacy arrangement goes tits up, it's going to cost you a lot more if you don't take advice from the start."

One of the proposed changes was getting intended parents' names on the birth certificate from the start. According to the University of Cambridge's Vasanti Jadva, a number of women she spoke to for her longitudinal study on surrogates not only didn't agree with their names—and their husbands'—being on the birth certificate but found it "bizarre" that it was even allowed. She said many intended parents were really anxious during those initial weeks not knowing whether the parental order was going to be granted. The whole situation created added stress for all parties involved in the surrogacy arrangement. "For surrogates, they don't want to keep the baby, it's not their baby," she said. "So for them, I think, it is reassuring to know that they are going to be able to give the baby to the parents and the parents will have legal responsibility for the child."[216]

Prof. Hopkins told me, "Parental orders and, more widely, legal parentage and recognition of intended parents of the child was very much at the forefront of the discussions we had." He added that the law commissioners were told stories of hospital staff insisting that a surrogate be called to give consent for medical treatment for a child brought in by intended—but not yet legal—parents. "There is also a significant symbolic importance to the intended parents of being recognized as parents of the child from birth and not feeling that in order to gain that they have to go off to court, then wait several months to get it," he added.

Unfortunately, the Conservative government announced in November 2023 that it would not be taking forward the recommendations by the Law Commission "at the moment." According to a piece in the *Independent*, Maria Caulfield, a health minister, wrote to the Commission that, "While we appreciate the importance of this work, parliamentary time does not allow for these changes to be taken forward at the moment." It remains to be seen what the newly elected Labour government plans to do with the report and recommendations.[217]

One of my father's greatest loves was the law: as an attorney he had great respect for the legal process and as an academic he loved the scholarship behind how laws were created in principle and how they were carried out in practice. It was little wonder that on my family's first trip to England in 1990 we found ourselves sitting up in one of the public galleries of London's Royal Courts of Justice. It was a thrill for my dad to see the very posh barristers in their white wigs debating the finer points of whatever the case was that we were witnessing. My brothers (who later both ended up as lawyers but no longer actively practice) and I were vaguely interested in the goings on for about fifteen minutes. But for three teenagers in Europe for the first time, there felt like so many other cooler things we could be doing so we headed off and left my dad to have his day in court.

Almost three decades later, I took my own children back to the Royal Courts, not to watch a case but to have our case heard in front of their family law court. Because ours was deemed an international surrogacy case, it was being held here and we had to appear in front of the judge with Ransom and Lexie. As we walked along the stunning stone corridors (there are said to be three-and-a-half miles of them in the building), my heeled boots making a click-clack noise on the decorated tiles, I thought of my father. He would have wanted, of course, to be there with me giving support, but also, he would have dearly loved the chance to be down in the courtroom trenches listening to all the legal minutiae. However, he would most definitely not have been happy to see me with a rather large legal chip on my shoulder.

It had been seven months since we'd initially begun the parental order process—something journalist and father through surrogacy Paul Morgan-Bentley told me he felt was "frankly a waste of public money"—and it felt like a costly paperwork exercise in futility. Our solicitor told us at the offset that technically at that moment under English law we did not have parental responsibility for our kids. For some reason that made my blood boil—this paradox that I was legally my children's mother in the United States but not in the United Kingdom.

One of the first things we had to do was to have our solicitor create a statement on our behalf discussing why we had chosen to do surrogacy. There were many parts of this parental order process that I found were quite intrusive and offensive, and this statement we had to give was most assuredly one of them. As if being an infertility survivor was not a hard and painful enough road to have battled, now I needed to explain myself to someone who would make a judgment on whether I should be allowed to parent my children in Britain. People who got pregnant naturally didn't need to explain themselves to a judge, so why did we? I felt like my infertility was being held against me and I was furious.

Also, the wording on the document—a form called A101A—that Julie and Chad had to sign really bothered me. Part of the form statement said:

> *If a parental order is made in respect to my child, I under-stand that I will no longer be legally treated as the parent and that my child will become part of the applicants' fam-ily [...] If I do withdraw my agreement and want my child returned to me, I understand I must notify the court that I have changed my mind and I must, at all times, act through the court and not approach applicants directly.*

I was so affronted that the British courts referred to my children as Julie's children. She did not want to mother them, she never viewed them as her children, yet the British courts were stating that my Ransom and Lexie were, in their view, her kids. As we sat down on uncomfortable wooden benches outside the court-room where our directions hearing was going to take place, my husband shot me a warning look when I asked the barrister hired by our solicitor if she thought the parental order was a stupid process. She hemmed and hawed and then told me that, yes, it was something of a legal conundrum considering that another jurisdiction ruled these kids as ours. She was the first to tell me that there was talk of the law changing.

Our case was soon called forward and as we entered the

courtroom, a pervasive sense of graveness and respect flooded over me. I had been taught by my dad—whom my brothers and I often paralleled to Atticus Finch from *To Kill a Mockingbird*—that a courtroom was something of a sacred place, that there needed to be deference shown much like others might do in a church, synagogue, or mosque. We sat down on the front bench, my husband holding Ransom and me with Lexie. I was a bit disappointed that the judge, a kindly grandfatherly figure, was not wearing a wig. Our solicitor told me later the reason being that since 2007 it was no longer a requirement for barristers and judges to wear them in family and civil court proceedings. The hearing was quite procedural, with our barrister presenting a bundle of paperwork to the judge and answering "yes" and "no" to the few questions he did ask. The judge then asked who each child was, and so we held them up individually. He smiled, queried a few more points and that was it.

The next step was for a parental order reporter assigned by the court to come to our home to assess us. After their evaluation as to whether we were suitable parents, they would file their report to the court and within three months we would have a final hearing. This also really unsettled me, having to invite someone into our home to also judge whether we were good parents. But it was another step along this seemingly never-ending process, so I decided to accept it as a mild hinderance. A few weeks after the first hearing, an email from the Children and Family Court Advisory and Support Service (CAFCASS) dropped in my email inbox. CAFCASS, a non-departmental public body that looks after children and families who are involved in family court, were charged with organizing the parental order reporter to come to the house. We arranged the meeting with a man called Thomas[218] and I sent him over the paperwork he required.

The morning he was set to arrive I spoke with our solicitor and she told me not to be nervous. I laughed, saying I wasn't stressed at all unless he wanted to critique how quickly I could change a diaper. By now, probably bored and tired of my irritability about the whole process, she good-naturedly said that it would be pretty painless and just to be honest with Thomas. When he knocked at the door and I let him in, I instantly relaxed. He was originally from Georgia (the state not the country) so I joked with him that if he found I was a terrible mom I'd just catch the first flight back to Detroit.

Somehow having a fellow American establish whether we were good parents here in England gave me something of an internal chuckle. I never saw his final report until I started working on this book, so it was intriguing not only to read how we characterized our kids' personalities at nine months (we'd thought Ransom would be the more social one and that Lexie seemed more hesitant about things, something that mostly flipped by the time they were toddlers) but also how he viewed us as parents. He wrote that we had a strong bond with the children and that both babies were attentive and "engaged in exploring their environment."

Thomas also noted a number of times in the report that we planned to be honest and open with the children that they were born via surrogacy. He also stated that I was "not threatened" that I wasn't the genetic mother, and that I spoke of "being very open to talking with the children about this as they develop." His final recommendation was that it would "be in the best interests" of the children to end the legal relationship between them and Julie and Chad, and to confer legal parentage to my husband and me. Several weeks later, now the middle of November, we had our final hearing. Our barrister told us beforehand how things were going to go: the judge, having read all the pertinent materials related to "reasonable expenses" as well as the CAFCASS report, might ask us a few general questions or make a statement. Some judges even offered to take photos with the family afterwards so that parents could add that to their scrapbook for their children, the last hurdle completed. I didn't really care either way, but it seemed like that was something that was usually done, so I said, "Great, yeah, if he's up for it."

She also told me that judges loved the final hearings on surrogacy cases because there was such a feel-good factor about them. Family court oftentimes delves into the deepest depressing depths of humanity—dealing with everything from children taken into care to abuse and abandonment—so surrogacy cases were happy ones, completing a family after a long, often sorrowful journey. I was told later that some judges like to group their surrogacy hearings together so that families who have been through similar circumstances can meet and exchange stories. The hearing was short and sweet, in part because Lexie and Ransom were none-to-pleased that it was close to their nap time.

The judge asked us if we were going to tell the twins that they were born through surrogacy, to which we replied that, yes, we would. He then stated that he was going to grant the parental order and how pleased he was for us. We then went up to take a photo in front of the Royal Seal of the United Kingdom, a golden lion and a white unicorn holding up a crown with a scroll underneath reading *Dieu et mon droit* (God and my right). My husband, dressed in jeans, was holding Ransom, who looked ever so bored by the process, while I'm holding Lexie, who was resplendent in pink-patterned dress and tights. The judge awkwardly stood between us in a gray suit and blue tie.

That picture is in their baby photo album now, a quirky addendum to their birth story.

Chapter Ten

Rules and Regulations

My former mother-in-law believes that if you do not have socks on your feet—no matter what the weather—you will die.

At first, I thought it was her quirk, and every time we would go visit her in Serbia, she would good-naturedly chase me around the house trying to get me to put on socks. While it also drove her stir crazy that I went out of the house with wet hair, it was the lack of the *carape* (socks) that truly set her off. So it was little surprise that when she first came to visit us in London in the late spring of 2018 after the kids were born, she constantly nagged me—in Serbian which I do not speak—about putting socks on Ransom and Lexie's feet. During her three-week visit it was hot and humid, and I didn't want the kids to get overheated, so every time she put socks on their feet, I would take them off when she would leave the room. It became a passive-aggressive mini-rebellion we fought against each other. My husband and I had also told her not to put blankets around the kids when they were in their cots because of Sudden Infant Death Syndrome (SIDS). Yet every time I would go in and check on them as they napped, blankets had mysteriously appeared, loosely wrapped around them. She also apparently thought drafts might kill them too.

A year or so later when we were in Serbia visiting with the kids, I found the book *Snippets of Serbia* in a chic shop in Belgrade. It was an illustrated guidebook with humorous keen observations about the Balkan country written by an American who had lived there for several years. One of the pages was entitled "Three Things that Guarantee Death in Serbia": not wearing socks, wet hair, and drafts. I let out a huge belly laugh in the shop, especially because as I had kissed my children goodbye earlier that morning—I was on a solo reporting trip for a few days in Belgrade—I noticed that my mother-in-law had surreptitiously put socks on their feet. As the car pulled away, I saw my husband fighting with her about it, the sock obsession driving him mad as well. "*Jebene carape*" ("those fucking socks"), I heard him yelling as I sped off down the potholed road.

This raging sock debate between my mother-in-law and me exemplified how different cultures can have completely contrasting views on things that are seemingly innocuous. Take, for example, birth certificates. Interestingly and confusingly, these documents represent different things in different countries, and this is something that sticks in the craws of those who take a stand against surrogacy and it has been the focus of countless international debates around parentage. While in the past a birth certificate had both social and medical meaning, in the age of assisted reproduction, in many countries it has become an exclusively social document. As was the case for our kids, many intended parents in countries like the US where surrogacy is legal have their names put automatically on the birth certificates, which according to academics Laurel Swerdlow and Wendy

Chavkin is "erasing" the gestational carrier from the document that "allegedly provides a record" of the baby's birth.[219]

Michigan judge Marianne Battani had set that precedence back in 1986 with her ruling on that first gestational carrier case. Some argue that this "deletion" not only alters the meaning of the document, "but also exclusively conveys the familial and national associations of the commissioning parents."[220] When the kids had been born, I was clueless about all of this but did ponder over the fact that these birth certificates weren't about who physically birthed the babies but who was going to parent them. "Birth certificates are legal documents, and they are supposed to be an accurate record of a child's birth," Jennifer Lahl from Stop Surrogacy Now told me, "not who the intended parents think the child is born to. We have a huge issue of falsification of records [that] magically erase women."

When I looked into this, I was told by legal experts that in the US, birth certificates are legal documents that reflect legal parentage, and they are not records of birth or biology. And they never have been, really. For example, marital presumption ensures that married parents are on the birth certificate but one or more might not be the genetic parent due to gamete donation, an affair, and so on. As Bruce Hale, a Massachusetts family lawyer, explained to me, a birth certificate reflects a child's legal parentage and is the key document used to prove the existence of a legal parent-child relationship, to prove identity, and access to a myriad of benefits. It's a reflection of who plans to parent the child. For a child born through assisted reproduction and surrogacy in the US, their intended parents, who may or may not be their genetic parents, become their legal parents through pre-birth orders or other legal means. Gamete donors and people acting as surrogates are not the parents of children born through surrogacy and should not be reflected as such on any birth certificate. Bruce added that in doing so, it would not only undermine the rights of the legal intended parents but would also create chaos and confusion for children who need clarity in legal parentage for reasons like health care and decision making for a minor. (Hey, Britain, listen up!)

Once we had the parental order for the children, I applied for them to get their British birth certificates. About two months later, with little fanfare, they arrived in the mail in a manila envelope. Tucked in at the bottom of the beige-and-red certificates was a sentence that read: "Certified to be a true copy of an entry in the Parental Order Register maintained at the General Register Office." At the time that sentence meant nothing to me, in fact I'm not even sure I even noticed it. It was just some legalese at the bottom of birth certificates that would only ever be used so that I could apply for their British passports. Their real birth certificates were the ones from the US where they were actually born.[221]

But what I found out later was that that sentence actually signaled that my children were born through surrogacy. "You have a document that discloses your children's procreational history without their consent," one international lawyer who works on cross-border surrogacy cases told me. "And so, what is a real challenge to me is that any law, which is framed proportionally to protect the rights and interests of all parties but particularly the child that is born of these arrangements, we shouldn't be discriminating in any aspect between children born of a surrogacy arrangement, IVF treatment in a non-surrogacy case, adoption or natural procreation."

The lawyer went on to tell me that while countries like France do not have markers like this on birth certificates, Britain and others do. This was done as a policy decision. "It was decided,

'Well, we need to make sure that these children when they grow up, if they want to have access to information relating to the birth, that they can contact the register," he told me, "and if we don't put a mark on their birth certificate, they'll never know." This all now made much more sense to me as to why Thomas from CAFCASS and the judge kept driving the point about whether we were going to tell Ransom and Lexie that they were born via surrogacy. That even if for some odd reason we decided not to tell them, the British government had forced our hand, pointing it out to all and sundry that this was the case. And therein lies the rub: legal parentage is something that has become one of the hotly debated international legal conversations taking place currently around cross-border surrogacy.

Another looming issue around cross-border surrogacy is that of jurisdictions. In many circumstances, international surrogacy operates in a "grey market that shops for opportunities" and benefits from the ambiguities in domestic laws, so as regulations may tighten in one jurisdiction, some operations just move on to another.[222] This is commonly referred to by many who study surrogacy as the "whack-a-mole" phenomenon. April Hovav, an academic who did her PhD on surrogacy in Mexico, told me that oftentimes you see the "same players" popping up in different countries. "You have these international players setting up but then you end up having local people kind of setting up parallel shops or subsidiaries," she said. "And it ends up being difficult to tie all the threads like, 'okay here is this one person but then who are they actually connected to? And is it one of the big international agencies and are they working for them?'"

There have been issues related to not only moving operations out of countries where cross-border surrogacy was stopped—for example India and Thailand—into neighboring countries where laws weren't in place or were more lax (Nepal and Cambodia), but also moving surrogates from one country where it isn't legal to another country where it is. Nepalese women, for instance, were not allowed to be gestational carriers so Indian women were brought to Nepal to be surrogates. Since the 2015 law banning cross-border surrogacy in Thailand, Thai gestational carriers for Chinese couples have been sent to Cambodia or Laos for the embryo transfer, go back home to Thailand for the majority of the pregnancy and then at the end of the third trimester are sent to China for the birth.[223]

Meanwhile after the cross-border ban in India, a Mumbai-based infertility specialist began recruiting Kenyan women to come to the country to be implanted with embryos of gay clients. The carriers then went back home and gave birth in designated hospitals in Nairobi where the babies' parents then came to pick them up. Legal loopholes are jumped over by moving the carriers "across borders, exposing [them] to greater risks while expanding and diversifying" the agency or clinician's global business.[224] Because of this, accusations of trafficking of women and the sale of children have dogged international surrogacy for years. "Women who are being moved across borders, say from Thailand to Cambodia or Laos, for me that is trafficking, but of women not children," said one expert who works on global surrogacy policy who wished to remain anonymous.

With the United Nations Optional Protocol to the Convention on the Rights of the Child (CRC)[225] stating that the sale of children means any act or transaction "whereby a child is transferred by any person or group of persons to another for remuneration," could surrogacy therefore be considered the sale of children? Not surprisingly when I asked Jennifer Lahl this she said, in a nutshell, yes. "Especially the commercial context of it [because] what is a surrogate being paid to do? Surrender a child," she said. "We say, 'We are not buying or selling children' but does she get to keep the money if she changes her mind and decides to keep the baby? I read surrogate contracts all the time and everything is punitive and ties to breach of contract in the money. We deceive ourselves by saying we are just doing nice things and 'oh by the way, we are going to pay you all this money, but we are not buying or selling children.'"

However, those who work in the international surrogacy sphere absolutely and vehemently disagree with her summation. The international lawyer I spoke with about my kids' British birth certificates told me that an exchange of funds does not imply the sale of children. He then gave me two reasons why he felt this was the case: "One is we accept in other areas of law that fertility treatments may be required for certain couples, and that there is a payment associated with that. The second reason is because no one is actually paying for the transfer of a child if the law in [that country] says that at the moment of birth [...] these people are the legal parents of a child. Provided that the surrogacy arrangement is lawful, there is clear law that has checks and balances for everyone along the way [and] provided the agent, the medical centers, the intermediaries are subject to regulation, it mitigates the risk of exploitation [and] I think it also combats this very notion of intended parents buying a child."

Some in the abolitionist camp have also tried to make the case that cross-border surrogacy could create a market for child sex trafficking and pornography, with babies being created just so they could be groomed for exploitation.[226] One oft-pointed-to case was of a gay American-Australian couple—who falsely claimed their son was born via a Russian surrogate—not only molested the boy but also offered him to pedophiles in a number of different countries.[227] To me, this case smacks of homophobic undertones, with the implication that gay dads have perverted reasons for wanting to be parents.[228] While there have been tragic stories where convicted pedophiles—including Baby Gammy's biological father—have had children via surrogacy, they are a miniscule but sad exception and in the future something that could be prevented if robust background checks by cross-border surrogacy agencies are made mandatory through international regulations.[229]

When I asked Barbara Collura from RESOLVE what she thought about accusations that surrogacy could be used for child trafficking she told me it was "pointless" to have these conversations. "You just have to start with what is the purpose and reason for somebody who is going through this method to build their family," she said. "As someone who has gone through IVF, I often say, 'no little girl dreams of having her babies via IVF or surrogacy.' How you get to this point, it is not easy, it is not a first choice, it is not something that people are rushing to do. You have to start with intent and the intent of the intended parents is the purest rationale for the desire to be a parent."

That intent and deep desire to have a child has, however, very often clouded the judgment of well-meaning intended parents, inadvertently leading their children to become stateless. "Stateless children are created when there is a difficulty in a nation state establishing or recognizing whom it considers the legal parentage of a child to be," writes Marsha Tyson Darling in her essay in *Babies for Sale?* She goes on to explain that the challenge is some children fail to acquire the nationality of their nation of birth or the country where their intended parents reside, leaving that child with no legal parentage and no state. While the United Nations Convention on the Rights of the Child states that every child has "the right to acquire nationality," in large swathes of the world, access to nationality is through *jus sanguinis*, with citizenship being settled or secured through the nationality or ethnicity of one or both parents.[230]

There is, at the moment, a dearth of international regulations on surrogacy arrangements and none of the existing instruments (like the Hague Adoption Convention) contain any provisions that might be adapted to regulate this developing area of international law.[231] What that means is that highly complex legal problems—like what American Bud Lake and his Spanish husband faced over the birth of their daughter in Thailand—have emerged over cross-border surrogacy cases, chief among them being legal parenthood and the child's nationality. Over the years, judges and national authorities in a number of countries have ended up facilitating requests by parents who have either violated surrogacy laws or dodged them by going abroad to have their babies.[232]

This is because once the birth of a child through surrogacy arrangements is a *fait accompli,* the child's best interests are "interpreted as requiring national authorities to cooperate with the intended parents" even if those parents have—according to those same authorities—gone against the rules of their own country.[233] "It's 'I will go to this country where I can effectively do what is unlawful in my own country [and] some poor judge has to deal with it,'" John Pascoe, the retired Australian family court judge, told me. "They are really difficult cases because often the child has come into the country, you do not know the circumstances of their birth, only what the parties are telling you, and you are in a position where your guiding principle is the best interest of the child."

Cross-border surrogacy throws up a ton of questions: Do the authorities issue birth certificates and give citizenship to the child suspected of being born through surrogacy in another country? Do they therefore recognize the intended parents as the legal parents? And by doing so, does it look like authorities are validating what is prohibited within their own borders? "I have parents from all over the world and they are lawyers, judges, police chiefs, fertility physicians who come [to the US] from countries where they are supposed to be enforcing the law against [surrogacy]," said Minnesota lawyer Steven Snyder, "but the desire to procreate supersedes their knowledge of their institutional prohibition of the process."

He added that they go back home to their own countries, are able to get citizenship for their children, and the courts rule in favor of naming them the legal parents. "The lawyers [in their home countries] have figured out how to present the cases with the proper documentation to get them through their court systems," he said, adding that's in part because of case law that has developed over the years in relation to cross-border surrogacy arrangements. Interestingly, he did add that it does matter to courts where the surrogacy took place, like for example, if it was in the US or Ukraine. "They do have that latitude to see them differently," he said, "and put them in different piles."

That's developed, in part, because of a number of problematic cross-border surrogacy court cases that have come out of prewar Ukraine. One case, *D and Others vs Belgium*, went all the way to the European Court of Human Rights (ECHR) in 2014. A married couple from Belgium—Mr. D and Mrs. R—had a son via a Ukrainian surrogate in 2013. As was consistent with the surrogacy contract, at birth the gestational carrier surrendered her responsibility to the child so therefore the boy could not get Ukrainian citizenship.[234] However Belgian officials refused to grant the child the right to travel back to the country with his parents as compensated surrogacy is outlawed in Belgium. This rendered the infant stateless. While his parents battled it out in the courts—with the ECHR rejecting the claim that Belgian authorities had interfered with their 'right to respect for their family life'—the baby was apart from his parents for almost four months.

In February 2021, I reached out to the couple's lawyer to ask what the update was on the case. I was told when they were finally able to return to Belgium with their son, the couple spent the next six years fighting in the courts to register his birth certificate. They were finally able to do so in 2020. Another Belgian boy, Samuel, born in 2008 also in Ukraine, was the biological son of Laurent Ghilain and an anonymous egg donor. When Laurent and his partner, Peter Meurrens, went to the Belgian embassy in Kyiv to get papers for their son, they were refused, even though a DNA test proved Laurent was the father. The boy was first put in foster care while his parents fought for a legal solution and as their money ran out, the boy was placed in an orphanage. Only after two-plus years did the Belgians finally issue the toddler with a passport.[235]

While this tragedy of statelessness does not happen to children born through surrogacy arrangements in the United States because of the Fourteenth Amendment, which confers all children born in the US with citizenship, it does not mean there aren't complications for those children when their parents try to bring them back to their home country. If a child doesn't have a registered nationality in the country where they are being brought up, not only does that mean that as a minor they might be barred from access to free health care and public education but when they turn eighteen, they won't be eligible to vote, get a job, or possibly even live in the same country as their parents. Such was the case of Valentina and Fiorella Mennesson. As surrogacy is illegal in France, their French parents, Dominique and Sylvie, commissioned a California surrogate to carry twins, who were created using Dominique's sperm and a friend's eggs.

When the girls were born in 2000, they were issued with US birth certificates listing Dominique and Sylvie as their parents. According to a conversation I had with Dominique, the trouble started with the French consulate in Los Angeles. "They refused to give us passports and they were looking to get information on proof of surrogacy," he told me. "Obviously I refused, and that was the starting point." It took over a decade for the French courts to finally rule that Dominique and Sylvie could be recognized as the girls' parents. But Valentina and Fiorella remained barred from being added to the French National Register, meaning that the girls were not granted French citizenship. This, despite their parents arguing that the interests of the twins should be paramount.[236] "My whole life was in France, I speak French, I eat French [food]," Fiorella, who when she spoke to me in 2020 was studying to be a graphic designer, said with a slight laugh. "I grew up with a big, big, big sense of injustice and something that impacts my life every day. I cannot stand injustice." After losing an appeal to the French Supreme Court, the couple's only recourse was to take their case to the ECHR in 2014, invoking a violation of the right to respect for private and family life, something guaranteed in Article 8 of the ECHR.[237]

While the court found that Dominique and Sylvie had not been prevented from enjoyment in France of their right to respect their family life, the denial of their daughters' status had been a violation. Following that judgment, French administrative law was changed, making it possible for children born abroad through surrogacy arrangements to obtain a French birth certificate if the genetic father was French.[238] However, it took another five years for Sylvie to finally be recognized under French law as the mother of the twins. "There is no question any more about my mother-hood," Sylvie told me soon after the ruling, adding that she, along with Dominique, co-founded Association Clara, which promotes the legalization of surrogacy in France. "I was feeling since the beginning it was an injustice and discriminatory to be obliged to adopt your own children. [We] fought for almost 20 years, and we did all the battle to make things change in France. We are entitled to say this harassment from the [Ministry] of Justice against us was really damaging for our family."

In June 2019, not long before the French government finally legally recognized Sylvie as the twins' mother, she along with Dominique and Fiorella took part in a conference on international surrogacy at the University of Cambridge in England. All three gave statements about how their legal battle had affected them as a family. Fiorella, with cotton-candy pink dyed hair, explained how frustrating it was to be "born and exist in a world that does not recognize us." Meanwhile, her father pointed out how important it was to understand how different surrogacy and adoption were, and that the legal issues between the two were distinct. Also in attendance at the conference was Maud de Boer-Buquicchio, who at the time was the United Nations' Special Rapporteur on the sale and sexual exploitation of children (2014–2020), who likely took note of this point. The Dutch lawyer had spent her career working in human rights, having at one point delved into the subject of illegal adoptions. Partly because of her experience on this subject and wanting to show her interest in the intersectionality of child's rights and bioethics when she took the job, she told me, "I decided it was important to address the [complex] issues of surrogacy."

And address it she did, releasing in 2018 a statement on the subject that rankled many within the surrogacy world. She warned that compensated surrogacy, as it was practiced in some countries, "usually amounts to the sale of children" and that there was an urgent need for surrogacy to be regulated. It was, said Circle's Dean Hutchison, "a harsh report" and there was concern by many that she was only hearing one side of the surrogacy story from those who opposed the practice. The Cambridge conference organizers—including Dean Hutchison, Steve Snyder, Richard Vaughan, and Bruce Hale—invited the UN Special Rapporteur to give a presentation on how she developed her initial findings. After she spoke, one father "went after her," said Dean. "He said, 'My daughter read in a newspaper that she is chattel and that I bought her. You have diminished the self-worth of these children.'" He felt that comment—along with side sessions with a number of participants, including Karla Torres from the Center for Reproductive Rights, who all gave their opinions on why they had issues with the 2018 report—appeared to have great impact as there seemed to be more nuance to her second report that was released later that year.

Karla told me that "we welcomed the shift in her findings" and that Ms. de Boer-Buquicchio had "sort of stepped back from saying that by default" surrogacy equated to the sale of a child. "[The 2019 report] instead seemed to call for more regulation around this so as to avoid potential sale of children," said Karla, "and then also address the rights of the person who acts as a surrogate." I asked Ms. de Boer-Buquicchio—after her tenure at the UN had ended—if it was true that her opinion on surrogacy had somewhat shifted because of the conference. She disagreed, adding that it was more that the second report had a wider scope. "One could say that my two reports were complementary," she said. "I know surrogacy occurs and it is going to happen more and more. So I think we have to address the reality and always with this perspective of the child's rights in mind." Stephen Page, the Australian lawyer who was also involved in organizing the Cambridge conference, agreed saying that she was "quite right" to say there should be international regulations around surrogacy. "Because at the moment there are not," he said. "Who are we failing? We are failing a number of people but particularly the children."

Ms. de Boer-Buquicchio's work has become part of the growing discourse over whether there should be international standards or regulations put in place on cross-border surrogacy. One of the organizations that has been at the forefront of many of these legal conversations is the Hague Conference on Private International Law (HCCH), as the recognition of legal parentage established as a result of a cross-border surrogacy is something that falls under private international law.[239] First convened at the end of the nineteenth century, the HCCH is a multilateral organization that counts over eighty-seven countries and the European Union as members (non-member countries can also be parties to its conventions) and covers the fields of family law, as well as civil procedure and commercial law. The HCCH might be best known in recent times for crafting the 1993 Hague Adoption Convention.[240]

It was New Zealand in 2009 that first reached out to the Secretary General of the HCCH, expressing concern "about the increasing number of international surrogacy arrangements with which its State authorities were having to deal" and the country queried if the Adoption Convention could be applied to the complexities that some of the cases posed.[241] The next year the HCCH concluded that the use of the 1993 Convention in cases of international surrogacy was "inappropriate" and an increasing number of member states, including Israel, called on the HCCH for multilateral action to be taken on cross-border surrogacy. [242] This led the HCCH to begin deliberating on whether to create some kind of international legal framework on the recognition of legal parentage arising from cross-border surrogate arrangements. "It is incredibly courageous of the Hague Conference to pick up this political hot potato and try to bridge the differences of opinion between the states," my international lawyer contact, who also advises the HCCH, told me.

The HCCH is at pains to make clear that their work in this area is not an endorsement of surrogacy but rather as a project intended to recommend a solution or solutions to address the issues of uncertain or "limping" parentage. That is when one state—say the United States—has legally established a parent-child relationship but another state—say France—doesn't recognize that ruling. "I think the [HCCH] are struggling a little bit because there are states that are very anti-surrogacy and those states are making it difficult," Prof. Sital Kalantry told me, adding that those countries have argued there is no need to resolve any issues regarding children because there should be no surrogacy. On the other side, some states worry that an HCCH treaty may include many safeguards, and this might be seen by some as regulation of the surrogacy market. So realistically, if an international treaty is "to have any chance of being ratified by many jurisdictions" it would have to be fairly basic and "presumably limited to mutual recognition of parental status across jurisdictions in cases of surrogacy."[243]

As of their 2023 report, the HCCH is trying to find a way to make one instrument, with the fallback being a general convention on legal parentage and then possibly a separate protocol on surrogacy. This would seem to be the way to try to take into consideration the very differing views on surrogacy among states. At center stage, of course, will be how parentage is determined in different states, which includes birth certificates. "There is this assumption that a birth certificate is a legal determination of who one's parents actually are," said my international lawyer contact. "It isn't. There is a legal presumption that two people who are named on the birth certificate are the legal parents, but in [many] surrogacy cases, because there is a judgment, the birth certificate is actually a reflection of the legal situation."

While it's feasible that some kind of international treaty on legal parentage could happen in the future, there are a lot of challenges because not only is the topic controversial, but it is also technically difficult. "When you try to have an international agreement of any kind, usually it takes a long time," said Judge John Pascoe, an Australian delegate to the HCCH's working group on surrogacy and former chief justice of the Family Court of Australia. "And you get very much into issues of national sovereignty, public policy, issues of that kind." He went on to add that there's a complete disconnect between the US and the rest of the world because the US takes the position that the Convention on Rights of Child doesn't apply to surrogacy. So there's the US view and then "there is the rest of the world," he said, where "you have gradation from open slather to not at any cost."[244] So, at the moment the international community is at a stalemate. While global cooperation on issues around surrogacy is "not only desirable but quite obviously necessary" there don't seem to presently be any viable approaches "to a truly globally accepted treaty or convention."[245]

In hindsight to all of this, my husband and I, of course, had been relatively lucky. Aside from the parental order being an administrative and logistical pain, we didn't face any major legal hurdles. My children had been born in a country where surrogacy contracts are legal—save, of course, Michigan at that point—and we resided in a country where surrogacy in general was also legal. Both countries recognized us as the legal parents of our children. However, Inge Sorensen, my Danish surrogate mom friend, faced an uphill battle on her legal parentage. The Danish government estimates that about one hundred children are born to Danish parents each year by surrogacy outside of the country, while about five children each year are born within Denmark in non-compensated surrogacy arrangements.[246] In that country, up until a recent law change that's expected to take effect in January 2025, it's been illegal to seek someone to be a surrogate—only family and friends can do non-compensated surrogacy in the country—and it's also illegal to have money involved.[247] Meanwhile, one of Denmark's Queen Margrethe's nephews, Prince Gustav, and his wife recently have welcomed two babies via surrogacy in the US.

Up until the law change, if Denmark found out that Inge and her husband had their child via surrogacy in the US, they'd have to go through a protracted legal case of limping parentage. Her husband would eventually be given full custody—as he is the genetic father—while Inge, who because of a pre-existing health reason could not bear children nor produce eggs, could try to adopt the baby after two and a half years, something specific in Danish law. "Maybe it would be accepted and maybe it wouldn't," she told me in 2020. "It's not something I think about constantly, but it does appear once in a while, like, 'did I do something wrong, was this unethical?' Because the law says something different over here and I can't tell my friends. I am a person who always tells the truth. So this was my first lie, and it was huge."

While Ms. de Boer-Buquicchio's 2019 report was partly intended to supplement the legal work that HCCH was doing on surrogacy, it was also done to complement the work International Social Services (ISS) were doing in relation to surrogacy and child's rights. Since 2016 ISS, a multilateral organization with 120 countries as members, had been holding numerous consultations to draw up a set of principles to guide global policy to protect children born through surrogacy arrangements. The work of ISS—which focuses on cross-border issues that affect children—has included centralizing policies and practices on the Hague Adoption Convention and creating the standards for the United Nations Guidelines for the Alternative Care of Children. It was natural that during the years as more and more cross-border surrogacy cases sprung up, member states began coming to ISS with policy questions. "Everybody is doing it on their own, like it's a cowboy's world," a former advisor to ISS who wished to remain anonymous told me in an interview. "As an organization, they are leaving the ethical questions aside, and they started saying that if the practice exists, it needs to make sure that human rights are upheld. Since they are an organization based on children, they want to do it from that perspective."

While the HCCH is concentrating mainly on answering the question as to who the legal parents are of a child already born, ISS' focus was on the broad picture, studying all the safeguards it believes should be in place for any surrogacy. Some of those protections include background criminal checks on intended parents and making sure that a child will have access to their origins, both in terms of knowing they were born through surrogacy but also their genetic history if they were donor conceived. ISS is also keen on defining when payments might be seen as leading to the sale of children as, "it is really important that we can tell the child that 'you were not sold,'" the former ISS advisor said.

However, this became a bone of contention for those who were involved in the talks around these ISS principles, arguing that their scope was too narrowly focused on child's rights. "They are coming at it from a social services perspective where they see a lot of children in distress," said Steve Snyder, who was initially involved in some of the working group meetings but dropped out because he felt it was futile. "And they are concerned about the adverse consequences of surrogacy on the children, which I don't see." He went on to ponder how an organization like ISS aims to create blanket regulations for totally disparate situations. "In developing countries where parties are allowed to take advantage of the system—women signing contracts in a language they cannot understand or they cannot read, clinics [where twins are born] telling the parents there was only one baby and then giving the other baby to someone else—these are baby selling instances that are human rights violations," he said. "The difficulty is that is not happening in the US. That is not what happens in Canada. A regulated system operates differently."

Isabel Fulda Graue from Mexico's GIRE told me that they also stopped participating in the discussions in part because they felt that ISS were making it impossible for a surrogacy situation to happen without it being interpreted as the sale of children. "The discussion about when the sale of children could happen in the context of surrogacy is important and we wanted to participate in that discussion," she told me. "However, we felt the document was being construed in a way that it was impossible to not come to the conclusion that all surrogacy was the sale of children." She also told me that they were uncomfortable with how one of the meetings they participated in turned into something of a shouting match.

One working group that was brought together by ISS included organizations like the Center for Reproductive Rights and Stop

Surrogacy Now, groups whose views are diametrically opposed. "There was no control over what was happening [and] there was no way to get consensus from both groups because we think opposite things," said Ms. Fulda Graue. "We felt it was more of a simulation basically to say, 'we consulted women's groups, they have no idea what they want, you know how feminists always fight between themselves.'"[248] Judge Pascoe, who has also served as an advisor to the ISS discussions on surrogacy, agreed that at times it has been hard to find common ground. "All you can do is come up with a principle position, and you can put them out there," he said. "And some people will agree, and some people will disagree but in my view at the very least it makes people look at the issue."

In early 2021 ISS released their Verona Principles, named after the Italian city where the first consultation took place. It is hoped by those who have worked on these principles that they become "customary international law," which is a general practice accepted as law.[249] Of the eighteen members of the UN Committee on the Rights of the Child, fifteen signed their names to the document, writing that it was "an important contribution" toward developing guidance for the protection of children born through surrogacy arrangements. "That is a massive message that you need to at least consider these principles when you are talking about surrogacy from a children's rights perspective," said my contact. But that could be as far as the UN will ever go on cross-border surrogacy. "The problem with surrogacy is that it's one of those human rights issues where there is no consensus amongst countries," Prof. Kalantry told me. "So there will never be a resolution that is pro-surrogacy. It could be an anti-surrogacy resolution but given that the United States is a big player, and we are a big market, you're not going to find the UN doing anything on it."

While international regulations on surrogacy are slow and remain controversial, unilateral attempts by countries like Britain, Denmark, Ireland, and New Zealand to change their laws continue to grind ahead. "There are a lot of people from different countries talking to each other about surrogacy," said Prof. Nicholas Hopkins from the England and Wales Law Commission. "Jurisdictions are trying to catch up to some extent and consider whether their legal regulation is appropriate. [So] that has been a worldwide trend." That is in large part because law often lags behind social change and technological advances, leading countries to address some of the gaps in their laws and rulings on surrogacy.

Canada is one such country. Their 2004 Assisted Human Reproduction Act prohibited payment to egg donors, paying surrogates for contract pregnancies, and for agencies taking a finder's fee.[250] Reimbursements to the surrogates were allowed—the only money that could change hands between the surrogate and the IPs—however those costs were never specified so that created issues. That led to questions of expenses related to things like grocery bills and mobile phone packages: could all the surrogate's groceries in the lead up to and during pregnancy be paid back or just the extra food she ate because she was pregnant? And would her entire phone bill be reimbursed or just calls related to the pregnancy like to the IPs and doctors? While some IPs were generous in repaying thousands of dollars in expenses others quibbled with their gestational carriers about parking tickets.[251]

Clarity was needed, especially after the owner of one agency, Canadian Fertility Consulting, was charged and convicted of flouting a number of these rules and had to pay $60,000 (Canadian) in fines. In June 2020 Health Canada—the governmental department charged with national health policy—finally released their regulations on reimbursement. "They passed a clarifying regulatory scheme that said 'Okay, for a long time, we didn't define what expenses could be paid and now we are going to define them and only those can be paid,'" Steve Snyder told me. "So instead of putting your mortgage and your car payment and your massage bills and your grocery bills and adding them all up into a number that equals the number you're willing to do surrogacy for, it's only things directly related to your surrogacy." So, for example, the guidance document states that pregnant women require an extra 350 to 450 calories a day so IPs can cover costs related to those extra calories but no longer the entire grocery bill.[252]

There has been recognition by many who work in the surrogacy space in Canada—where between 2013 and 2017 upwards of 800 children were born via surrogacy arrangements—that the 2004 law has become problematic in large part over the illegality of surrogacy compensation. In February 2020 Canadian Senator Lucie Moncion initiated a bill to end compensation bans (however due to COVID-19, the bill had to be reintroduced to Parliament again that October).[253] Her revision proposals included protections that prohibit anyone from coercing someone to be a donor or a surrogate if they are unable to consent or if there is reason to believe they have been bullied into making the decision. "How do we protect women from exploitation? How do we protect women's health? How do we protect children? How do we find a way of making this a healthy practice that is working within a framework?" Senator Moncion asked rhetorically during a video call with me. "Right now it is in limbo. There are too many things that are unwritten, there are too many things that are prohibited. It is not a well put in place system." As of May 2024, nothing has happened with the bill after its second reading.

Meanwhile the Mexican Supreme Court in 2021 examined a

challenge by the country's National Human Rights Commission (a federal institution) to the 2016 Tabasco law that ended cross-border surrogacy. The court ruled that surrogacy was a protected medical procedure but not all jurisdictions have taken up the court's directive.[254] However, in some states now intended parents can be listed on their child's birth certificate. Though numbers are of course hard to come by, academics and activists reckon between 2013 and 2016 as many as 500 babies a year were born via surrogacy arrangements in the Mexican state. Of those, about 70 percent were believed to be gay foreigner arrangements.[255]

While surrogacy had not been at the center of public debate for a number of years in Mexico, the discussion at the Supreme Court certainly helped give surrogacy more visibility in general, "both within the feminist movement (with both our perspective and the abolitionist one giving way to heated debates) and among conservative groups, which are very likely to oppose the practice publicly," Ms. Fulda Graue explained to me over email after our initial interview. So though "Mexico can definitively be categorized among the states that authorize surrogacy"—at least in some of its states—the existing regulations "leave much to be desired" and since the federal government has not decided to legislate on the matter "the courts will continue to have an active and dominant role in the evolution of surrogacy in Mexican law."[256]

After a complaint by a collection of LGBTQ rights organizations, Israel's Supreme Court in February 2020 gave the country's parliament, the Knesset, twelve months to end discrimination in surrogacy. It took another two years, but now gay and trans Israelis can also pursue surrogacy in the country. As mentioned earlier in this book, gay couples in Israel have not been able to work with Israeli surrogates, hence why my friends Ben and Offir and Nir and Or had to go to the US for their surrogacy journeys. According to the Association of Israeli Gay Fathers, gay couples can spend upwards of $100,000 for surrogacy arrangements, including travel and accommodation, in the US or Canada.[257] The organization argued that that cost would be halved if gay dads could stay in Israel. "I have surrogate friends who said they were done doing surrogacy," Israeli surrogate Orit Chorowicz Bar-Am told me before the court ruling, "but if the law will change, they would do it again because it's important for them to do it for gay couples."

This is not the first time the Knesset has been called to look into laws around surrogacy. In 2018 the country expanded surrogacy rights to single women but continued its ban for same-sex couples and gay men. And thousands took to the streets in protest including a number of gestational carriers. "A lot of surrogates 'came out of the closet' in the protest and went on TV shows, got interviewed on radio and I think we made the movement because during that time there were so many conversations around surrogacy," Orit told me, admitting that she herself had not been very vocal before those debates. "People were talking about surrogates saying they were poor women being exploited. No. You want to understand? Talk to us. Because it is very clear that people when they talk about surrogacy, pardon my language, don't know shit."

There are also moves to create accreditation organizations in the US around surrogacy. In 2023, SEEDS adopted a set of standards for agencies.[258] Part of that grew out of concern over agencies that were willing to take on IPs who wanted a number of kids from a number of surrogates at the same time. "We need to make a standard," Wendie Wilson-Miller told me. "Because this is truly going to make the rest of the world look at us and think we are a baby factory." She said that while there is nothing they can do to make this kind of practice unlawful, "we can as attorneys, as agencies, as clinics, as mental health professionals collectively come together" to try and convince agencies those practices are not a good idea and that it taints the entire industry.

Internationally, I hope that practices will evolve for the better. And while I don't think we will ever see a transnational regulatory agency like what academics like France Winddance Twine have called for, I do agree that the global fertility industry does need some kind of regulation and accountability. There continues to be potential for abuse and exploitation in this growing global industry that operates, "with virtually no government or international oversight" and where the stakeholders—including IPs, children, and surrogates—have often little or no legal recourse from those less than ethical operators in the surrogacy industry.[259] For countries where surrogacy is practiced but there is still no law, I do hope that governments address this rationally and swiftly before problems arise. "I was at a conference in Cape Town and this man stood up and said, 'I'm from Ghana and surrogacy is happening in Ghana. What can we do?'" said Australian lawyer Stephen Page. "I said, 'get laws.' You have got to have laws in place." Maybe the Verona Principles will serve as something of a global blueprint as it relates to child protection and that the HCCH will continue to debate and make strides when it comes to issues around legal parentage.

For intended parents and surrogates who participate in cross-border surrogacy—or any kind of surrogacy for that matter—I wish that they'll do their due diligence by examining the number of difficult and complicated ethical, medical, social, and legal arguments around the practice. "Look at the legal framework, look at the cultural acceptance in the country," advised Bud Lake, who had such drama when his daughter was born in Thailand. "Obviously there are trade-offs and if you want something that is super secure, well nothing is ever 100 percent."

Chapter Eleven

The Kids Are Alright

One of the most profound pieces of wisdom I ever got on mother-hood came from a rock star.

Six weeks after Lexie and Ransom were born and I was still in Michigan, I interviewed Emily Saliers, one-half of the folk-rock duo Indigo Girls. I'd been a huge fan of their music since 1989 when I saw them open for R.E.M. in Detroit during my senior year of high school. Their single "Closer to Fine" became a theme song for my college friends and me; we'd feverishly dance around to it at dorm parties, and, sunroof open, we'd blast the chorus from the top of our lungs on weekend road trips. (New life was breathed into that great song when it was introduced to a new generation after being featured in the *Barbie* movie and soundtrack in 2023.) So when an opportunity came for me to interview Emily Saliers about her new solo album, I took it.

As a freelancer—and also a working mother on maternity leave—there's a constant worry about being forgotten and not even three weeks after the twins were born, I was emailing various editors I wrote for with story ideas. One of them told me she didn't want to hear from me for at least a month. "Ginanne, don't worry, we won't forget about you, just go love those babies," she said in an email. And while I appreciated her sentiment, I was going slightly stir crazy. For years, even on vacation, I would do work, as often there is no rhyme or reason when edits come back on filed stories or editors are fishing around for ideas. And as a new mom, I wasn't sure what I was "supposed" to be doing once the babies had been fed and were sleeping. I was exhausted physically but mentally my mind was running at a million clicks per minute.

I happened to mention all this to Ms. Saliers when we started the interview as I knew she was also a parent. Me as a frazzled new mom possibly veering down an unprofessional path with a famous singer/songwriter. It was my initial toe dipping into the parental waters, trying out the feel of bonding with someone about motherhood. It felt slightly odd, but she took the bait when I told her my kids were newborns. "Becoming a parent takes the selfishness out of you to a great extent because these little creatures, you want to put them first," she told me. Sagely, she went on to say that a lot of parenting was based on doing something with or for your kid even when you weren't in the mood or you were busy. "But you do it anyway," she said, before adding jokingly, "like I will not always give them my last bite of pizza, but it is a huge shift and that is a wonderful thing to experience."

I told her how I was stressed over things like them getting enough formula, that Lexie seemed colicky while Ransom had acid reflux. I felt fully immersed and like it would never end. She then told me something that I reflected on a lot over the next year: that raising kids comes in stages. Just when you feel like you can no longer take the particular struggles of a phase—the biting, the tantrums, the food throwing, the sleep regression, the curious hands into everything, climbing out of cribs, the refusal to try new things—they move on to a new one. All that angst from my side, and then it's gone in a flash. Now with six-plus years under my mommy belt, it seems pretty obvious advice and something I'd very likely share with new moms. But during those early fraught days, getting parenting advice from one of my musical heroes wasn't only cool—it was also just really helpful.

I struggled in my role as a new mother, and I felt really guilty about it. I had wanted these children for so long; my primeval howling into the wind every time there was a fertility setback. But now that motherhood had arrived, it was like I was supposed to forget all that trauma and just be happy. Be satisfied. That I should take to motherhood with poise and ease. I wasn't supposed to gripe about midnight feeds or how grating a baby's cry could be when you had tried everything in your toolbox to fix it. I felt very alone in these feelings, though I learned later it's actually universal. "There's a lot of postpartum depression among [infertility] survivors," Jennifer White, co-founder of the US surrogacy agency Bright Futures Families, told me in one of our many Zoom conversations. "You have tried so hard for so long to be parents and then you feel like you can't complain about it. Parenting is hard too."

It all came to a head over lunch with a friend in London not long before we had our final parental order hearing. My Hong Kong-based pal was in town for a few weeks, and she suggested lunch at one of my favorite cafes in Primrose Hill. I walked there with the twins and, after stealthily maneuvering the green double-wide stroller into a quiet corner, we instantly got to talking. She was in the harrowing throes of IVF. Her descriptions of being depressed about how the pregnancy test stick was always negative—that one horrific thin blue line that represented "NO!!!" every time—resonated so loudly with me that I wondered if other diners could hear it too.

Our conversation churned back up all the stuff that I had gone through for several years when I was struggling with my broken eggs and my barren womb. I started telling her that it had been very hard for me to adjust to being a mom. It wasn't just the regular stuff, like the loss of identity and the lack of sleep, but also how strange it was to no longer be consumed by worrying about my infertility and the surrogacy. I felt like there was a hole where that pain and worry had nestled and gnawed for so long, and I didn't know what to fill it up with now. My friend paused before she took a bite of her sandwich, me having strong-armed her into getting the reuben which was the café's specialty. "I think," she said looking into my eyes, "you are having an identity crisis."

I was blindsided by her comment and asked her what she meant. "Here you are with your gorgeous twins right there," she said pointing over to them snoozing, "and you are going on about infertility as if you have no kids. You still see yourself as an infertile woman and not as a mom." And that comment totally hit me sharp across the face. She was right. I felt like I had much more in common with my friend (who eventually went on to have a little boy) than I did with new moms. I hadn't emotionally been able yet to make that transition. "Infertility is just so traumatic, especially long-term infertility with multiple losses, which most people who end up having to use surrogates have experienced," Kim Kluger-Bell, who has written a number of children's books on infertility and surrogacy, told me two years later in an interview. "It doesn't just go away. The trauma and the grief around spending so much time and money and emotional energy, [it] stays with you."

When I asked her if it made sense that some people suffered from PTSD after surrogacy, she said that of course there is lingering trauma and that can surprise people. "When you are going through infertility you think, 'well once I have my baby everything is going to be fine,'" said Ms. Kluger-Bell. "And it is in many ways but at a deep emotional level it's not." I also spoke with Inge about this. She said that while she was ecstatic when she first became a mom to Carolina, she had moments where she felt her husband was "more the real parent" because he was the genetic father. "I went through years of infertility treatments, and I never succeeded," she told me, adding that she too felt like she suffered for a time from PTSD. "I became a mom and while I am so happy to have this opportunity, there is something inside of me that still makes me angry with my body. Self-pity. Yes, I think that is the right word."

Elly Teman writes that like obese people who undergo drastic weight loss and have to redefine their identity from "fat" to "thin" so too do infertile women who become mothers. That identity change from a "childless woman" to a "mother" is massive and sometimes the collateral damage is intended mothers distancing themselves from their surrogates to fully create their new identity, status, and role.[260] Zsuzsa Berend told me that many couples redefined their relationships with their surrogates after the birth.

One surrogate Dr. Berend wrote about in her book chronicled how painful it was to get an email from her IPs saying that there was no further need for contact and that "this has always been a business relationship and should not be construed as anything more."[261] That may be in part, she told me, because gratitude can sometimes become a burden. "Gratitude, it's not just about being appreciative," Dr. Berend said, "it's knowing that someone did such an enormous thing that you can never pay back, and people confuse that with owing." While the idea of cutting out your surrogate horrified and disgusted me, I did ponder for months after the twins were born how my relationship with Julie was supposed to move forward.

Turns out, so did Julie. "I do not have the emotional stamina for friends that need constant maintenance," Julie told me when we talked about those early days after the twins were born and the redefining of our relationship. "I was cool if we did not talk for two months but also you weren't the personality of, if I were to text you and say, 'hey, I was just thinking about the twins, how are they doing?' it wasn't like you were going to block my number from your phone." Because of Julie's age and the fact that the twin pregnancy was a lot more work than her other three pregnancies had been, she decided that she would not be doing surrogacy again. But she told me, "on the emotional side of things, there was just something about being in a position to be a blessing to somebody else" that had made the experience of great value to her. To this day, Julie and I keep in touch a few times a year through texts, emails, and video calls.

Other surrogates and their IPs have carved out similar relationships post-birth. Callie Kolkind, my Circle coordinator who has been a gestational carrier for a Swedish couple who had twins and a Norwegian couple who had one child, told me a similar thing. That there was "pure gratefulness" from all sides over the two surrogacies she did. The summer after she gave birth to the twin boys, Callie and her entire family went to Sweden to visit the IPs and their children. "I walked away from that [surrogacy] experience," she told me, "with so much more than I ever thought I would gain."

Orit, the Israeli surrogate, told me that she believes she will always be connected to her intended mother. "But I don't have the need to call her and talk to her because we are not friends," she said, adding that they occasionally send texts to each other. "But what we two have experienced together, it is like something that is tattooed in your body." Kim Cotton, meanwhile, says that after the trauma of her traditional surrogacy experience back in 1985, later becoming a gestational carrier for twins was a cathartic experience. "I needed a way to [offset] the negativity," she told me, saying that she's still in close contact with the parents and twins who now live in New Zealand. "That ongoing pleasure that I got sort of made it better. It balanced my psyche, really, because I was quite hurt before."

For gay dads and their surrogates, the post-pregnancy relationship is probably easier to navigate. That's in part, says Dr. Berend, because there are no complications in terms of jealousy or control during the pregnancy. She told me that a lot of women who choose to be carriers for gay couples "aren't exactly cutting edge" in terms of living more traditional lives so "they get a kick out of men who want to raise children without a woman." Nir, Or, and their carrier, Briana, are still very close. When she was pregnant with their second daughter during COVID-19, the couple and their eldest daughter stayed with Briana and her family for two months in Minnesota waiting for the birth. Nir told me that while their older daughter, who was born in 2017, has been told that Briana gave birth to her, she understands Briana's not her mom. "She asks a lot why she doesn't have a mother," Nir told me. "And I explain that families come in different formats and I say, 'but if you need to call someone a mother, I'm happy to be the one.' [Besides] pregnancy, giving birth and breastfeeding, we fulfill everything else about motherhood."

On Nir's Instagram feed, he often posts pictures of his girls with the hashtag #themotherIam and to be honest, it's made me think a lot about what motherhood means. Who is a mom? Who can be a mom? What is the definition of motherhood? What qualifies someone to have the moniker of mother? It parallels Dr. Teman's thoughts on how surrogacy is a cultural anomaly because it shakes up what notions we have of things and makes us ponder preconceived ideas of parenthood. Like Nir and Or's daughter, my kids have started to ask questions. So far, I just tell them that I had broken eggs and a broken belly, and two nice women helped me out. They seem content with that answer at the moment.

Much research has come out in the last several years about how important it is for children to be told from an early age their conception and birth stories. The longer parents wait to tell their kids, especially about being donor conceived, the kids may begin to feel like it's something shameful. Wendie Wilson-Miller told me that the reason why some parents wait to tell their children is because they themselves haven't quite gotten their heads around it yet: "Intended moms going into [egg donation] are very nervous about 'Will I really feel like the mom? Will the donor try to take my child away?' There is a lot of fear." She advises IPs to be very firm in their decision before they move forward and to be comfortable with the idea of sharing their procreative history with their children pretty much from the start.

While I was decisive on doing an open donation and had already begun reading Lexie and Ransom books about it—a favorite still is Kim Kluger-Bell's *The Pea That Was Me*—I was taken aback when a little over a year after the twins were born, our egg donor Dani asked if she could get a photo of them. While it had been included in our contract that she would receive confirmation if there was a live birth, she had never asked during the negotiations to get any more than that. My initial Mama Bear reaction was a strong "No!" I wrote back to Circle:

I just wanted to say that I am not comfortable sending pictures of the kids to the egg donor. I cannot really explain it, but I had a very visceral reaction when I read the email and while I appreciate her curiosity about how the kids look, it just doesn't sit well with me.

Circle came back to me saying it was fine and that's how I left it for a year. But working on this book and speaking with a number of people who have been egg donors, IPs who have donor-conceived children, and children who are surrogate-born donor-conceived kids, my opinion started to change. Liz Scheier from We Are Egg Donors told me that as a younger woman she had done anonymous egg donation and at the time she hadn't thought much about it. But later, when she became a mother herself, she started thinking what if the children born through her egg donation were not being treated well by their parents or were being lied to?

"We've seen a handful of cases where people have been contacted by now adult children, and they're hearing horror stories about how those kids were raised," she said. "That is a guilt I do not know how to get over. And that is my greatest fear: that one day I am going to be reached out to by these kids saying, 'why did you deliver me into this house?'"

She went on to point out that while recipients know a lot about who their anonymous donors are, those donors are not given any information about the potential parents. Meanwhile, no country makes it mandatory for parents of donor-conceived children to tell them they were conceived in this way. However, in a number of countries, including Sweden, Britain, Switzerland, and Australia, people who are donor-conceived have the right to find out who their donor is at the age of eighteen.[262] For gay dad Paul Morgan-Bentley, he and his husband "can't wait" to one day meet their anonymous egg donor if their son Solly wants to. "We want to give her the biggest hug," he told me. "We want to say thanks."

Meanwhile, Inge told me that their egg donor has been involved in Carolina's life from the beginning. "I was selfish on behalf of my child just to be on the safe side," she said, adding that from the start they informed their donor that they wanted some kind of relationship. "I have never felt any jealousy and she saw pictures of the pregnancy and childbirth. I have been involving her all the way through it." Carolina, who now has a full biological brother born via the same surrogate, has also spent time with her egg donor. "I thought it was fun to see them together," Inge told me. "It is important for me to have Carolina look at someone and see, 'We have the same genes.'"

This conversation with Inge was the final push that changed my mind. Plus, as Ms. Scheier and Ms. Wilson-Miller had both emphasized to me, while the vast majority of egg donors don't want anything to do with children born from their donations, they just want to make sure that the kids are alright.

In the late summer of 2020 I wrote to Dani:

> I wanted to write to you to say, first of all, thank you! Seems a strange thing to say but I never thanked you before, in part because I was processing a lot of stuff during and after our surrogacy. But I am writing a book about surrogacy ... I have been speaking to a lot of experts ... and they all say how important it is that not only that people do open

donations (what we did) but also that kids feel like if they want to reach out, they have a way some day to do so . . .

I then apologized for not sending the photos the year before, saying it was something I needed to get my head around. I then went on:

[The twins] are the best things that ever happened to me. I never thought I would love being a mom as much as I do. Lexie is blonde with blue eyes (I call her eyes Lake Michigan Blue because I know you live near the lake and I grew up on Lake Michigan and it will always be the most special place in the world to me) and she is BOSSY!!!! She is also kind and incredibly intelligent and empathetic (though can be a bit sneaky and cheeky at times!). Ransom also has blueish eyes . . . and he has a funny sense of humor, I think he might be the cutest boy who ever lived, and he is just an absolute sweetheart. He melts me with his giggle and his kindness. They are both so happy, so active and very, very, very much loved.

I then went on to say that her gift was the greatest one ever imaginable and asked her if we could keep in touch periodically and, if the kids ever wanted to meet her, we could reach back out to her. I also sent her a photo of the kids sitting in the sand on Lake Michigan from the previous summer.

Two hours later she replied:

I cried!!!! Thank you so much! They are both precious!!! I appreciate it so much! I always think about the kids that have been born from me donating and it truly melts my heart. I'm so glad you got your perfect babies! Being a mom is the best!

While short and sweet, her reply made me giddy, in part because it felt huge that she was open to communication. We emailed a few more times and while I stopped short of saying I wanted to meet with her in person with the kids, primarily because at their young age it wouldn't mean much to them, I felt a sense of relief. I had done this for my kids out of respect for their future selves in case they ever needed to work through any questions about their identity. Plus, at some point I would have had to confess to the kids what I had done, admitting that I had shut her request down. And that just sounded pretty petty and self-indulgent to my ego. If I was trying to raise my kids to be generous, resilient, and gallant human beings, what then would that lesson in hypocrisy teach them?

I spoke to a few donor-conceived surrogate-born kids about this and asked them how they had worked through questions around their conception and birth. Fiorella Mennesson, who wrote a children's book on surrogacy called *Ma famille, la GPA et moi* (*My family, surrogacy and me*), finds it "really inappropriate" when people ask her if she ever has doubts as to who her parents are. "I am not really comfortable with the question because it is absurd and it hurts," she told me. "It is so weird to be questioned about my parents and who my 'real' mother is." Meanwhile, Gee Roberts, a British medical student who was born through traditional surrogacy in 1998, says that it gives you a different view on family. "For me," she told me, "family, it's not really about genetics." She has always known the background of her birth, and it was something that her parents had made natural from the start.

When she was in her first year in school, her teacher gave the class an assignment to draw a picture of their families. Gee drew a picture of her mom, dad, and her "tummy mummy," Suzanne, who has always remained a part of her life. The school's head teacher asked Gee's parents who this mystery extra woman was in the artwork and when they explained, the teacher got emotional because she had been adopted. She told Gee's parents how fantastic it was that they had normalized it for Gee from such an early age. "I think we really underestimate how clever children are," Gee told me in an interview after doing her medical rounds in a clinic. "Children are not innately anything, we teach them everything they know. So for me [my circumstances are] just as normal as having one mom and one dad to other people."

Gee has been very vocal about her background not only with her friends and fellow students but has also served as something of an ambassador for donor-conceived surrogate children in the United Kingdom. She has briefed the law commissions on her opinions and was also invited by the UN to speak in Geneva on a panel with other donor-conceived children on the thirtieth anniversary on the Convention on the Rights of the Child. One of her biggest takeaways from the event was how different her childhood experience had been to the others—none of whom were surrogate born—and there was an anger there. "They feel that their rights have been betrayed, they feel so passionately about it," said Gee, when I told her about a few brusque emails I had exchanged with one of them because they did not approve of surrogacy. "I am in a group chat with a lot of donor conception people, but I find it quite challenging because they are so hurt. A few times I have tried to put the line there and say, 'Look I value your opinion as donor-conceived people but please don't try and speak for [us] because you are not born through surrogacy."[263]

Jill Rudnitzky Brand, that first gestational surrogacy baby

born in Michigan in 1986, told me that she has always known her birth story. "I'd like to say there was some well-conceived moment when they told me, but I just grew up always knowing," she said. "I think the first time that it struck me as being really amazing was when I was a freshman in college. There was a fundraiser at the Cleveland Clinic to help fund the procedure for families who couldn't afford it." She said the event was also to honor her parents for their bravery and courage. "There was just couple after couple after couple coming up to me saying, 'Because of your family, because of you, we have a child of our own, and you don't know what that means,'" she said. "And that was the first time that I felt like I understood, 'Wow, like, this is my story.' It changed the world, yet I had never felt that before."

For years there have been arguments around potential long-term ramifications for surrogate-born children: Would they be confused? Would they be angry? Would they wonder who their "real" parents were? Would they feel like they were chattel? And for years, there wasn't much research conducted so assumptions were that children born through surrogacy would, like research that came out on adoption, possibly struggle with grief, loss, or issues of abandonment.[264] The outlier is the research that has been done by Dr. Susan Golombok, professor emerita and former director of the Centre for Family Research at the University of Cambridge. She did a twenty-year-long longitudinal study—the only one of its kind in the world—examining what impact surrogacy has on children born through those arrangements. She writes in *Modern Families: Parents and Children in New Family Forms* that with surrogacy differing from other types of assisted reproduction it could "conceivably result in greater problems for surrogacy families" than for those created through more traditional procedures like sperm or egg donation.

However, her research, which has followed forty-two British families at different times throughout the children's lives, found the opposite: that children born through surrogacy were doing well and had good relationships with their parents. "And the answer to the question of who they saw as their 'real' mother was crystal clear," Dr. Golombok wrote in *We are Family: What Really Matters for Parents and Children,* published in 2020. "It was the one who raised them."[265] In their first assessment when the kids were one-year-olds, contrary to numerous concerns that have been voiced about surrogacy, "the differences identified between surrogacy families and the other family types indicated greater psychological well-being and adaptation to parenthood by mothers and fathers of children through surrogacy" than by a comparison group of parents through natural conception.[266] Parents through surrogacy showed greater warmth and attachment toward their children and a greater enjoyment overall than those natural conception parents. They also reported lower levels of stress associated with parenting with mothers specifically showing lower levels of depression.

Dr. Golombok and her team of researchers—which includes Vasanti Jadva who did the longitudinal study on surrogates' post-birth—found that overall, the kids at fourteen weren't troubled by the fact that they had been born through surrogacy. "They would say things like, 'this doesn't really mean a lot to me and there are much more interesting things going on in my life than how I was born,'" she told me in an interview. Others meanwhile talked more positively about it, saying it made them special or it was something different about them. "It just turned out to be not at all true, the things that people were predicting about the angst that these children would be suffering in adolescence," Dr. Golombok said. "Because they actually, genuinely, weren't very interested in the whole thing. It just wasn't a big deal to them."

While Dr. Golombok and her researchers did not specifically ask the fourteen-year-olds about money or compensation for the surrogate, they were asked about the way they were born and how that made them feel. "They were completely fine about it," she said. "They certainly did not seem obsessed, ruminating over these kinds of issues." That research runs contrary to the rhetoric put out by those who have issues with surrogacy who claim children born through these arrangements will feel like purchased products. "This child is specifically produced, for which money is being exchanged under the guise of fees," said Arun Dohle, who works for the Dutch organization Against Child Trafficking. "This is clear, a sale of children."

What troubles me greatly about these kinds of comments is how that makes children born through surrogacy feel—will my Ransom and Lexie feel like they are weird or freaks? Dr. Golombok said that children can feel stigmatized if their family is different. "They don't have problems within their family, but sometimes this kind of stigma, teasing or bullying, whatever they experience from outside the family," she said, "that is what is emotionally damaging to children." Dr. Golombok was in the midst of doing the twenty-year interviews when we spoke in 2021 and added that the world needs much more research on long-term implications of surrogacy on children and surrogates, especially in terms of cross-border surrogacy.

That research, which was released in 2023, found that, "the absence of a biological connection between children and parents in assisted reproduction families does not interfere with the development of positive relationships between them or psychological adjustment in adulthood." Interestingly, those findings were consistent with previous assessments at age one, two, three, seven, ten and fourteen.[267] The report, released in *Developmental Psychology*, also found that families benefitted when parents of children born through third-party assisted reproduction spoke to their children early on about the circumstances of their birth in an age-appropriate way, ideally before they started school.[268]

Meanwhile, Barbara Collura from RESOLVE told me that there is a lack of awareness by those who speak out against surrogacy, that the very children they are saying they want to protect are actually being upset by what they are hearing and taking in. "How are you making people feel by basically delegitimizing their life?" she asked. "These folks are saying that publicly all the time, and that there needs to be some sort of reckoning around that."

Jill, Gee, and Fiorella articulated their feelings on this to me. Gee told me she finds it very upsetting that people "almost disapprove of me innately" because of how she happened to be born. Most of them, she assumed, had never been through surrogacy so it felt a bit rich for them to be "speaking" on her behalf. "If people are saying things like that from a place of opinion, where they have experienced something, then I can validate that," Gee said. "But if people are saying it from conceptual abstract things that they just decided with no experience, like where have you got that from? You don't know."

Fiorella, meanwhile, said she's often found that those against surrogacy aren't interested in getting the opinion from surrogate-born kids, yet they claim to talk for them. "We have a lot of extremist people in France who fight against surrogacy," she said. "They claim that it's in the children's interest and it's really ironic because there is nothing towards the children in what they do." Jill, who had to use IVF to have her second child, said it's important for people to understand the motivation of why people choose surrogacy in the first place, as it's not anyone's first choice. "You are giving a viable option for people who otherwise couldn't have a biological child," she said. "And making [a] blanket statement is just like whenever you make a broad, gross generalization: you miss the nuance, you're going to make a lot of really cataclysmic errors."

Surrogates, too, are annoyed that those against the practice claim they are speaking up for them and carriers are becoming increasingly vocal about it. Many of them are not only proud—one American blogger had a slogan on her blog page stating, *"I make families, what's your super-power?"*[269]—but there is also a real sense of empowerment that many women have gotten from being surrogates. Some are writing books and blogs about their surrogacy experiences while others have become educators and advocates, going on to work for agencies or organizations that support fertility health care. Orit said that being a carrier "changed me from the inside and from the outside" and that's why she decided to switch careers and do a doctorate focused on surrogacy. Meanwhile, according to Sarah Jones, a four-time surrogate who runs the non-profit SurrogacyUK, British carriers historically "didn't have a big voice" and the people campaigning for reforms used to solely be lawyers and IPs. But these days, she said, "we've been called quite militant."

Karen Smith Rotabi and Nicole F. Bromfield write in their book *From Intercountry Adoption to Global Surrogacy* that American surrogates portray themselves online as being "empowered, knowledgeable, and in control of their experiences as surrogates, not exploited, uneducated, or deceived women" who are not capable of giving consent, which is often how they have been portrayed. The lived experience of these women is that not only do they feel *au fait* about what they went through but also "they feel sufficiently empowered with this knowledge to be able to provide advice and guidance" to not only those who are going through the experience but also those thinking about it.[270]

Those were some of the reasons why Callie Kolkind decided to testify in front of Minnesota state legislators about her surrogacy experience. In her testimony she spoke of how she didn't fit the stereotype of being an "uneducated, low-income, sub-class breeder" and that handing the twins to the Swedish family she carried for was "the greatest gift of all."[271] She told me that after she left the hearings at the state capitol someone spit on her. "I was completely berated," she told me. "I remember shaking when I drove away and I was crying so much I pulled over and called my dad and said, 'tell me that I am a good person.' Looking back, I have no idea how another human can make someone feel so inferior and horrible."

Despite awful stories like Callie's, there are also very positive ones for surrogates, especially in how it relates to their own children. One of the interesting findings in Dr. Jadva's longitudinal research on both traditional and gestational carriers was how the children of carriers reacted to them being surrogates.[272] The overwhelming majority said not only had it been a positive experience for their family but also that they were very proud of their mothers for doing what they did. British surrogate Tracey Sims told me that her daughter, who was ten at the time, would tell people that her mommy was having a baby for another women whose tummy was broken. "She was so clear cut, so black and white and she'd tell people who asked, 'Mummy is a surrogate,'" Tracey laughingly recalled. "I'd then have to swoop in behind her and explain it a bit more to people."

Julie and Chad had been very open with their kids when she became our surrogate. "We prepared them emotionally from the very beginning," Julie said. "We wanted to give them more knowledge and information about why we chose to do this." She said they used it as a teaching tool to explain that some people cannot have children on their own. "It was a good conversation piece for the kids," she said. "And to introduce them to something entirely different." She paused and then said with a laugh that she doesn't think the experience scarred her kids and, "so I think we are doing okay." She told me that one of her daughters to this day often asks about the twins and Julie shows her the pictures and videos that I send.

Orit told me a similar tale, that they used her surrogacy also as a lesson for her boys and that the whole family took ownership of the experience. She cycles every day with her boys to school but in the last month of her pregnancy, she felt too heavy to do it. Her boys understood that everyone in the family was making sacrifices. "They said, 'When you give birth, we will go back to it,'" she recalled as her younger son moved around on her lap. "And the first thing I did after coming back from the hospital was taking my children by bicycle to kindergarten."

The perceptions around surrogacy have seen a seismic shift since those early days back in mid-1970s Michigan when Noel Keane drafted that first compensated surrogacy contract. A lot of that has to do with how it's portrayed in popular culture and the media. Assisted reproductive technologies in general and surrogacy specifically has long been a firm favorite for dystopian writers. Aldous Huxley's 1932 novel *Brave New World* introduced the term "test tube" babies, with the British writer describing a world where babies were fertilized and incubated in artificial wombs.[273] Meanwhile, I often hear people refer to Margaret Atwood's *A Handmaid's Tale* as being about surrogacy, something I strongly disagree with because from a legal perspective surrogacy does not involve intercourse. What that book and popular television series is actually about is rape, kidnapping, child trafficking, and sexual assault, but surrogacy it ain't.

While Joanne Ramos's 2019 novel *The Farm* has some dystopian undertones with surrogates forced to live in a luxury retreat for the duration of their pregnancies and monitored 24/7, there's a nuance to it, examining a number of ethical and class issues that surrogacy raises. British science journalist and novelist Susan Spindler's 2021 novel *Surrogate,* is also a deeper examination, focused on a mother who becomes her daughter's gestational carrier. She told me that when she first started working on her novel in 2014, she often had to explain what surrogacy was because it was not so mainstream. She said that people didn't believe her that it was something that really was done and when she would read comments under stories that had been written about surrogacy they would be, "very numerous and disproportionally negative." These days she says there is still "some of that" on stories but nowhere near the volume because "I think it has been normalized."

The television world, meanwhile, is seemingly obsessed with surrogacy. American soap operas like *The Young and the Restless* and *General Hospital* have taken on surrogacy as a plot line as have popular British television soap operas like *EastEnders,* *Coronation Street* and the long-running BBC radio serial *The Archers.* Streamed series like the BBC's 2020 offering *The Nest* looked at embryo switching and cross-border surrogacy between Ukraine and Scotland while *Little Fires Everywhere,* based on the popular novel by Celeste Ng and starring Reese Witherspoon and Kerry Washington, featured traditional surrogacy as a subplot. The popular Israeli television drama *Shtisel*—one of my all-time favorite shows—in its third season has a surrogacy subplot as well. Another Israeli series *A Body That Works*, streamed on Netflix and starring Lior Raz, from *Fauda*, was the country's highest-rated show in 2023 and has been renewed for a second season. The popularity of surrogacy as a plot is very likely because although it's such a small part of the overall landscape of assisted reproduction, with Dr. Jacobson telling me, "there's something about surrogacy that really fascinates people."

The big screen has also been intrigued by the topic. Indian filmmakers have found surrogacy ripe as a subject for celluloid, starting in 1983 with *Doosri Dulhan*, where an intended father hires a prostitute to carry his child, to *Mimi, Baba Baby O...* and *Dukaan*, all of which have a mixed bag of stereotypical plotlines. Hollywood, meanwhile, has been doing films on the subject since the 1970 release of *The Baby Maker*, a movie starring Barbara Hershey as a hippie who becomes a traditional surrogate. Over three decades later in the not-very-funny comedy *Baby Mama* Tina Fey plays a single woman who hires a gestational carrier. Amy Poehler's character, a surrogate desperate for money and in an unstable relationship, tries to then swindle her by faking a pregnancy. "We play 'Surrogacy Bingo' whenever a new show or series comes out about surrogacy," joked Sarah Jones from SurrogacyUK. "She's a psycho? Check. She falls in love with the father? Check. She goes on a killing spree? Check. It's so unbelievably frustrating [and] IPs are looking at it and going, 'this must be the norm, so we are not going to choose surrogacy as an option because this is what is going to happen.'"

While several people I interviewed for this book told me they've been approached by filmmakers to help guide and educate them to make productions more realistic and authentic, it has mostly fallen on deaf ears because no one is interested in the mundane arc of a normal surrogacy. New York-based filmmaker

Jeremy Hersh—who I discovered also happens to be the nephew of someone I went to college with—defied that when he made his 2020 film *The Surrogate*. He posted on a surrogate site asking if anyone would be willing to speak with him for the film about a Brooklyn-based Black woman, the daughter of a Yale University dean, who becomes a surrogate for her gay friends. "I wrote, 'I want you guys to tell me everything, like what's your nightmare surrogacy movie so I know not to do it,'" he told me, adding that throughout the writing process he often would send parts of the script to one of the surrogates he befriended.

His film received good reviews, in large part because he was willing to tackle several topics around surrogacy, including race, that others have chosen to sweep aside. In most films, books, and television programs on infertility in general and surrogacy specifically, it's often portrayed as being something that primarily affects white middle- and upper-class women thus normalizing the image of "infertility as a white woman's issue."[274] Women of color who suffer from it aren't seeing themselves onscreen, in books, or the media so their feelings of alienation are reinforced because their stories are simply ignored or not depicted. Reverend Stacey Edwards-Dunn, the founder of Fertility for Colored Girls, told me that when high profile Black women like Michelle Obama or Gabrielle Union speak about their infertility, it gets lots of media attention for a few weeks but then it drops off again. "There's some surface conversation that is going on," she said. "And we have to unwrap this onion and really get to the core of some of the issues, particularly that Black women and couples are dealing with as it pertains to issues of race and disparity around reproductive health and infertility."

Dr. Jacobson writes that in both fictional and non-fictional media presentations of surrogacy, it's often whittled down so that some of the complexities are "highly digestible and easily recognized" with the hook being often around exploitation. "Many stories on surrogacy," she writes, "[use] caricatures that symbolize an exploitative relationship to explain surrogacy: the victimized infertile woman versus the swindler; the privileged, entitled, upper-class woman obsessed with a genetic child versus a poor baby machine forced to breed to feed her own children."[275] It is the horrible or sad elements of surrogacy that make the headlines—Black French parents incredulous when their Ukrainian clinic insists that the white baby born via their surrogate is genetically theirs; the Cambodian surrogates forced to raise their surro-babies when surrogacy is made illegal in their country; the Chinese actress who decides she no longer wants her American-born babies. "It's slow, slow, slow overcoming bad news," said Jennifer White, who told me that one of the reasons she and her sister decided to start the podcast *I Want to Put a Baby in You* was because they wanted to show another side of surrogacy. "Good news isn't sexy."

Meanwhile, the LGBT+ community has played a major role in helping to normalize surrogacy. Over the past number of years there has been huge growth in family building within the community. The Family Equality, a US non-profit, found in a 2018 survey that 77 percent of LGBTQ millennials (aged 18–35) are either parents or are considering having children, a 44 percent increase over the previous generation.[276] Interestingly, I had several experts tell me they felt that many people seem to struggle more with straight couples having babies through surrogacy than gay men because it's not so black and white. "Obviously there is no woman, they want a baby, and they need a surrogate," Gee told me. "People have been really quick in many ways to accept gay guys [doing] surrogacy over straight couples." Sara Matthews, my gynecologist, agreed with that sentiment. "I still think there is a bit of stigma attached," she said. "It's like 'if you're not persevering with carrying your own child, there is something terribly wrong with you' or 'why not accept you can't and move on?' [I] think part of the anti-surrogate thing is all to do with being sexist actually."

According to Lisa Schuster, formerly of Men Having Babies, there is "definitely a growing number of guys" who have applied for the organization's finance programs and going to their conferences, and its skewing younger and younger these days. "Guys in their twenties have grown up going 'it's possible for me, I'm gay, but there are avenues out there for me to become a parent,'" she said. "They never thought that they wouldn't be a dad." Older gay personalities like Anderson Cooper and Ricky Martin have talked about how when they were growing up, they thought it would never be possible to have biological children. Meanwhile, other celebrities too like Nicole Kidman and Keith Urban, Priyanka Chopra and Nick Jonas, Angela Bassett and Courtney B. Vance, Shilpa Shetty, Elizabeth Banks, and Lucy Liu have not only shone a spotlight on surrogacy but raised awareness around infertility as well.

Actress Kristin Wiig, who had twins via surrogacy with her husband in 2020, told *InStyle* magazine that it helped reading and talking to other people who had gone through similar experiences. "It can be," she said, "the most isolating experience." Judith Daar has written that these public displays "can help shape perceptions" around infertility and this attention to things like surrogacy "nudges the practice into the mainstream, opening hearts and minds to the myriad of ways" that people can become parents.[277] That being said, I'd argue that the voices of celebrities who have become parents through surrogacy have so far been conspicuously absent when it comes to lobbying for changes in legislation around surrogacy, most notably recently in New York state.

I also think that COVID-19 has helped to shape and hone public perceptions for the better, in particular cross-border surrogacy, which seemed to be news to many people that it even existed as a practice. The heartbreaking footage by Ukrainian agency BioTexCom of forty-six surrogate newborns—whose parents, because of 2020 pandemic border closures, were stuck at home in Spain, France, Ireland, and other countries—lined up in rows in their cribs led to international public outcry for their well-being. More positive tales like that of Toronto-based Zimbabwean/Nigerian couple Patrick and Enitan Goredema, who charmingly related to BBC World Service how they missed the birth of their son in Georgia and what it was like to finally meet him, was an uplifting broadcasting highlight.

Meanwhile, Emily Chrislip, the Idaho carrier who for over a year had to take care of her surro-baby because the parents were stuck in China, was featured on a number of US breakfast news shows where she was heralded as a hero. "We have surrogates who are willing to take the babies for a week if the parents are in a bind to get here as are prior surrogates or IPs from across the country," Dean Hutchison from Circle told me during that first global lockdown. He added that from the start, they were working with the US State Department to get foreign IPs allowed in to be with their newborns. "It's very cool to see the internal work not only of Circle but the whole surrogate community," he said.

I started working on this book right before those first cross-border surrogacy lockdown stories began appearing in the international media. It had been two years since Ransom and Lexie had been born and over a year since our parental order had come through. Our surrogacy journey was indeed over and not soon after my conversation with my friend from Hong Kong, I hit my stride as a mother. While certainly not the best mom—but really who is?—as they got bigger and more communicative, I found myself growing increasingly more adept in my role and falling in love with them more every single day. We had our inside jokes, quirky nicknames for each other, and my beloved bedtime ritual of reading books and playing silly games that they concocted for me.

What I didn't realize until I put proverbial pen to paper was that there were still a few underlying things that I hadn't come to terms with that sort of shocked me. One, of course, was Dani. But the other was how I still had visceral emotions over a number of things that I was chronicling about our journey. And that felt quite strange because how could I be sad and crying about the pregnancies I never achieved, the eggs that never developed, the embryos that didn't take but yet still love my children so wholly and with such relish? I knew that Ransom and Lexie were the children I was always supposed to mother so why did these things still tug at my heartstrings years later? "You do have these complicated feelings, right? And I am sure you do think about the miscarriages," said Evan Ryan, as we bonded over the complicated and sometimes incongruous emotions around motherhood after surrogacy. "Because I do feel like, 'These two, I was meant to be [their mom].' The whole thing, yeah, is very fraught."

I felt guilty, confused and it jumbled up so much inside me that I decided I needed to untangle this with my therapist. And what he said really struck me: that it was perfectly normal to feel both sorrow for the babies that didn't get a chance to be born while also being in absolute bliss and love with Ransom and Lexie. It didn't have to be either/or and it was okay to feel both things.

And it didn't take away any love that I had for my children that I also still carried with me that sense of loss. That had also become a part of who I am and a part of their story too.

In fact, he said, it would be strange if I didn't feel some residual sadness for what might have been while still being so grateful that my surrogacy journey had led me to be able to raise these two remarkable humans. As it turns out, that piece of my heart that I thought had died that night in Tanzania had merely lain dormant, waiting. The birth of my children had been the elixir, slowly allowing it to come back to life with fresh vigor and meaning. And now it was filled up with a love that is so overpowering that just writing about it makes me catch my breath.

Julie not only gave birth to my twins that day, but she also gave birth to me as a mother.

Chapter Twelve

We Fought the Law, and We Won

Sitting close to the podium in the basement of the Royal Oak Public Library, I feverishly typed away on my laptop.

I was trying to get our Michigan Fertility Alliance (MFA) newsletter, which I was responsible for as the voluntary communications and research director of the grassroots organization, out to let the world know that our Michigan Family Protection Act (MFPA) legislation had, moments earlier, been signed into law. I then noticed a commotion in my peripheral vision and just when I looked up, Governor Gretchen Whitmer, flanked by her security and her press team, started leaning down toward me. With a bright red lipsticked smile she said to me earnestly, "Thanks for all your hard work on this bill." I stammered and said, "Thank you, Governor, for signing it."

With the signing on April 1, 2024, of the Michigan Family Protection Act, things had come full circle between Big Gretch and me. Governor Whitmer likely didn't know the significance of thanking me because I doubt she even remembered that six years previously she and I had had a conversation about surrogacy in Michigan. It was two months after Lexie and Ransom were born. At the time, I was running a website with a friend that was focused on female empowerment; I had interviewed Emily Saliers from Indigo Girls for the site, and I wanted to interview Gretchen Whitmer, who was a relatively unknown former state legislator running for governor. The primaries hadn't happened yet and Big Gretch, a nickname she got from Detroit-based rapper Sada Baby in his song "Aktivated," was one of several people vying for the job. I reached out to her press people for an interview and was invited to Lansing to meet her.

We talked about everything from Michigan politics to the problems with the state's public education system. After the interview, I briefly explained why I was back in Michigan: that my twins had been born through surrogacy in Illinois because in Michigan there was still a civil and criminal ban on the practice. She asked me why that was and at that point, I didn't know. But we both agreed it was something worth looking into and that the law should be changed. I don't remember if she said whether she knew that surrogacy contracts were null and void in the state, but I do remember she found it strange that they were. I had completely forgotten about that specific part of our after-interview conversation until about three weeks before the MFPA was to be signed. It had slipped my mind over the years and only when I recalled another conversation I had had around that same time in early 2018, did it come back to me that she and I had spoken on how the surrogacy law needed to be updated.

That other conversation had taken place a few weeks after Lexie and Ransom were born, when we were still at my mom's house. The phone rang one afternoon while they were napping so I dove for the phone to stop its ring from waking them up. It was a woman—I don't recall her name—who was running for the Michigan legislature, and parched for adult conversation, I started asking her some policy questions, including why surrogacy was still illegal in Michigan. I think I threw her for a loop because she hemmed and hawed and finally said that she thought it was because of the Catholic Church. I could tell she didn't really know the answer but then Lexie cried so I ended the conversation. With time, I got even busier with my growing babies and never investigated it any further. However, once I started working on this book, I finally found out what a rich and complex history Michigan has with surrogacy.

As it turns out, that potential legislator wasn't alone in not knowing much about the historic reasons why Michigan was the first and last state to make compensated surrogacy a felony. When I asked retired Michigan Judge Marianne Battani—the one who ruled back in 1986 that Jill Rudnitzky should have her biological parents listed on her birth certificate—about the state's draconian surrogacy laws, she was shocked. "This comes as a complete surprise," she said.

What I took away from that conversation was that if a former US district judge didn't know about the broad criminal and civil ban on surrogacy in her home state, it was little wonder that others like me were shocked to find out the same once we started down what can be a long and harrowing road. I had so much wanted to work with a surrogate in Michigan for a number of reasons, but my home state pretty much prevented me from doing so because there was no way to adjudicate surrogacy contracts. While it was only a disappointing stumbling block for us when we started our surrogacy journey since we lived internationally anyway, over time it has increasingly angered me that countless couples in Michigan were either forced to go out of state to pursue surrogacy or have to do surrogacy in state with the risk of legal loopholes and heartbreaks.

While the 1988 Surrogate Parenting Act was both a civil and criminal ban, there was a loophole where uncompensated surrogacy could be pursued. But the problems were vast, including that potential surrogates didn't have to go through the rigorous medical and psychological checks that carriers did in states where surrogacy was legal. Plus, even finding a surrogate was like a needle in a haystack. There were Facebook groups with intended parents sharing their harrowing stories in hopes that a surrogate would find their story compelling enough and agree to be their carrier, but with no binding contracts and potential looming legal dramas once the babies were born.

That happened to Tammy and Jordan Myers, a couple from Grand Rapids whose story in 2021 made national news. Tammy, a breast cancer survivor and a mother of one daughter, was not able to carry another pregnancy and so they decided to pursue surrogacy in state. However, the couple happened to live in a more conservative part of Michigan and the judge refused to grant a pre-birth order for their twins. This was unlike in other parts of the state where judges were sporadically granting pre-birth orders, a document which declares that the intended parents are the legal parents of the child. That meant that the Myerses had to adopt their children so their names could be put on the birth certificates, the exact converse of Judge Battani's 1986 ruling. (And while the story garnered a lot of media attention in the US, it's not dissimilar to what countless intended parents have to do in places like Britain and Ireland—including my husband and me through a parental order.)

The backwardness of Michigan's criminalization of surrogacy

didn't sit well with Stephanie Jones either. In mid-October in 2018 Stephanie had just survived a second near-death experience with an ectopic pregnancy. Her doctor came in to tell her that she didn't think Stephanie, a mother of one, could survive another pregnancy. In that same conversation, her doctor mentioned surrogacy.

Stephanie, a former automotive executive and small business owner, then did the only thing that felt logical after such heart-breaking news—she started Googling. And she found out pretty quickly that surrogacy in Michigan was a rough, tough road. She put her phone down, cried, and decided that all needed to change. Stephanie, who is also from the Flint area where I had grown up, not only began looking to find an out-of-state surrogate (her daughter was born in Kentucky in 2020) but she also started investigating to see if there were Michigan-based groups working to change the outdated 1988 Surrogate Parenting Act, as well as supporting people with infertility. And there were none. And so, from her hospital bed, the Michigan Fertility Alliance was born.

Two years later, during a global pandemic, not long after Stephanie's daughter was born and I was starting work on this book, I connected with her via Jennifer White and Ellen Trachman, that sister duo of the *I Want to Put a Baby in You* podcast. After an initial interview for this book, Stephanie and I kept in touch because we were both so passionate about surrogacy generally and changing the law in Michigan specifically. I told Stephanie all about the history of surrogacy in Michigan and exchanged several contacts with her. Before I knew it, we were conversing pretty much every day and a few months later she asked me if I wanted to help her do communications and research for MFA. I said yes. "Changing laws is hard, time-consuming, complicated work," she told me in one of our initial conversations on the subject. "A lot of people want to see the law change in Michigan. It's just a matter of finding the right combination of available resources and the bandwidth to do so."

Her words were foreshadowing for what we were both about to learn.

As the pandemic started to wind down, our work with MFA started to ramp up. In early 2021, I reached out to Susie Alfred Schechter, who had lived across the street from me growing up. She sometimes babysat for my brothers and me, and she was inherently cool. Turns out, Susie also was one of the driving forces behind changing Michigan's law to ban smoking in public places. So, I naturally got in touch with Susie to get some advice on how one goes about changing a state law. Susie, now a lawyer in suburban Detroit, was encouraging but warned me it would be a long, hard-fought battle. I also reached out to other childhood friends, former state lawmakers, and neighbors who had all in one way or another had insights into state politics.

During the summer of 2021, we also took on our first cohort of interns, all from the University of Michigan, who helped work on MFA's website, blog, and newsletter. They also helped prepare for MFA's first Michigan Infertility Advocacy Day (MIAD) in September, where over one hundred MFA advocates who had joined the cause spoke to fifty state lawmakers about why the surrogacy law needed to be repealed. One of those was Rep. Samantha Steckloff, a Democrat who represented Farmington Hills. She was a breast cancer survivor who understood that IVF and surrogacy were likely the only ways she would be able to expand her family. "Being able to carry my own child," she told me later in an interview, "was probably never going to happen."

When she had joined the legislature in 2020, keen to work on surrogacy and infertility legislation, Rep. Steckloff was passed a surrogacy bill that had never really gained much traction in the Michigan House of Representatives. It was far from model legislation and was more symbolic than anything, but it was a signal that she was now charged with the responsibility. "It was a personal connection to me," she said. "And we know that personal connections are the things that truly allow bills like this to move." Once we made our personal connection with Rep. Steckloff—who learned from us that there was also another surrogacy bill that didn't include compensation that was being worked on by Democrats in the Senate, which at the time, like the House, was in the Republican majority—we started having meetings, discussing the best way forward on a potential bill.

We all were intent that a bill had to not only make it equitable for intended parents, surrogates, and children born through surrogacy but that it also needed to include compensation, which followed best practice across the United States. That was important because it felt like that put everyone on a level playing field. That the physicians, clinics, lawyers, psychologists, nurses, and social workers all got paid in a surrogacy agreement but the one person who was doing all the literal and figurative heavy lifting, the surrogate, didn't, wasn't fair in our books.

A year later, on the exact day of the second MIAD, that Senate bill was introduced, which took Stephanie and me both by surprise. The bill lacked several things that were non-negotiables—including compensation—and so as an organization, MFA decided not to support the bill. That potential legislation ended up going nowhere, in part because 2022 was an election year. After that legislation dropped, two months later in November, for the first time in forty years, the Democrats gained the majority in both the Michigan House and Senate. With a Democratic governor—Whitmer—in office, who had decided to make reproductive justice a cornerstone of her gubernatorial policy, it looked like the time might be right for MFA to press forward with an inclusive surrogacy bill.

A few weeks after the legislature sweep, Stephanie and I reached out to Bruce Hale, who was also on the American Bar Association's Assisted Reproductive Technologies committee, who I had originally connected with while working on this book. We all started talking about what needed to be included in a law and Bruce suggested that Stephanie and I start going over the Uniform Parentage Act of 2017 (UPA), which was model legislation that included best practice for surrogacy law. It was decided that things needed to remain hush-hush because we didn't want groups like Right to Life, Stop Surrogacy Now, and Catholic Conference to know we were working on broader legislation as they had, in other states like New York, tried to pervert potential legislation.

As we inched toward Christmas and began fine-tooth combing over the Act, another contact, Karla Torres, reached out to us. She too was inspired by what this change in the Michigan Legislature could mean for a potential law and asked how we'd feel about creating a working group to help craft legislation. (Michigan had also just passed Proposal 3, which enshrined reproductive rights, including access to abortion, in the state's constitution.) Stephanie and I were enthused, in part because, with neither of us being lawyers nor having any background in drafting legislation, we felt out of our element. We were soon introduced to Polly Crozier, the director of family advocacy for GLBTQ Legal Advocates & Defenders (GLAD) and Courtney Joslin, a law professor at University of California Davis School of Law, who also happened to be the reporter for the UPA 2017.

By early 2023, we combined our two working groups, which now also included representatives from Family Equality and the National Center for Lesbian Rights. In doing so, the group decided that our legislation should also include updates to parentage laws in Michigan as well, in large part because there were several court cases pending over same-sex couples and child custody in Michigan. One case, *Pueblo v. Haas*, which the Michigan Supreme Court was going to be hearing, dealt with a birth that took place before Michigan's ban on same-sex marriage ended. In 2008, the lesbian couple had a child together and there was no way for the family to secure their child under Michigan statutes. When the couple separated, Ms. Haas, the genetic parent who had carried the pregnancy, denied Ms. Pueblo all contact with their child. Ms. Pueblo sought shared custody, but both the trial court and the Michigan Court of Appeals ruled that she was not a parent to her child.

In another heartbreaking case, Lanesha Matthews and Kyresha LeFever had twins together also before same-sex marriage was legal in Michigan. Ms. LeFever was the genetic mother, and Ms. Matthews was the birth mother. After co-parenting their children for several years, the couple separated, and a protracted battle began over whether Ms. Matthews should be stripped of her legal parentage and her name removed from the birth certificate. A lower court ruled that Ms. Matthews acted as a surrogate to her own children. Thankfully, in 2021 the Michigan Court of Appeals overturned that ruling and appropriately concluded that Ms. Matthews was an equal legal parent.

These cases, as well as others, made our working group feel it was integral that every family in the state should have equal access to secure parent-child relationships from birth. This was a slight change in mindset for Stephanie and me because we had been for so long solely focused on just repealing the surrogacy bill, and as two heterosexual women, we didn't know about a number of implications that children born through assisted reproduction faced in same-sex families. But we understood that a bill that protected all children born through assisted reproduction, like IVF and surrogacy, was more inclusive and the right way to go. "There were some early moments where there was a decision point and it was clear that we're not just going to work on a surrogacy repeal," Polly Crozier told me in May 2024. "So that was the trust building part. So it's like, 'Are you grassroots people going to be open to a vision that protects more people?' Because [everyone in the working group] is so busy, and there's so many fires to put out and so many horrible things happening. Like we can't just repeal a surrogacy ban, you have to protect all the kids."

Everyone in the working group was assigned various responsibilities within which to focus and during weekly meetings the coalition updated and debated what things should go into a bill. I was busy doing research, logistics and writing up several blogs to argue for why the 1988 Surrogate Parenting Act needed to be repealed. The lawyers, meanwhile, were busy drafting the legislation. "My initial take was 'Holy shit, they want us to do this fast,'" Polly said to me with a laugh. "I could tell that it was going to be a lot of work. So one thought I had was 'this is really going to demand a lot of my energy.'"

By late February 2023, Polly and Courtney had put the final touches on the bill. Our best practice legislation included ensuring that all children in Michigan born through assisted reproduction had clear paths to parentage, meaning that there was no question at birth who the people would be who were planning to parent the child. For unmarried couples who used donor gametes and for lesbian couples, that would mean a Voluntary Act of Parentage form, which would state from birth that the non-genetic parent of the child was also legally a parent. Our bill would provide clear protections for everyone involved. With everyone's signoff, the bill was sent to Michigan's Legislative Service Bureau (LSB), a non-partisan arm of the Legislature that provides legal counsel, bill drafting, law compilation, and publishing.

It took months for the LSB work to be done. In a quirk in how Michigan bills get approved, our surrogacy and parentage bill needed to be broken down into different parts to create a nine-bill package that was inclusive of existing legislation including parts of the Public Health and Estates codes, which needed to be updated if the bill passed. Polly told me that Michigan is "totally weird" in this aspect of breaking the bill up and that "it's not how it is done in any state" where she has worked on bills before.

For months, Polly would haul around paper copies of all nine bills with her so that if LSB edits came in, she could quickly coordinate with Brendan Johnson, Rep. Steckloff's legislative director, on the changes. "I couldn't call LSB myself, so he was the conduit," Polly recalled. "I remember sitting in a gross little parking lot overlooking my child's field hockey game with the nine bills, being on the phone with Brendan. Then he would get the person from LSB on the phone. And we would just sit there and figure it out. And that happened more than once."

While Polly was busy on revisions, MFA started working with a Lansing lobbying firm, Public Affairs Associates, as well as a communications firm, Alper Strategies and Media, to help grease wheels in Lansing and beyond. They also guided us on getting prepared for hearings, helping us draft our documents and statements, as well as helping Stephanie and me figure out who we wanted to have testify. Our coalition, as well as our advisors, also finally settled on a name for the bill—the Michigan Family Protection Act (MFPA). And, after much back and forth with LSB, the bill package was ready in the early autumn. In October, Rep. Steckloff introduced the bill to the House.

Soon after, the House Judiciary Committee held two hearings on the bill, with Stephanie, as well as a number of our advocates including Leah Zientek, a gestational carrier who is a development officer for University of Michigan Health, primed and ready to share highly personal and emotive stories around infertility, surrogacy, and parentage. (Funny enough, the uncle of the filmmaker Jeremy Hersh, who made the film *The Surrogate*, happened to be in the committee room that day giving a witness statement on unrelated legislation, and we had a laugh about how small a world it was that I had interviewed his nephew for this book.)

Representatives from COLAGE, the only national organization that empowers youth in LGBTQ+ families and Mothering Justice, a Detroit-based non-profit policy advocacy organization providing resources for mothers of color, also rounded out MFA's testimony. "I didn't feel nervous about the experience until the day of the hearing," Leah, who was a carrier for her friend who had a congenital heart defect, told me after the hearing. "I think the gravitas of the moment hit me, in the best kind of way, and I recognized that I was about to speak about something and someone I cared about so much."

I flew in for the hearings, missing Halloween with my kids in London. Even though I didn't give a statement in the end because of time, I knew I had to be there in person to be support for Stephanie and our advocates but also to run interference. Rep. Steckloff and I joked after the hearing that she was worried she was going to have to pin me down because she could tell I was so agitated by the inaccuracies and scaremongering that

Catholic Conference and Right to Life kept spewing during their statements. It did take a lot of willpower for me not to get up and say something, in part because having worked on this book for such a long period of time, I felt I was extremely well-versed in all the debates and conversations around surrogacy and IVF. So to listen to the purposeful misinformation and inaccuracies really rankled me.

I wasn't the only one who was vexed by their statements. Leah, whose story we felt was important to share to counterbalance the narrative that surrogates are women who have no agency, was also gobsmacked by their misleading rhetoric. "When I started to hear the approach and tactics the opposition was using to argue against the MFPA, and how they described gestational carriers, I experienced a moment of pause," she wrote to me later in an email. "I had that kind of moment when you're playing a game, a match, and you know you have the winning shot, or the winning hand, or the winning move ahead of you. I know that I am representative of gestational carriers in the state and country, who believe in supporting friends and family members, or even strangers, grow their families."

She added that as a mother of a child with intellectual and developmental disabilities, their approach was offensive with some of the tactics they used. "I fight for my child to have access and choices and be able to grow safely and successfully, just as I will fight for families to have access to reproductive health tools such as IVF and gestational carriers," she wrote. "The opposition couldn't have picked a better approach to light a fire in me, at the same time knowing that the narrative was unequivocally false, contrived, and harmful."

While I kept my mouth shut, especially with Right to Life conflating surrogacy in the US to surrogacy in Ukraine and India, I did finally have my say after the legislative director for Right to Life Michigan incorrectly used an example to try and convolute the debate. In the question-and-answer part of the hearing, she made a statement that "in Africa" women were "chained to beds" and put in jail for being surrogates. This, I knew was not true and so after the hearing, I sprinted over to her. After introducing myself as a journalist I said, "Can you tell me what country this was in Africa and also what your source is? Because there are fifty-four countries on the continent, and I have never heard this happening in any of the countries. I have spent four years writing a book on global surrogacy so I feel like this is something I would have known about."

I think I freaked her out because she got flustered and said that "I have read a lot on surrogacy globally and I just don't remember where it was." I gave her my email address and said I looked forward to her fact checking these details with me. Turns out that what I think she was referring to was the case in Cambodia—which is most assuredly not in Africa—where gestational carriers were arrested by the government and later forced to raise the children, who were not their own.[278] I am still waiting for her clarification email.

What bothered me so much was not only did she try and compare surrogacy practices in two disparate parts of the world, a common tactic used by those in the anti-surrogacy space, but her example fell back on itself because Cambodia did not have proper laws in place on surrogacy. Hence that was why the horrific story unfolded in the first place. With laws that give everyone agency in the situation and include contracts that are legal, and valid documents recognized by the state, these kinds of problems would be prevented from happening. So to fight against updating surrogacy laws using an example of a place where there were no surrogacy laws created an argument which was nonsensical.[279]

Luckily, the bill passed through both the Committee and the House—with not a single Republican voting for our bill. A few months later, the Senate Civil Rights, Judiciary and Public Safety Committee also held hearings, ironically, in the Binsfeld Building, named after Sen. Connie Binsfeld, who had been the lawmaker responsible for the 1988 ban on surrogacy. A lot had happened in the surrogacy and IVF space since the MFPA had passed through the House in November. In February 2024, the Alabama Supreme Court had ruled in a case that that embryos should be considered children and that a person could be legally responsbile for destroying them. It put panic through the fertility health care community, in part because it was seen as an attack on assisted reproduction. For all of us who had frozen embryos that we were no longer going to need, it was shocking and disturbing. A GIF I saw around that time succinctly and touchingly summed it up: "No one cares more about embryos than fertility patients. And no one understands more than fertility patients that embryos are not children."

Luckily, the MFPA passed through committee after two hearings, where we again had a stellar team of advocates speaking on behalf of the bill. I had been at the first Senate hearing, but I had to get back to my kids in London and so couldn't stay around for the second hearing or the Senate vote. But Stephanie and I streamed it online together over Facetime. And when the votes were coming in, the two of us cried fat ugly tears of joy. It's hard to explain what that felt like—relief, release, happiness, incredulity, bitterness, sadness, shock—all the emotional roller coaster of feelings I had felt for years just pouring out of me in heaving sobs. My kids, who were downstairs, came up and hugged me. I had explained to them earlier what was happening and while they didn't get it, they understood vaguely that it had something to do with them and that I was, despite my wet cheeks, so very happy.

On March 19, 2024, our bill passed on the Senate floor, sadly with only two Republicans voting in favor of the bill. But we had done it, we had changed the law. (In another quirk in state law, if a bill does not pass by two-thirds in both houses, the bill goes into effect ninety days after the end of the legislative session. So that looks to be in early March 2025.) And it felt so huge. "I was confident the entire time," Rep. Steckloff told me a month after the MFPA was signed into law. "I knew from the moment we won the trifecta [of the House and Senate becoming Democratic majorities and a Democratic governor] in November 2022. I knew once that happened, we just got surrogacy legal in the state of Michigan."

Governor Whitmer released a TikTok video soon after, announcing that she was looking forward to signing the bill into law, making it the first law on parentage and assisted reproduction since that disaster in Montgomery in February. "I've never met a coalition as well-educated, thought out and powerful as this group was," Rep. Steckloff told me after the MFPA signing. "I mean, without you guys, this wouldn't have been as successful. So it was because of the coalition and being able to work on it in a silo that also helped because we didn't have to worry about the outside noise."

I flew back to the US at the end of March for the bill signing. Stephanie had desperately tried to get me a slot to speak at the signing but the governor's office, worried about time, said no. But Leah did give a speech about how momentous and important this law was. Sitting next to my mom and my older brother, who had been there when Lexie and Ransom were born, and across from

Polly, who had also flown in for the signing, I quietly wept when Stephanie went up to the podium to speak about our journey and to introduce Governor Whitmer. "We had no roadmap and no idea where this journey would take us," Stephanie said during her speech. "But we never wavered. When one door closed, we found another and kicked it down. Proof that we took our sorrow and turned it into our superpower."

But our battle isn't over. The Supreme Court of the United States' (SCOTUS) decision to overturn *Roe v Wade*—the landmark 1973 ruling that gave women the right to have abortions—in June 2022 was a huge blow to those who work in reproductive rights in the United States. It also was perceived as grave concern to those in the surrogacy industry in the United States. The *New York Times* in August 2022 published a piece "The Surrogacy Industry Braces for a Post-Roe World" that examined how some agencies were concerned that surrogates who lived in states where abortion was banned would be "forced to go to extreme lengths to access abortion or miscarriage care in the event of fetal abnormalities" or if the surrogate's life was at risk.[280]

Abortions are exceedingly rare during surrogate pregnancies. Dean Hutchison and Sam Hyde, who is now the president and owner of Circle, told me in an interview in September 2022 that in the fourteen years that Circle has kept statistics on this, with over 3,600 cycles and about 1,400 children born, there have been only fourteen terminations, seven of which were reductions. The *New York Times* article quotes Kristen Hanson, the co-founder of Simple Surrogacy out of Texas, which arranges about eighty-five surrogacies a year, saying in their twenty-one-year history they have only had four surrogates who had an abortion. In the article, five other agencies agreed that the numbers are minimal.

However, while they are rare, it's something that must be

discussed and agreed upon, which was what we had to do with Julie and Chad. IPs and carriers are matched, in part, for how their views align on the subject and nearly everyone agrees that if the carrier's life is in danger, a termination should take place. The same holds true in most cases if there are severe genetic irregularities that could impact the quality or length of the child's life.[281] In the end, it should be the surrogate's ultimate choice over her bodily autonomy, something specifically written into the MFPA.

Yet in some states, including Texas and Oklahoma, agencies could be vulnerable to heavy fines or even prosecution for helping carriers access abortion care. Some agencies, therefore, have adjusted their practice requiring genetic testing of embryos or implanting only one embryo per cycle. "It's definitely made a small number of surrogates more hesitant to proceed if they're in a state with far more draconian laws," Dean said about the Dobbs decision and its possible ramifications. "That's because number one, they don't want to violate law. Number two, they don't want their life in jeopardy over [needing] a termination and not having the ability to get the care." He added that a small number of parents asked to restrict the matching states they would go to based on laws.

On the other side of the coin, said Sam, who resides in Michigan, "you might think 'oh, it's going to reduce the number of women who are interested in becoming surrogates'" but it was definitely not the case in August 2022, as it was Circle's best month of all time in terms of recruiting potential carriers. "So," he added, "it's not dampening enthusiasm amongst potential surrogates in the least bit." While macroeconomics may play some small role, it might be because surrogacy, as he said, is now in the "collective zeitgeist" of the United States. In terms of the concern of how the SCOTUS ruling will affect surrogacy, Sam said: "It's a product of heightened ambiguity and in the whole fertility environment right now a lot of IVF clinics are very worried about embryos being destroyed and things like that," he said. "For the most part, all those things are really unlikely to come to fruition. But you have to kind of plan for all possible externalities."

While it was impossible for Sam to know at the time of our conversation, his words rang terribly true after the Alabama Supreme Court ruling. When Stephanie and I attended a global conference on surrogacy in Copenhagen in June 2023, a lot of the conversations were around how lawmakers were coming for IVF, and by default, surrogacy too. Later that summer, a group of anti-surrogacy activists met in Morocco to sign the *Declaration of Casablanca for the universal abolition of surrogacy*. It is believed that the group, which met again right after the MFPA was signed into law, may have had some sway over the Pope who, in a text released in April 2024 called *Dignitas Infinita*, declared that surrogacy was a "violation" of both women and children born through it. (I did reach out to the press people behind the Casablanca Agreement for an interview but I was told that their spokesperson was "too busy" at the moment.)

While most people in the surrogacy space that I talked with do not take this group seriously, it does show that global debates on IVF and surrogacy are far from resolved. This was exampled clearly in June 2024 when the Southern Baptist Convention, the world's largest Baptist organization, at their convention in Indianapolis, voted to oppose IVF, something that the *New Republic* stated signalled, "a dangerous shift in conservative stances on the procedure." *Politico*, meanwhile, noted that the move could be the "beginning of a broad turn on the right against IVF, an issue that many evangelicals, anti-abortion advocates and other social conservatives see" as the anti-abortion movement's "next frontier—one they hope will eventually lead to restrictions, or outright bans, on IVF at the state and federal levels."[282] The very next day, Republicans in the U.S. Senate voted to block a bill to protect access to IVF. President Joe Biden said in a statement that, "The disregard for a woman's right to make these decisions for herself and her family is outrageous and unacceptable."

The conversations around IVF became an increasingly huge topic in the US presidential race. Gov. Tim Walz, during the Democratic National Convention, spoke in a heartfelt manner about he and his wife's personal experience with infertility while Donald Trump claimed during a campaign stop in Michigan—with absolutely no plan put forward—that, if elected, he would make the government or insurance companies pay for IVF. A few weeks later he made the incredulous claim that he was the "father of IVF." That led Vice President Kamala Harris, as she departed Detroit, to slam his comments. She said, "What he should take responsibility for is that couples who are praying and hoping and working towards growing a family have been so disappointed and harmed by the fact that IVF treatments have now been put at risk." Taylor Swift, meanwhile, also weighed into the debate, stating on Instagram that one of the reasons she was supporting the Harris/Walz ticket was because Gov. Walz has "been standing up for LGBTQ+ rights, IVF, and a woman's right to her own body for decades."

So while my tale has a happy ending—with two beautiful children and model legislation now making surrogacy legal in my beloved home state—I worry for the millions of others out there globally whose IVF and surrogacy story is just beginning.

Stephanie Jones, founder of Michigan Fertility Alliance; Michigan Governor Gretchen Whitmer; and me on April, 1, 2024, at the signing of the Michigan Family Protection Act.

Acknowledgments

It takes a village to raise a child and also, as it turns out, to write a book about IVF and surrogacy.

I interviewed almost one hundred people for this book, several of whom graciously allowed me to keep peppering them with questions and comments as I wrote and did research. In particular, I want to thank Dr. Elly Teman, Dr. Heather Jacobson, and Dr. Zsuzsa Berend for their time, and for their integral research that helped me better understand the motivations and personalities of surrogates. My deep appreciation as well to Bruce Hale, Karla Torres, and Dean Hutchison, who I interviewed at the very beginning of this project and helped give me some great recommendations of people I should speak to and research that was important to broaden my approach. A big thank you to Dr. Sara Matthews for her humor, insights, and pep talks that someday, somehow, I would become a mother. I also tip my hat to Jill Rudnitzky Brand and Dr. Wulf Utian for sharing their stories and memories.

A massive thank you to all the people in our Michigan Family Protection Act (MFPA) coalition that tirelessly worked on the bill—Karla Torres and Jorie Dugan from the Center for Reproductive Rights, Polly Crozier (who has the Patience of a saint!) from GLAD, Courtney Joslin from UC Davis, Shannon Minter and Nesta Johnson from the National Center for Lesbian

Rights, and Meg York from Family Equality. There is no way we could have climbed this mountain without you. To our Michigan Fertility Alliance Leadership board members—LeAndrea Fisher, Cherish Paska, Alex Kamer, Kevin O'Neill, Sue Johnston, Chelsea Lantto, Aubrey Gojcaj, Laura Muysenberg, and Leah Zientek—who have cheerleaded this book throughout the process, I am forever grateful. Huge kudos to Rep. Sam Steckloff, whose passion and humor helped us get this bill passed. And, of course, my MFPA ride-or-die Stephanie Jones—whenever I hit empty, you somehow reached full throttle, and vice versa. What a journey this has been and there is no way I would have wanted to have done it with anyone else.

My friends have all been incredible sounding boards throughout this whole process, but there are several I want to particularly highlight in no particular order—Bari Shaffran, Erika Dimmler, Sara Latham, Kate Hilton, Gina Dafalia (I am spelling it right this time!), Monica Ellena, Kirsten Fear, Will Morgan, Megan Royle Carrella, Annie Walsh Norton, Alyssa Husby, Sarah "Buddha" Brown, Clothilde Ewing, Caryn Mendoza, Mary Forrest Engel, Silvia Spring, Emily Flynn Vencat, Kit Maloney (and Renaud Notaro), Debbie Berger Fox, Brooke Stroud Carnot, Noa Zingher, and Suzanne Murphy Heath. Thanks to Rachel Stewart Reinders for your book cover ideas and to Aurelie Baudry Palmer for your whimsical illustrations. Thanks to Darcy Sherman for the author photo and for capturing my monsters every summer in all their wholesomeness.

Huge shoutouts, of course, to Tracy Gatrell for keeping me (somewhat) sane and making me constantly laugh with our sober-yet-drunken conversations about logistics, and to Barbora Satkova for keeping things organized. And to Olivia Sherman, who started out as the twins' babysitter and has now become like a twenty-five-year younger #bestie. Thanks, Simon Kariuki Ndungu, for always being there for us and being a calming source of light when it sometimes seemed very stressful and dark. Thanks to Julie for sharing her reminiscences about her surrogacy experience (and of course for being our incredible gestational carrier—the greatest gift from a stranger who became a friend) and a massive shout-out to Ben and Offir for walking me through my initial questions and freak-outs around surrogacy. Thanks to Jennifer Olsen for always focusing on the details. And Daniela Burani, appreciate you for stalking your cousin for a quote.

Thanks to my family—my mother, who is my best friend, and the person who I model my parenting after, and my brothers Reb Brownell and Joe Brownell, who have listened and advised on many aspects of this book. I may not have always agreed, but I very much appreciate your counsel. Thanks for being two fantastic uncles who are wonderful role models, except when it comes to Pac Man and salvaging anchors.

And, of course, to Ransom and Lexie—my Boo-Boo Bear and No-No. This book is a love letter for you, so that you can catch just a glimmer of how much you were wanted and loved before either of you even stepped foot in this world. I love you both more than all the water in Lake Michigan—even when you chicken bok and nima-nima me repeatedly. You have completed me, and my life is blessed because of you.

Notes

1 "ART and Gestational Carriers," U.S. Centers for Disease Control, accessed August 8, 2024, https://www.cdc.gov/art/key-findings/gestational-carriers.html, 4.

2 A note on names: to protect my children's identities, I am using a variation of their names. For people I interviewed in a professional capacity, I have used formal surnames after a primary reference of their first and last names. For people that I have developed relationships with—a number of lawyers, academics, and surrogates for example, as well as my friends—I have used first names after initial reference.

3 Leslie Morgan Steiner, *The Baby Chase: How Surrogacy is Transforming the American Family* (New York: St. Martin's Press, 2013), 246.

4 "Eggs from Elsewhere," *The Economist*, July 22, 2023, 10.

5 "The Most Personal Technology," *The Economist*.

6 "The Most Personal Technology," *The Economist*.

7 Years later when I interviewed Sara Matthews for this book, I asked her to tell me exactly what the term meant. She said, "'Unexplained' means that we are morons and we have not found the reason because we are simple creatures." (She said this jokingly and then got more serious.) "Anything that we don't know, we call it 'unexplained.' Basically, when you look at causes for people not being able to get pregnant you look at: Are you producing an egg? Is the egg good quality? Are eggs and sperm able to get together? Anything stopping that happening like mucus at the cervix so it makes it harder? Is the sperm okay? Is it the right shape? Genetically normal? Then comes the womb things. This is the hidden thing; it is the one aspect of pregnancy that we know least about. We are pretty good at sperm, and IVF will get over ovulation issues. Genetic tests weed out the good sperm, bypass the tubes. With wombs, aside from the obvious anatomical problems—a heart shape, division down the middle, you have scarring in the womb or previous surgery—investigating womb things, that is the bit we know the least about. [So] a large part of unexplained infertility is either a combination of small factors or it is something we just are not clever enough to diagnose. Your womb was trouble from the start. [When]

you started talking about surrogacy, I thought that was the answer. We got the eggs, we got the embryos, but your womb was always an issue. I was worried about you."

8 Susan Golombok, *We Are Family: What Really Matters for Parents and Children* (London: Scribe Publications, 2020), 133.

9 Elly Teman, *Birthing a Mother: The Surrogate Body and the Pregnant Self* (Berkeley: University of California Press, 2010), 21.

10 Teman, *Birthing a Mother*, 135.

11 Zsuzsa Berend, *The Online World of Surrogacy (Fertility, Reproduction and Sexuality, Vol. 35)* (New York: Berghahn Books, 2016), 39.

12 Heather Jacobson, *Labor of Love: Gestational Surrogacy and the Work of Making Babies* (New Brunswick, NJ: Rutgers University Press, 2016), 87.

13 Jacobson, *Labor of Love*, 53.

14 Karen Smith Rotabi and Nicole F. Bromfield, *From Intercountry Adoption to Global Surrogacy: A Human Rights History and New Fertility Frontiers* (London: Routledge Press, 2017), 134.

15 Elly Teman, "My Bun, Her Oven (or: Surrogacy as a Cultural Anomaly)," *Anthropology Now* 2, no. 2 (2010): 33–41.

16 Teman, "My Bun, Her Oven," 29.

17 Teman, "My Bun, Her Oven," 3.

18 Teman, "My Bun, Her Oven," 30.

19 Jacobson, *Labor of Love*, 91.

20 Jacobson, *Labor of Love*, 91.

21 The reason that a large number of Israeli gay men go to the US is that only until recently, surrogacy was not open to them in their own country. I discuss this further in Chapter 8.

22 Jacobson, *Labor of Love*, 51.

23 Debora Spar, *The Baby Business: How Money, Science, and Politics Drive the Commerce of Conception* (Cambridge: Harvard Business School Publishing Cooperation, 2006), 74.

24 Judith Daar, *The New Eugenics: Selective Breeding in an Era of Reproductive Technologies* (New Haven, CT: Yale University Press, 2017), 128.

25 American Society for Reproductive Medicine, accessed August 2024 https://www.asrm.org/globalassets/asrm/asrm-content/news-and-publications/ethics-committee-opinions/consideration_of_the_gestational_carrier-pdfmembers.pdf.

26   France Winddance Twine, *Outsourcing the Womb: Race, Class and Gestational Surrogacy in a Global Market* (New York: Routledge, 2011), 14.

27   Balaram, the seventh child of Krishna's parents Devaki and Vasudev, was transferred as an embryo into Vasudev's first wife, Rohini. This was to prevent the baby from being killed by Devaki's brother Kamsa. Accessed August 3, 2024, https://www.shethepeople.tv/news/surrogacy-in-mythology/.

28   In Judith Daar's book, *The New Eugenics: Selective Breeding in an Era of Reproductive Technologies,* she states that in 1785 a Scottish surgeon named John Hunter successfully impregnated a woman with her husband's sperm using a warm syringe. However medical journals were "bereft of information" for the next one hundred years until the Philadelphia artificial insemination by Dr. Pancoast.

29   Elizabeth Yuko, "The First Artificial Insemination was an Ethical Nightmare," *Atlantic,* January 8, 2016, https://www.theatlantic.com/health/archive/2016/01/first-artificial-insemination/423198/.

30   Ann V. Bell, *Misconception: Social Class and Infertility in America* (New Brunswick, NJ: Rutgers University Press, 2014), 6.

31   Twine, *Outsourcing the Womb,* 6.

32   Bell, *Misconception,* 6.

33   Bell, *Misconception,* 6.

34   "The Most Personal Technology," *The Economist.*

35   "Selling Hope," *The Economist,* July 22, 2023, 7.

36   "Selling Hope," *The Economist.*

37   "Selling Hope," *The Economist.*

38   Spar, *The Baby Business,* 75.

39   Spar, *The Baby Business,* 75.

40   Spar, *The Baby Business,* 75.

41   Jacobson, *Labor of Love,* 18.

42   Steiner, *The Baby Chase,* 61.

43   Sandye Rudnitzky, "One Beautiful Egg: The First Gestational Surrogacy," *Hadassah Magazine,* April 2024, https://www.hadassahmagazine.org/2024/04/03/one-beautiful-egg-the-first-gestational-surrogacy/#:~:text=It%20was%20unexpected%2C%20to%20say,parents%20in%20a%20surrogate's%20womb.

44   Rudnitzky, "One Beautiful Egg."

45   At the bat mitzvah Sandye made a speech. "She called me up to stand next to her," Dr. Utian told me, "and she was crying, everybody was crying and I had

tears running down my face." He was also invited to her wedding but he and his wife were in South Africa so they could not attend.

46   Golombok, *We Are Family,* 125.

47   According to a few sources, no one has ever been prosecuted on this law.

48   Larry Gostin, ed., *Surrogate Motherhood: Politics and Privacy* (Indianapolis: Indiana University Press, 1988), xi.

49   James Risen, "Michigan Outlaws Surrogate Maternity Contracts; Ban Aimed at 'Baby M' Clinic," *Los Angeles Times,* June 28, 1988, https://www .latimes.com/archives/la-xpm-1988-06-28-mn-5095-story.html.

50   Risen, "Michigan Outlaws Surrogate Maternity Contracts."

51   Risen, "Michigan Outlaws Surrogate Maternity Contracts."

52   Spar, *The Baby Business,* 71.

53   Bruce Hale, Esq., et al., International Surrogacy Forum paper (University of Cambridge, June 27–28, 2019), 14.

54   Hale, International Surrogacy Forum paper, 15.

55   Hale, International Surrogacy Forum paper, 15.

56   Hale, International Surrogacy Forum paper, 15.

57   In Judith Daar's *The New Eugenics: Selective Breeding in an Era of Reproductive Technologies*, she writes that Jack Skinner, a thrice-convicted armed robber, challenged the constitutionality of the Oklahoma Habitual Criminal Sterilization Act of 1935, "during the heyday of the eugenics movement." The law, based on a scientifically unsupported idea that criminality was a heritable trait, allowed state officials to sterilize persons convicted two or more times for felony crimes of "moral turpitude." In the unanimous decision, William O. Douglas wrote that the case touched "a sensitive and important area of human rights ... the right to have offspring," (p. 3).

58   But, as Heather Jacobson points out, for a country that has a history of contentious religious and ethical debates around these issues, surrogacy raises questions "regarding procreative liberty, parentage, and parental rights."

59   Hale, International Surrogacy Forum paper, 14.

60   Steven H. Snyder, "Reproductive Surrogacy in the United States of America: Trajectories and Trends," in *Handbook of Gestational Surrogacy*, ed. E. Scott Sills (Cambridge: Cambridge University Press, 2016), 276–86.

61   Snyder, "Reproductive Surrogacy," in Sills, *Handbook of Gestational Surrogacy*, 277.

62   American Society for Reproductive Medicine, "Consideration of the Gestational Carrier: An Ethics Committee Opinion," https://www.asrm.org

/practice-guidance/ethics-opinions/consideration-of-the-gestational-carrier
-an-ethics-committee-opinion-2023/.

63   Daar, *The New Eugenics*, 73–74.

64   Jacobson, *Labor of Love*, 38.

65   Sharmila Rudrappa, "India's Reproductive Assembly Line," *Contexts* 11, no. 2 (2012): 22–27.

66   Rudrappa, "India's Reproductive Assembly Line," https://journals.sagepub.com/doi/full/10.1177/1536504212446456.

67   Since the interview in 2021, that number now hovers between $40,000 and $50,000.

68   Jacobson, *Labor of Love*, 36.

69   For obvious reasons, most surrogacy agencies will not take on surrogates who have ever suffered themselves from infertility. However, many surrogates, including Julie, when working with infertile couples, often begin to get a slice of the reality and pain of infertility when they are unable to get pregnant. "Surrogates come to gestational surrogacy with the expectation that their own fertility would transfer to their IPs," Heather Jacobson writes, "and some are shocked that this does not happen." She told me in an interview that for some of the surrogates she interviewed, "this was their first real foray into the world of infertility and that was highly meaningful for them."

70   America Tonight digital team, "Outsourcing Surrogacy: It Takes a Global Village," Al Jazeera, May 15, 2014, http://america.aljazeera.com/watch/shows/america-tonight/articles/2014/5/15/outsourcing-surrogacyittakesa globalvillage.html.

71   Spar, *The Baby Business*, 85.

72   Spar, *The Baby Business*, 86.

73   Alison Bailey, "Reconceiving Surrogacy: Toward a Reproductive Justice Account of Indian Surrogacy," *Faculty Publications - Philosophy*, Illinois State University, 2011, https://ir.library.illinoisstate.edu/fpphil/1.

74   Spar, *The Baby Business*, 86.

75   Sital Kalantry, "Regulating Markets for Gestational Care: Comparative Perspectives on Surrogacy in the United States and India," *Cornell Journal of Law and Public Policy* 27, no. 3, article 8 (2018).

76   Surrogacy 360, https://surrogacy360.org/considering-surrogacy/current-law/. Like in the US, surrogacy in Mexico is regulated on the state level.

77   Miranda Davies, ed., *Babies for Sale?: Transnational Surrogacy, Human Rights and the Politics of Reproduction* (London: Zed Books Ltd., 2017), 9.

78   GIRE, "Surrogacy in Mexico: The Consequences of Poor Regulation," 2020, https://gire.org.mx/wp-content/uploads/2020/02/Surrogacy-in-Mexico .-The-Consequences-of-Poor-Regulation.pdf.

79   GIRE, "Surrogacy in Mexico," 16.

80   Nicolás Espejo-Yaksic, Claire Fenton-Glynn and Jens M. Scherpe, eds., *Surrogacy in Latin America* (Cambridge, UK: Intersentia, 2023) 6–12.

81   Espejo-Yaksic, Fenton-Glynn, and Scherpe, *Surrogacy in Latin America*, 11.

82   Espejo-Yaksic, Fenton-Glynn, and Scherpe, *Surrogacy in Latin America*, 9.

83   Espejo-Yaksic, Fenton-Glynn, and Scherpe, *Surrogacy in Latin America*, 9.

84   With global surrogacy laws changing constantly, I have gone with the most accurate I could find, which is the Cornell study mentioned below. In the past few years, Russia has banned cross-border surrogacy while Georgia and other countries are contemplating prohibiting it. Meanwhile, Thailand, as of April 2024, is possibly opening back up to cross-border surrogacy after a several-year ban.

85   Cornell Law School and International Human Rights Policy Advocate Clinic and National Law University, Delhi, "Should Compensated Surrogacy Be Permitted or Prohibited?," Cornell Law Faculty Publications (2017).

86   According to GIRE's report, "Surrogacy in Mexico: The Consequences of Poor Regulation," despite the fact that surrogacy in Tabasco has been possible for over two decades, the number of IPs who traveled there only really took off after 2012. That was because India's cross-border surrogacy trade began to shut down. Two years later, when Thailand also shut down, even more IPs came to Tabasco. "Thus, changes in the international framework had an important impact for Tabasco to become (although to a lesser degree) a national and international destination." The report goes on to say that with the increase in cases, problems with the legal framework started to become more obvious.

87   Soraj Hongladarom, "Surrogacy in Thailand," in *Eastern and Western Perspectives on Surrogacy*, ed. Jens Scherpe, Claire Fenton-Glynn, and Terry Kaan (Cambridge, UK: Intersentia, 2019), 502.

88   Sally Howard, "Wombs For Hire," *British Medical Journal*, November 1, 2014, cached May 2020, https://www.bmj.com/bmj/section-pdf/779068?path =/bmj/349/7981/Feature.full.pdf.

89   Daniel Hurst, "Japanese Man Wins Sole Custody of 13 Surrogacy Children," *Guardian*, February 20, 2018, cached May 13, 2020.

90   Hurst, "Japanese Man Wins Sole Custody."

91   Hurst, "Japanese Man Wins Sole Custody."

92   Hannah Beech, "They Were Surrogates, Now They Must Raise the Children," *New York Times*, November 26, 2022, accessed April 2024.

93   Howard, "Wombs For Hire."

94   Kalantry, "Regulating Markets for Gestational Care."

95   Marcy Darnovsky and Diane Beeson, "Global Surrogacy Practices" (working paper, International Institute of Social Studies, The Hague, Netherlands, 2014).

96   Kalantry, "Regulating Markets for Gestational Care."

97   Amrita Pande, "Mapping Feminist Views on Surrogacy," in Davies, *Babies for Sale?*, 328.

98   Prabha Kotiswaran, "Surrogacy in India," in Scherpe, Fenton-Glynn, and Kaan, *Eastern and Western Perspectives on Surrogacy*, 377.

99   Shonottra Kumar, "India's Proposed Commercial Surrogacy Ban Is an Assault on Women's Rights," Undark, November 11, 2019, https://undark.org/2019/11/07/india-commercial-surrogacy-ban/.

100   Soumya Kashyap and Priyanka Tripathi, "The Surrogacy (Regulation) Act, 2021: A Critique," *Asian Bioethics Review* 15, no. 1 (published online September 20, 2022): 5–18.

101   Elly Teman, "The Power of the Single Story: Surrogacy and Social Media in Israel," *Medical Anthropology* 38, no. 2 (November 2018): 1–13.

102   Teman, "The Power of the Single Story," 284.

103   Teman, "The Power of the Single Story," 284. Dr. Teman writes in this paper a fascinating account about how surrogates in Israel, connected through social media, became very interested in the concept of the "single story." The ultimate surrogate journey was supposed to have three elements: a close bond between surrogate and IM/IPs, an epic birth story, and a "happily ever after" performed in a public way. If that did not play out as they envisioned, some would even sign up to be a surrogate again to get that experience they could then play out on Facebook and Instagram.

104   Lei Shi, "Surrogacy in China," in Scherpe, Fenton-Glynn, and Kaan, *Eastern and Western Perspectives on Surrogacy*, 360.

105   Nicola Davison, "China's surrogate mothers see business boom in year of the dragon," *Guardian*, February 8, 2012, https://www.theguardian.com/world/2012/feb/08/china-surrogate-mothers-year-dragon.

106   Davison, "China's surrogate mothers see business boom in year of the dragon." See also M. Rivkin-Fish, "Conceptualizing feminist strategies for Russian reproductive politics: Abortion, surrogate motherhood, and family support after socialism," *Signs: Journal of Women in Culture and Society* 38, no. 3 (Spring 2013).

107   C. C. Weiss, "Reproductive migrations: Surrogacy workers and stratified reproduction in St. Petersburg" (doctoral dissertation, De Montfort University, Leicester, 2017), https://www.dora.dmu.ac.uk/handle/2086/15036.

108   These interviews in relation to Russia and Ukraine were done pre-Russian invasion in February 2022. The surrogacy landscape in both Russia and Ukraine changed drastically after the war began and as of 2024, the surrogacy landscape remains in a state of flux, unless otherwise noted in the text.

109   This tends to be the case for Ukrainian surrogates as well, according to Polina Vlasenko, a researcher in medical anthropology who has done research on surrogates in Ukraine.

110   Christina Weis, "Workers or mothers? The business of surrogacy in Russia," openDemocracy, 2015, https://www.opendemocracy.net/en/beyond -trafficking-and-slavery/workers-or-mothers-business-of-surrogacy-in-russia/.

111   Konstanin Svitnev, "Gestational Surrogacy in the Russian Federation," in Sills, *Handbook of Gestational Surrogacy*, 232–40.

112   Natalia Khvorostianov and Daphna Yeshua-Katz, "Bad, Pathetic and Greedy Women: Expressions of Surrogate Motherhood Stigma in a Russian Online Forum," *Sex Roles* 83, no. 2 (January 29, 2020), https://link.springer .com/article/10.1007/s11199-020-01119-z.

113   Khvorostianov and Yeshua-Katz, "Bad, Pathetic and Greedy Women," 3.

114   Not her real name.

115   New Life has been a very controversial agency over the years and there will be more on this in a later chapter related to their time in Thailand. The "Baby Broker Project," a work by the investigative news website Finance Uncovered, found, "Some New Life surrogates, tempted by life-changing amounts of money, signed up to undergo risky pregnancies in jurisdictions where surrogacy is often unregulated. These women agreed to become surrogates seemingly without the benefit of legal support, potentially leaving them open to exploitation and abuse … from low-income countries in Eastern Europe, Asia, Latin America, and Africa." Read more at: https://www .financeuncovered.org/stories/new-life-surrogacy-agency-baby-broker-project.

116   Rhona Schuz, "Surrogacy in Israel," in Scherpe, Fenton-Glynn, and Kaan, *Eastern and Western Perspectives on Surrogacy*, 175.

117   Renate Klein, *Surrogacy: A Human Rights Violation* (Victoria, AU: Spinifex Press, 2017), 31.

118   "Eggs from Elsewhere," *The Economist*, 9.

119   Teman, *Birthing a Mother*, 113.

120   "The Most Personal Technology," *The Economist*, 4.

121 Steiner, *The Baby Chase*, 117.

122 Steiner, *The Baby Chase*, 231.

123 "Eggs from Elsewhere," *The Economist*, 9.

124 Golombok, *We Are Family*, 88.

125 Diane Beeson and Abby Lippman, "Gestational Surrogacy: How Safe?," in Davies, *Babies for Sale?*, 84.

126 Spar, *The Baby Business*, 43.

127 For an excellent understanding of IVF and how the procedure should work but sometimes, as in the cases they highlight, doesn't, check out "The Retrievals" in *New York Times*, https://www.nytimes.com/2023/06/22/podcasts /serial-the-retrievals-yale-fertility-clinic.html.

128 Spar, *The Baby Business*, 43.

129 Spar, *The Baby Business*, 43.

130 Spar, *The Baby Business*, 43.

131 Steiner, *The Baby Chase*, 232.

132 Beeson and Lippman, "Gestational Surrogacy," in Davies, *Babies for Sale?*, 84.

133 Beeson and Lippman, "Gestational Surrogacy," in Davies, *Babies for Sale?*, 90.

134 Beeson and Lippman, "Gestational Surrogacy," in Davies, *Babies for Sale?*, 90.

135 Amy Speier, *Fertility Holidays: IVF Tourism and the Reproduction of Whiteness* (New York: New York University Press, 2016), 73.

136 "Eggs from Elsewhere," *The Economist*, 9.

137 Ms. Scheier did add in a follow-up email that since most of these respondents were either current or recent donors, the numbers skewed toward unhappy/neutral. But, "generally speaking, the older donors get, the happier they are to be contacted" as they have more distance from the experience, become moms themselves, and so on.

138 Emily Bazelon, "Why Anonymous Sperm Donation is Over and Why That Matters," *New York Times Magazine*, December 3, 2023, https://www .nytimes.com/2023/12/03/magazine/anonymous-sperm-donation-genetic -testing.html.

139 Bazelon, "Why Anonymous Sperm Donation is Over."

140 Bazelon, "Why Anonymous Sperm Donation is Over." I will touch on this more in the last chapter but some donor-conceived people and LGBTQ groups worry that, according to the *New York Times*, "laws that require the end of

anonymity pose an unanticipated threat" as lesbian couples and single parents make up 70 percent of the people "working with sperm donors." And, "some of these families fear that disclosure laws will open the door to recognizing biological donors in some way as parents—possibly granting them parental rights and more broadly undermining the legitimacy of LGBTQ families."

141   Teman, *Birthing a Mother*, 113.

142   Not her real name.

143   Elle Hunt, "There's a crisis in male fertility. But you wouldn't know it from the way many men behave," *Guardian*, March 12, 2024, accessed June 2024, https://www.theguardian.com/commentisfree/2024/mar/12/men-fertility-falling-sperm-counts-conceive-problem.

144   Not her real name.

145   Female Fertility Figure (Akuaba), 19th–20th century, wood, beads, string, Metropolitan Museum of Art, New York, https://www.metmuseum.org/art/collection/search/312279.

146   Female Fertility Figure.

147   Emma Maniere, "Mapping Feminist Views on Surrogacy," in Davies, *Babies for Sale?*, 313.

148   Maniere, "Mapping Feminist Views on Surrogacy," in Davies, *Babies for Sale?*, 316.

149   Spar, *The Baby Business*, 77.

150   Maniere, "Mapping Feminist Views on Surrogacy," in Davies, *Babies for Sale?*, 320.

151   Daar, *The New Eugenics*, 63.

152   Susan Markens, *Surrogate Motherhood and the Politics of Reproduction* (Berkeley: University of California Press, 2007), 17.

153   Amrita Pande, *Wombs in Labor: Transnational Commercial Surrogacy in India* (New York: Columbia University Press, 2014), 9.

154   Darnovsky and Besson, "Global Surrogacy Practices."

155   Markens, *Surrogate Motherhood*, 17.

156   Klein, *Surrogacy: A Human Rights Violation*, 3.

157   Kajsa Ekis Ekman, Linn Hellerström and the Swedish Women's Lobby, "Swedish Feminists Against Surrogacy," in Davies, *Babies for Sale?*, 308.

158   Markens, *Surrogate Motherhood*, 17.

159   Spar, *The Baby Business*, 77.

160   Markens, *Surrogate Motherhood*, 108.

161   While surrogacy is still controversial politically in a number of European countries, a 2023 US National Institutes of Health report showed that in many of those countries, there has been a softening of views around surrogacy. https://www.ncbi.nlm.nih.gov/pmc/articles/PMC10239602/.

162   Dr. Nayna Patel, who has been featured in films like *Google Baby* and on *The Oprah Winfrey Show* counterargues this point. "When they say 'this womb is for sale' well, it's nothing like an organ transplant. It is very different; you are not removing an organ," she told me in a phone interview.

163   Bell, *Misconception*, 6.

164   Bell, *Misconception*, 14.

165   Bell, *Misconception*, 15.

166   Teman, *Birthing a Mother*, 5.

167   Jacobson, *Labor of Love*, 101.

168   Teman, *Birthing a Mother*, 123.

169   Steiner, *The Baby Chase*, 240.

170   Ann Carrns, "Tech Companies Get High Marks for Covering Infertility Treatments," *New York Times*, November 15, 2017, https://www.nytimes.com/2017/11/15/your-money/infertility-treatment-coverage.html.

171   Rakshitha Arni Ravishankar, "Does Your Employer Offer Fertility and Family Planning Benefits?," *Harvard Business Review*, March 10, 2022, https://hbr.org/2022/03/does-your-employer-offer-fertility-and-family-planning-benefits.

172   Steiner, *The Baby Chase*, 107.

173   Daar, *The New Eugenics*, 89.

174   Daar, *The New Eugenics*, 81.

175   Bell, *Misconception*, 2–3.

176   Karen Purcell et al., "Asian ethnicity is associated with reduced pregnancy outcomes after assisted reproductive technology," *Fertility and Sterility* 87, no. 2 (February 2007): 297–302.

177   Monica Luhar, "She Didn't Tell Her Family About Her Infertility Diagnosis. Now She's Helping Those Struggling to Conceive," NBC News, November 2, 2017, accessed March 2024, https://www.nbcnews.com/news/asian-america/she-didn-t-tell-her-family-about-her-infertility-diagnosis-n812846.

178   Bell, *Misconception*, 90.

179   Bell, *Misconception*, 91.

180   Bell, *Misconception*, 92.

181   Bell, *Misconception*, 81.

182   Steiner, *The Baby Chase*, 176.

183   Teman, *Birthing a Mother*, 157.

184   Teman, "My Bun, Her Oven," 33–41.

185   Teman, *Birthing a Mother*, 114.

186   Not her real name.

187   Steiner, *The Baby Chase*, 246.

188   Beeson and Lippman, "Gestational Surrogacy," in Davies, *Babies for Sale?*, 86.

189   Lisa M. Shandley et al., "Trends and Outcomes of Assisted Reproductive Technology Cycles Using a Gestational Carrier Between 2014 and 2020," *JAMA*, published online October 18, 2023, doi:10.1001/jama.2023.11023.

190   Teman, *Birthing a Mother*, 24.

191   Teman, *Birthing a Mother*, 241.

192   Steiner, *The Baby Chase*, 124.

193   Bell, *Misconception*, 7.

194   Steiner, *The Baby Chase*, 66.

195   Twine, *Outsourcing the Womb*, 78.

196   Angela Giuffrida, "Italian parliament approves bill to criminalise surrogacy abroad," *Guardian*, July 26, 2023, accessed March 2024, https://www.theguardian.com/world/2023/jul/26/italian-parliament-approves-bill-criminalise-people-seeking-surrogacy-abroad.

197   Katarina Trimmings and Paul Beaumont, eds., *International Surrogacy Arrangements: Legal Regulation at the International Level* (London: Hart Publishing, 2013), 501.

198   According to an article in the *Guardian* (https://www.theguardian.com/world/2016/apr/26/gay-couple-win-custody-battle-against-thai-surrogate-mother), Mariam Kukunashvili said that Patidta knew from the beginning that they were a gay couple. When I asked her how things broke down, she told me: "When the couple arrived before [the] baby delivery, one out of the couple was very rude … he was constantly crossing the [surrogate's] boundaries, and like very pushy and very aggressive messages. And I kept telling him that 'it will not work, don't give orders because it doesn't work in Thai culture.' [And] I think it was just her revenge." When I asked Bud about this, he told me he completely disagreed with her version of events.

199   The Protection of Children Act now rules that at the time of birth, children born through surrogacy will be considered the legal offspring of the commissioning parents. The new law is also clear that the birth certificates will indicate the baby's parents are the commissioning parents and they

do not require that it's noted if it's a surrogate birth. (Soraj Hongladarom, "Surrogacy in Thailand," in Scherpe, Fenton-Glynn, and Kaan, *Eastern and Western Perspectives on Surrogacy*.) Bud told me that part of their problems arose because they had to wait for the law to pass in order to enter their plea in family court. "Because the military government forbid [surrogacy] it caused a lot of confusion," he told me in a follow-up text. Once the law was passed, it cleared the way for Bud to be legally acknowledged as the father.

200   Zsombor Peter, "Thailand Prepares to Lift Commercial Surrogacy Ban," *VOA*, March 10, 2024, https://www.voanews.com/a/thailand-prepares-to-lift -commercial-surrogacy-ban/7521512.html.

201   Though in Orit's case the intended mother already had a child. She, however, was unable to have another one. So while Orit did not birth her as a mother, she did birth her as a second-time mom.

202   Teman, *Birthing a Mother*, 266.

203   Teman, *Birthing a Mother*, 193.

204   I became a dual national in 2009. According to the US State Department, "dual nationals owe allegiance to both the United States and the foreign country. They are required to obey the laws of both countries, and either country has the right to enforce its laws. It is important to note the problems attendant to dual nationality. Claims of other countries upon US dual nationals often place them in situations where their obligations to one country are in conflict with the laws of the other," https://travel.state.gov/content/travel/en/legal/travel -legal-considerations/Advice-about-Possible-Loss-of-US-Nationality-Dual -Nationality/Dual-Nationality.html.

205   The father or the second parent, according to "Building Families Through Surrogacy: A New Law" by the Law Commission and the Scottish Law Commission, can be either the surrogate's spouse or the intended father if his sperm is used.

206   Since it was an international family law case, it goes to a high court judge. Most domestic surrogacy cases are dealt with in magistrate's court.

207   *Report of the Committee of Inquiry into Human Fertilisation and Embryology*, HMSO, London, 198, (reprinted 1988), CM 9314 ('Warnock Report'), 8.10.

208   Davies, *Babies for Sale?*, 166.

209   Golombok, *We Are Family*, 104.

210   Golombok, *We Are Family*, 104.

211   Teman, *Birthing a Mother*, 11.

212   Fenton-Glynn, *Eastern and Western Perspectives on Surrogacy*, 119.

213 "Parental Orders Granted, Our Exclusive Findings," My Surrogacy Journey, https://www.mysurrogacyjourney.com/blog/surrogacy-trends-for-uk-nationals-our-exclusive-findings/.

214 Espejo-Yaksic, Fenton-Glynn, and Scherpe, *Surrogacy in Latin America*, 16.

215 Fenton-Glynn, *Eastern and Western Perspectives on Surrogacy*, 121.

216 Very rarely in Britain the surrogate decides not to give consent to the Parental Order. One case that came before the family courts was of a couple (C and D) whose biological twins (A and B) were born via surrogate (E). For reasons that are unclear, though she has no desire to parent the children or have anything to do with them, E refuses to allow the biological parents who are raising them to have legal custody (https://www.bailii.org/cgi-bin/format.cgi?doc=/ew/cases/EWHC/Fam/2016/2643.html&query=(surrogacy)+AND+(fottrell)). As stated in the International Surrogacy Forum in Cambridge paper, "In the current parental order process, the balance of power is tipped toward the surrogate in that she can tie the judge's hands and completely block the grant of the parental order for whatever reason," (p. 13).

217 Aine Fox, "Proposed changes to surrogacy law 'will not be taken forward at the moment,'" *Independent*, November 10, 2023, accessed March 2024, https://www.independent.co.uk/news/uk/government-maria-caulfield-law-commission-surrogacy-wales-b2445264.html.

218 Not his real name.

219 Laurel Swerdlow and Wendy Chavkin, "Motherhood in Fragments: Disaggregation of Biology and Care," in Davies, *Babies for Sale?*, 28.

220 Swerdlow and Chavkin, "Motherhood in Fragments," in Davies, *Babies for Sale?*, 28.

221 Bruce Hale, a Massachusetts-based lawyer who focuses much of his work on surrogacy told me that, "in the UK they do not believe birth certificates from any other country, so they are not going to take a birth certificate from any other country, period. So you have to re-adjudicate parentage over in the UK. That's a weird thing for them to do so that is why they are revisiting it."

222 Carmel Shalev, Hedva Eyal, and Etti Samama, "Global Babies: Who Benefits," in Davies, *Babies for Sale?*, 62.

223 Preeyapa T. Khunsong, "Thai police to probe surrogacy operation's Chinese links," *Associated Press*, February 14, 2020.

224 Sophie Lewis, *Full Surrogacy Now: Feminism Against Family* (London: Verso, 2019), 4.

225 For full summary see: https://www.ohchr.org/EN/ProfessionalInterest/Pages/OPSCCRC.aspx.

226 While a few abolitionists will talk of surrogacy as child trafficking—which under the Palermo Protocol (https://www.ohchr.org/en/professionalinterest

/pages/protocoltraffickinginpersons.aspx) includes any intention to exploit the child, the bigger concern by people who focus research on surrogacy is the sale of children, where there is an exchange for money or other considerations like a promise of a new house. That is not trafficking.

227   American Mark Newton and his Vietnamese-Australian partner Peter Truong claimed their son was born via surrogacy in Russia, when in fact the little boy was sold to Newton by his mother for $8,000 and his papers falsified (https://www.abc.net.au/news/2013-07-10/gorman-second-thoughts/4809582). While a stomach-turning case, it was one of child selling and illegal adoption versus surrogacy.

228   For more on this see: https://archive.crin.org/en/library/un-regional -documentation/concluding-observations-69th-israel-report-opsc.html.

229   Marilyn Crawshaw et al., "What are the children's 'best interests' in international surrogacy?," in Davies, *Babies for Sale?*, 171.

230   Marsha Tyson Darling, "What about the children?: Citizenship, nationality and the perils of statelessness," in Davies, *Babies for Sale?*, 186.

231   Tyson Darling, "What about the children?," in Davies, *Babies for Sale?*, 186.

232   Britta van Beers and Laura Bosch, "A Revolution by Stealth: A Legal-Ethical Analysis of the Rise of Pre-Conception Authorization of Surrogacy Agreements," *The New Bioethics* 26, no. 4 (2020): 351–71, https://doi.org/10.1080 /20502877.2020.1836464.

233   van Beers and Bosch, "A Revolution by Stealth."

234   Tyson Darling, "What about the children?," in Davies, *Babies for Sale?*, 194.

235   Tyson Darling, "What about the children?," in Davies, *Babies for Sale?*, 194.

236   Tyson Darling, "What about the children?," in Davies, *Babies for Sale?*, 193.

237   Walter Pintins, in Scherpe, Fenton-Glynn, and Kaan, *Eastern and Western Perspectives on Surrogacy*, 24. Note: this was the same argument used by the Belgian couple in *D and Others v Belgium* https://hudoc.echr.coe.int /eng#{%22itemid%22:[%22002-10163%22]}.

238   Sonia Allan, a law professor in Australia, wrote in *Babies for Sale?* that the decision by the ECHR in the Mennesson case "does not require countries to change their laws prohibiting all, or particular kinds, of surrogacy," (p. 369).

239   While public international law regulates the activities of governments in relation to other governments (as well as corporations and international organizations), private international law has developed to settle private non-state disputes—like divorces, birth rights, and commercial disputes—involving

more than one jurisdiction of foreign law element. See "Working Paper No. 661: Global Surrogacy Practices" by Marcy Darnovsky and Diane Beeson.

240   Circle Surrogacy's John Weltman told me in 2020: "Well, I'm one of the very few heads of a surrogate parenting agency that believes that we should create an international world that's accepting of surrogacy. There is only one way to do that. And that is the one thing that exists internationally that is authorized by every country, which is adoption. And if you followed the rubric of adoption in surrogacy, then you will be completely acceptable everywhere in the world, because you'd have intended parents screened before they could be in the program, you'd have surrogates screened before they can be in the program, you would have egg donors screened before they could be in the program. All kinds of protocols that made sure that there were home studies done before the placement occurred. And to me, that is the only way to do this."

241   Trimmings and Beaumont, *International Surrogacy Arrangements*, 412.

242   Trimmings and Beaumont, *International Surrogacy Arrangements*, 413.

243   Espejo-Yaksic, Fenton-Glynn, and Scherpe, *Surrogacy in Latin America*, 16.

244   An informal Australian expression that means the freedom to act without restriction.

245   Espejo-Yaksic, Fenton-Glynn, and Scherpe, *Surrogacy in Latin America*, 16.

246   Ellen Trachman, "Denmark Passes New Pro-Surrogacy Regulations," Above the Law, February 14, 2024, https://abovethelaw.com/2024/02/denmark-passes-new-pro-surrogacy-regulations/.

247   One of the reasons for a change of law came after a Danish court ruled in 2020 that the intended mother of twins, who was not the biological mother, could not adopt her children because money had been exchanged with their Ukrainian surrogate. Meanwhile, because her husband was the biological father, he was acknowledged as the legal parent. The family took the case to the European Court of Human Rights. It found that Denmark's refusal to recognize the parent-child relationship between the mother and child was a human rights violation—not a violation of the mother's human rights, but of the two children, to have a recognized legal relationship with their mother. The government of Denmark decided to change the law, which will recognize from birth the parents of children born through surrogacy abroad. https://abovethelaw.com/2024/02/denmark-passes-new-pro-surrogacy-regulations/.

248   The former advisor told me that the aim of the meeting was to make sure that the proposed principles did not go against any human rights of women and added, "I do not think it is the ISS' role to try and find consensus on the issue of women's rights in surrogacy."

249   See https://www.icrc.org/en/war-and-law/treaties-customary-law/customary-law.

250   Alison Motluk, "After pleading guilty for paying surrogates, business is booming for this fertility matchmaker," *Globe and Mail*, February 28, 2016, https://www.theglobeandmail.com/life/health-and-fitness/health/business-is-booming-for-fertility-matchmaker-leia-swanberg/article28930242/.

251   Motluk, "Business is booming."

252   Ellen Trachman, "Are the New Canadian Surrogacy Rules Good Or Bad, Eh?," Above the Law, June 17, 2020, https://abovethelaw.com/2020/06/are-the-new-canadian-surrogacy-rules-good-or-bad-eh/.

253   Trachman, "Canadian Surrogacy Rules."

254   Espejo-Yaksic, Fenton-Glynn, and Scherpe, *Surrogacy in Latin America*, 16.

255   Laura Perler, "'Trafficked' into a better future? Why Mexico needs to regulate its surrogacy industry (and not ban it)," Opendemocracy.net, December 17, 2015.

256   Espejo-Yaksic, Fenton-Glynn, and Scherpe, *Surrogacy in Latin America*, 16.

257   France 24, "Israeli same-sex couples seek end to surrogacy discrimination," August 8, 2020, https://www.france24.com/en/20200819-israeli-same-sex-couples-seek-end-to-surrogacy-discrimination.

258   https://seedsethics.org/seeds-standards/.

259   Twine, *Outsourcing the Womb*, 82.

260   Teman, *Birthing a Mother*, 199.

261   Berend, *The Online World of Surrogacy*, 193.

262   Susan Golombok, *Modern Families: Parents and Children in New Family Forms* (Cambridge: Cambridge University Press, 2015), 94.

263   Gee was quick to point out that she wasn't speaking on behalf of all donor-conceived surrogacy-born children and that as one person "we need loads more people to come forward and talk about it." But, she added, grouping all the donor-conceived kids together, "it doesn't fit right with me."

264   Rotabi and Bromfield, *From Intercountry Adoption to Global Surrogacy*, 133. Note: However, the parallels between adoption and surrogacy have real limits. They add that the "conflation between adoption and surrogacy" probably came about because as intercountry adoption started to diminish, surrogacy arrangements were on the rise. They extrapolate that "adoption researchers turned to surrogacy research" and that assumptions must be tested before any firm conclusions can be made.

265   Golombok, *We Are Family*, 149.

266   Golombok, *Modern Families*, 127.

267   University of Cambridge, "Assisted reproduction kids grow up just fine—but it may be better to tell them early about biological origins," April 13, 2023, https://www.cam.ac.uk/research/news/assisted-reproduction-kids-grow-up-just-fine-but-it-may-be-better-to-tell-them-early-about.

268   Susan Golombok et al., "A Longitudinal Study of Families Formed Through Third-Party Assisted Reproduction: Mother–Child Relationships and Child Adjustment From Infancy to Adulthood," *Developmental Psychology* 59, no. 6 (2023): 1059–73, https://doi.org/10.1037/dev0001526.

269   Rotabi and Bromfield, *From Intercountry Adoption to Global Surrogacy*, 138.

270   Rotabi and Bromfield, *From Intercountry Adoption to Global Surrogacy*, 139.

271   Chris Steller, "Surrogacy policies need more thoughtful development, committee votes," Minnesota House of Representatives, March 5, 2015, https://www.house.leg.state.mn.us/SessionDaily/SDView.aspx?StoryID=5558.

272   Dr. Jadva told me that while many surrogates she interviewed were very open about their surrogacies, one carrier had not told her neighbors because she thought it would be difficult to explain so she just decided to say it was her baby. And after the baby was born, she told them that the baby had died because "she just thought that was easier."

273   Twine, *Outsourcing the Womb*, 6.

274   Bell, *Misconception*, 55–56.

275   Jacobson, *Labor of Love*, 50–51.

276   Family Equality, "LGBTQ Family Building Survey," 2019, https://www.familyequality.org/resources/lgbtq-family-building-survey/.

277   Daar, *The New Eugenics*, 17.

278   Beech, "They Were Surrogates."

279   During the hearings, Jorie Dugan from the Center for Reproductive Rights tackled the questions around whether surrogacy is human trafficking, something that the groups against surrogacy constantly brought up. MFA's consistent refrain was that "Surrogacy (in the context of the US) is not human trafficking because it involves consenting adults who freely enter into a legal agreement to carry a pregnancy for someone else. A surrogacy agreement is an agreement, between one or more intended parents and a surrogate, in which the surrogate agrees to become pregnant by assisted reproduction for the purpose of bringing a child into the world that the intended parents will parent from birth.

The US Department of Justice provides that human trafficking is a crime involving the exploitation of a person for labor, services, or commercial sex, and the US Department of Homeland Security, in its 2023 Factsheet on DHS Efforts to Combat Human Trafficking, notes that "human trafficking generally involves the use of force, fraud, or coercion to obtain labor or a commercial sex act." Our argument was that, "While surrogacy agreements are not human trafficking, comprehensive laws" would only "strengthen the legal protections of all parties involved in safeguarding against situations of force, fraud or coercion."

280   David Dodge, "The Surrogacy Industry Braces for a Post-Roe World," *New York Times*, August 23, 2022, https://www.nytimes.com/2022/08/23/well/family/surrogacy-pregnancy-roe-abortion.html.

281   Dodge, "Post-Roe World."

282   Megan Messerly, "Why the Southern Baptists' vote opposing IVF could change national politics," *Politico*, June 12, 2024, https://www.politico.com/news/2024/06/12/ivf-southern-baptist-convention-evangelical-00162994.

Ginanne Brownell is an award-winning writer and journalist. Raised in Michigan and based in London, she has covered stories on six continents and in over forty-five countries. Her work has been published in outlets including *New York Times*, *Wall Street Journal*, *Financial Times*, *Washington Post*, *Foreign Policy*, and *Scientific American*. She has worked on staff for CNN, *Newsweek*, and UNICEF. Ginanne is also the author of *Ghetto Classics: How a Youth Orchestra Changed a Nairobi Slum*.

She has a BA in history from Albion College and an MA in history from the London School of Economics.